Remember the 80s

Remember the

80s

now that's what I call nostalgia

Richard Evans

PORTICO

First published in the United Kingdom in 2008 by
Portico Books
10 Southcombe Street
London
W14 0RA

An imprint of Anova Books Company Ltd

ISBN 9781906032128

A CIP catalogue record for this book is available from the British Library.

10 9 8 7 6 5 4 3 2 1

Reproduction by Dot Gradations Ltd., UK
Printed and bound by SNP Leefung Printers Ltd., China

This book can be ordered direct from the publisher.
Contact the marketing department, but try your bookshop first.

www.anovabooks.com

Contents

Foreword

Martin Fry (ABC)

Ten years. One Decade. One helluva ride.

What kind of 80s did you have? Was it a Strawberry Switchblade or Johnnie Hates Jazz 80s? A Todd Terry or Frankie Knuckles 80s? A Simon Le Jon Bon Jovi 80s? Some or all of the above?

When people talk about the 80s they mention leg-warmers, purple eye-liner and asymmetrical hair. Loads of hair. Loads of hairspray. Then they say 'and that was just the boys'. They're right. It was a flamboyant, innocent and defiant time. Something of a struggle. Lurid and day glo. What no-one remembers is how boring, intolerant and ugly the world was before the 80s arrived.

The 80s was the party. A lot of what we consider classic 80s was homemade. Clothes bought from a jumble sale to create a look audaciously stolen from a movie still. Carefree not corporate. A lot of what we call classic 80s was chaotic and experimental, a wind up. A chance to turn heads in a violent pub. Amateur was everything and meant that anything was possible. The 80s fashion-music-art-video scene has a ramshackle charm that lives on today.

If nothing else the decade we dare to call the 80s was about as diverse as it gets. A mass of contradictions. What a swell party it was. Pre-digital analogue fun. Let's face it, the 90s was pretty anonymous in comparison.

Nostalgia, as we all know, is a very powerful thing and part of the enduring appeal of something like 'Don't You Want Me' is remembrance of times past. A golden age. A time before mortgage payments and midlife crisis. A time before all the boring adult stuff, before all the responsibilities.

The 80s is now a state of mind and no-one knows the cultural shifts of this bygone age better than Richard Evans. Richard knows that the story of the 80s can only be told through the big picture and the minute details. Somewhere between the then and the now. By the people for the people.

Richard Evans, we salute you!

Martin Fry, March 2008.

Introduction

Richard Evans

I'm not sure where the story of this book really starts. It might have been 18th June 2006 when the *Observer* newspaper profiled my website RememberTheEighties.com with a whole page of editorial, the headline 'Wham! Big Hair & Eighties Pop Make Internet Comeback', and an inevitable picture of a Rubik's Cube. That piece was seen by the publishers of this book and was enough for them to get in touch to see if I was interested in writing something about the eighties for them.

On the other hand the *Observer* would never have run the story if I hadn't set up my RememberThe Eighties.com website in the first place, and that takes us back to 2002 when I decided to set up the site to feature the latest news of the bands and artists I had loved in the eighties – many of whom are still working, recording and touring today – who rarely got any sort of coverage in the mainstream media.

Of course I would never have set up the website unless I had so thoroughly lost my heart to music as I grew up through the eighties, so I suppose – although I obviously didn't know it at the time – the story of this book really starts in 1980 when I was twelve years old and in my first year at secondary school.

Back then the events of 1952, just twenty-eight years earlier, would have seemed like ancient history to me; about as relevant to me and my life as the Battle Of Hastings or the Roman Empire. Now, twenty-eight years later, 1980 feels like yesterday. The difference, I suppose, is in living through something makes it very personal. As the American reformer John W. Gardner once said, 'history never looks like history when you are living through it'.

The eighties was the first decade I could call my own; ten years of making the choices about what I liked,

disliked, wanted and didn't want, that truly laid the foundations of who I am today. It was a decade of musical discoveries, of friendships, of fitting in and standing out; a decade of parties, concerts, girls, experiences, films, books and television. It was ten years of growing up.

It's at this point that I should probably apologise to everyone I was friends with in the eighties because it's extremely likely that at some stage in the writing of this book I tried to get inside your head to imagine what the decade looked like to you, which might seem a little creepy. Equally, I suppose I should apologise to everyone I wasn't friends with in the eighties because I didn't creepily try to get inside your head, and therefore may have completely omitted aspects of the decade that you consider essential.

I owe more thanks than I can adequately express here to all the RememberTheEighties.com readers who took the time to share their eighties with me for this book. I received literally hundreds of thoughts, reminiscences, suggestions and pictures – many of which you'll find in the book – and I loved going through them all. Thank you everyone for your support; your memories were honest, touching, inspiring, funny, frequently quite sad and often very embarrassing! This is your book as much as it is mine.

Thank you to Polly Powell at Anova for spotting the opportunity for this book and for introducing me to Portico Books, and to Portico's Tom Bromley, Barbara Phelan and Gemma Wilson who not only gave me the chance to do this, but who – with the help of the whole Anova team - magically transformed my ramblings into the book you are now holding in your hands. Thanks also to Blueprint Management, Peter Coyle, Peter Duncan, Sarah Foster, Martin Fry, Mike Hall, Sally Stratton, Simon Watson,

Clayton Wehrle, mum, Rozz, Ali and Phil... all for helping in so many different ways.

To finish, I would like to dedicate this book to the two people I love most in the world: my wife Beverly (whose eighties mostly revolved around Duran Duran) for keeping the real world at arms length while I worked on it, and for all her love and support always; and my daughter Arianne (who's only four and therefore doesn't remember the eighties and still thinks I'm teasing when I tell her that Boy George is a man) for her regular – and very welcome – interruptions, love and hugs.

Richard Evans, May 2008.

PS. I still can't believe that Martin Fry has written the foreword! It was only the second time we'd met when I told him about this book and he immediately offered to help in whatever way he could. What a gent. Thanks Martin, but I bet you'll be more careful about who you give your mobile number to in the future!

1980

Snapshot

As 1980 dawns, Pink Floyd are number one in the singles chart with 'Another Brick In The Wall' and Rod Stewart has the number one album with his *Greatest Hits (Vol.1)*. ● Margaret Thatcher is in her first year at 10 Downing Street ● The Rubik's Cube goes on sale outside Hungary for the first time ● If you bought a new car before August it would be a V-reg ● As 1980 progresses Ireland's Johnny Logan wins the Eurovision Song Contest with 'What's Another Year', West Ham beat Arsenal to become the FA Cup Winners, and Bjorn Borg defeats John McEnroe at Wimbledon ● A pint of milk costs 17p ● Ronald Regan is elected US President ● The music world loses John Lennon, AC/DC's Bon Scott and Joy Division's Ian Curtis, while the acting world mourns the passing of Peter Sellers ● The bestselling single of the year is The Police's 'Don't Stand So Close To Me' ● The first Sony personal stereo goes on sale under the name of Sony Stowaway ● Pirate radio station Radio Caroline's ship Mi Amigo sinks and the station is forced off the air ● 'Space Invaders' makes the transition from the arcades to Atari's home game system ● The *Voyager 1* space probe discovers that both Saturn and Jupiter have two more moons than originally thought ● The 'Who Shot JR?' episode of *Dallas* attracts the largest TV audience ever ● *Post-It* notes are invented ● Unemployment reaches 2 million ● As the year closes St Winifred's School Choir are number one in the singles chart with 'There's No One Quite Like Grandma' and ABBA are number one in the albums chart with the year's bestselling album, *Super Trouper*

> 'We were taking dance music on one side of the fence; disco records like Chic and people like that, and mixing it with punk and rock, and David Bowie and people like that, and the combination of rock music and dance music was really the fundamental marriage of music that created the eighties sound.'

GARY KEMP, SPANDAU BALLET

Sounds like...1980

31 DECEMBER 1979. In a warehouse above Woolworths in Manchester's Oldham Street, Joy Division are playing Factory Records' New Year's Eve party. Adam & The Ants are onstage at London's Electric Ballroom. Blondie's show at Glasgow's Apollo is being recorded for The Old Grey Whistle Test while a fledgling Simple Minds are performing at the city's Technical College. In Chelmsford I'm twelve and I have been allowed to stay up to see in the new decade with my parents and my Grandma and the evening almost certainly involved the four of us playing Scrabble. On the television David Bowie is playing an acoustic version of 'Space Oddity' on Kenny Everett's New Year's Eve TV special. I don't know that the song is already over ten years old, but I do know that Bowie looks like – and sounds like – the future, and as we enter a whole new decade it turns out that I'm not the only one.

Unbeknown to me at the time, Bowie is already a figurehead for an emerging generation, his influence is already at the fore in 1979 with two number one hits ('Cars' and 'Are "Friends" Electric') from self-confessed Bowie fanatic Gary Numan, and the experimentation of Bowie's 'Berlin' trilogy of albums – *Low*, *Heroes* and *Lodger* – is influencing records from a number of up and coming acts

including the Human League and Ultravox, then led by John Foxx. In 1980 Bowie Nights are springing up in clubs around the country as an alternative to an increasingly stale punk scene and a mainstream club culture that is still serving up a steady diet of disco. Similarly minded clubbers who want to be different, who want to embrace their own individuality, are coming together, dressing up and dancing to Bowie, Roxy Music, Chic and Kraftwerk. The most famous Bowie Night of all is Steve Strange and Rusty Egan's Blitz, which started as a Bowie Night 'Club For Heroes' in 1978, outgrew its original venue and moved into London's Blitz Club in early 1979. 'Club For Heroes' became simply the Blitz, a celebration of individuality and creativity attracting a crowd of London's brightest young things, and the Blitz's influence will go on to reach legendary proportions.

The media – spearheaded by a fledgling style press in the form of *The Face* and *i-D* (both of which launch this year) – struggle to label this emerging movement, offering up The Blitz Kids, The Cult Without A Name and The Now Crowd before eventually settling on New Romantics, a movement whose style will dominate music over the next couple of years before the term becomes watered down and synonymous with eighties

i-D Magazine
The i-D magazine logo, when turned sideways, looks like a winking face, pre-dating text message 'emoticons' by some twenty years.

'Visage's "Fade To Grey" is an iconic, classic record that changed music forever.'

MICKY JOCK

'Adam & The Ants brought style and glamour back to the boring rock scene. More importantly, the messages in the songs were refreshing and positive, be proud of who you are, have fun.'

NIK BRASIER

'My favourite eighties band would be Spandau Ballet. From the first time I heard "To Cut A Long Story Short" I was hooked really. I loved the newness of it, it was just something I hadn't heard before.'

MARK FINNEGAN

cliche, with synthesisers, men in eyeliner, frilly shirts and kilts. Those effects won't really be felt in the mainstream (or by me!) until later in the year, with the debut singles from Japan ('Gentlemen Take Polaroids'), Spandau Ballet ('To Cut A Long Story Short') and Visage ('Fade To Grey'), but it's Bowie himself who neatly reclaims his futurist crown in August of this year by presenting the New Romantic look to the mainstream for the first time in the video to his chart-topping 'Ashes To Ashes' single (which even went so far as to feature a cast of extras hand-picked from Blitz by Bowie, including Steve Strange but – much to his own disappointment – not the Blitz's cloakroom attendant, the then unknown Boy George).

But if 1980 is the start of a new era it is also the end of an old one, and an increasingly stagnant and directionless punk scene hits new depths when the Sex Pistols release a posthumous version of Paul Revere & The Raiders' '(I'm Not Your) Stepping Stone'. Punk is not without its survivors, however, and the post-punk impact is wide-ranging; punk innovators Siouxsie & The Banshees have their most commercially successful year ever with 24 weeks in the charts spread across a trio of classic singles ('Happy House', 'Christine' and 'Israel'), and a further six weeks in the album chart with *Kaleidoscope*. Billy Idol's Generation X release 'Dancing With Myself', which fails to ignite much interest at the time but will later reach classic status when he revisits the song later in the decade as one of the eighties' most successful rock artists. Adam & The Ants release three singles in 1980, finishing the year with 'Antmusic', which goes to number two and represents not only the commercial start of one of the eighties' biggest music successes but launches a

true eighties icon in Adam Ant. The post-punk rock movement, meanwhile, is going strong; The Cure make their singles chart debut with the superbly atmospheric 'A Forest', and Joy Division release a single, 'Love Will Tear Us Apart', and an album, *Closer*, which, I would argue, rank among the most important releases of not just the year, but of the decade.

A new wave (the New Wave!) of rock mixes some of the attitude of punk with elements from other genres, and sees both The Police and Blondie release three classic singles each: The Police's 'So Lonely', 'Don't Stand So Close To Me' and 'De Do Do Do, De Da Da Da' (and a number one album *Zenyatta Mondatta*) and Blondie's number one singles 'Atomic', 'The Tide Is High' and 'Call Me'. Martha & The Muffins enjoy their sole UK hit with 'Echo Beach', and the classically trained Joe Jackson releases his most commercially successful single, 'It's

Different For Girls'.

Much of this passes me by however, as I have nailed my personal colours to the mast of heavy-rock and spend far too many hours this year planning how the patches and embroidery will look on the back of my denim jacket, should I ever get one. In retrospect I will find this venture into the world of rock a bit odd. My real fascination is with the punks hanging around Chelmsford's shopping precinct, so I can only later assume it to be a peer-pressure thing; some of my friends have older brothers who were into rock and I think their tastes were handed down to us as the benchmark of musical sophistication. I have no older siblings, and no friends with brothers with an interest in punk.

To be fair, 1980 is a great year for rock. It's the year when Motorhead will release what is perhaps the ultimate rock single of all time, 'Ace Of Spades' (which I will always love, and it was Motorhead's skull logo which took pride of place on the back of my hypothetical denim jacket!); Deep Purple and AC/DC will top the album charts with *Deepest Purple* and *Back In*

Black respectively, and a flurry of rock singles that will go on to be classics are released, including Judas Priest's 'Breaking The Law', Rainbow's 'All Night Long', Saxon's 'Wheels Of Steel' and Rush's 'Spirit Of Radio'. But it's Status Quo who are my favourites, whose logo I will carefully copy onto the covers of my school exercise books, and whose *12 Gold Bars* compilation is released in March this year. *12 Gold Bars* becomes the album I covet most, the album I will always pick up in record shops and examine in minute detail before finally getting my own copy on cassette at Christmas – my first album – and spending the festive season playing it over and over again on my dad's enormous 'portable' cassette player.

Rock doesn't mix well with other genres, however, and lunchtimes at school will become a daily battleground of scuffles between gangs nominally dubbed mods and rockers. Playground politics dictate that as a rocker I must close my ears – and my heart – to mod music, and consequently to some of the most exciting and enduring music to emerge from the year. The Specials will take one of the year's first number one single positions with their five-song 'Live EP' (rather inexplicably released with the name 'The Special AKA' on the sleeve and 'The Specials' on the label), featuring 'Too Much Too Young' as the lead track and giving the now-legendary 2-Tone label its first UK number one. The Specials will go on to score another three top ten singles this year:

Sounds Like 1981
The Year as a Mixtape

SIDE ONE

Human League 'Being Boiled', Gary Numan 'We Are Glass', Ultravox 'Sleepwalk', The Vapors 'Turning Japanese', Spandau Ballet 'To Cut A Long Story Short', Dexys Midnight Runners 'Geno', Adam & The Ants 'Antmusic', The Jam 'Going Underground', Motorhead 'Ace Of Spades', Rainbow 'All Night Long', The Stray Cats 'Runaway Boys', The Selecter 'Three Minute Hero', The Specials 'Rat Race', The Beat 'Mirror In The Bathroom', Madness 'My Girl'

SIDE TWO

The Gap Band 'Oops Up Side Your Head', Kool & The Gang 'Celebration', The Police 'Don't Stand So Close To Me', Michael Jackson 'She's Out Of My Life', Blondie 'Atomic', David Bowie 'Ashes To Ashes', Visage 'Fade To Grey', The Cure 'A Forest', Japan 'Gentlemen Take Polaroids', OMD 'Enola Gay', John Foxx 'Underpass', Siouxsie & The Banshees 'Israel', Joy Division 'Love Will Tear Us Apart', Martha & The Muffins 'Echo Beach', Bob Marley & The Wailers 'Could You Be Loved'

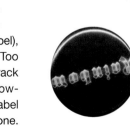

1980

Number One Albums

Rod Stewart Greatest Hits (Vol. 1), The Pretenders Pretenders, Various Artists The Last Dance (Motown Compilation), The Shadows String of Hits, Johnny Mathis Tears And Laughter, Genesis Duke, Rose Royce Greatest Hits, Sky Sky 2, Boney M The Magic Of Boney M, Paul McCartney McCartney 2, Peter Gabriel Peter Gabriel, Roxy Music Flesh And Blood, The Rolling Stones Emotional Rescue, Queen The Game, Deep Purple Deepest Purple, AC/DC Back In Black, Gary Numan Telekon, David Bowie Scary Monsters And Super Creeps, The Police Zenyatta Mondatta, Barbra Streisand Guilty, ABBA Super Trouper

'Rat Race', 'Stereotype' and 'Do Nothing', plus a second top-five album (*More Specials*), and Madness will have their most active year ever in the UK singles charts (with 'My Girl', 'Baggy Trousers', 'Embarrassment' and the 'Work Rest & Play EP', featuring 'Night Boat To Cairo', all taking top ten places). Years later I will still remember standing at the lockers outside the school maths rooms and confessing to a friend how much I liked The Beat's single 'Mirror In The Bathroom' – a treacherous admission for a fledgling rock fan!

The Specials' politically charged output was probably wasted on me and my pre-teen peers but the image was a great influence on school fashion. Despite only a few of us having the necessary resources to adopt the full regalia of our chosen side the distinction is easy; the mods wear their school ties with small, tight knots while the rockers wear the biggest, loosest knots they can produce.

Sartorially I have it easy, the standard uniform for rock fans being leather or denim jackets adorned with badges, patches and embroidery, beyond which pretty much anything scruffy goes. But it's a lot more difficult on the other side of the playground; parkas, blazers (school blazers, naturally, do not count!) or Harrington jackets adorned with Union Jacks, RAF targets and 2-Tone badges are the mod staples, worn over Ben Sherman or Fred Perry shirts with skinny ties, drainpipe Sta-Prest trousers, white socks and loafers, brogues or bowling shoes.

Occupying an uneasy place between the two factions are the skinheads. Style-wise it's kind of an extreme version of mod – bleach-splashed jeans and denim jackets, braces and Doc Marten boots being the main wardrobe – but musically the skins are pulling from a vast range of influences, some predominantly from ska, reggae and 2-Tone and others from the rock and punk Oi sounds of bands like Sham 69, Angelic Upstarts and Cockney Rejects. Given skinheads' fearsome reputation for violence and hooliganism it's no real surprise that only a tiny number of my twelve-year-old peers dare align themselves with this particular movement and those that do try are treated with some derision: it's a tricky look to pull off convincingly at twelve years old!

Then there's disco. Not a style generally associated with the eighties but as we enter the decade the charts are still chock-a-block with disco survivors. 1980 is in fact the year of Ottowan's anthemic 'D.I.S.C.O', not to mention number one singles for Odyssey ('Use It Up And Wear It Out') and Kelly Marie ('Feels Like I'm In Love'), while hits compilations from Rose Royce and Boney M take the top spot in the album charts. There are also key hits from the patron saints of disco, The Village People, with 'Can't Stop The Music', as well as Liquid Gold ('Dance Yourself Dizzy'), Kool & The Gang ('Celebration') and The Gap Band's 'Oops Up Side Your Head', which comes complete with its own curious dance moves, involving sitting down on the floor in long rows, swaying from side to side and making vague rowing actions for no apparent reason. But by 1980 the seventies' disco followers, formerly resplendent in their flares, their lycra and their sparkles, seem to have been left behind and disco is just part of a mainstream that this year also includes hits from people like Barbra Streisand, John Lennon, Michael Jackson and Sheena Easton.

New Wave

A genre from the first half of the eighties, which mixes rock music, a punk attitude and a pop sensibility with elements from other genres (for example ska, reggae, disco or soul).
KEY ACTS: The Police, Blondie, Talking Heads, Elvis Costello.

Post Punk

A diverse genre of rock music influenced by the punk movement but rejecting the simple, stripped-down chord structures of early punk in favour of more complex and often more experimental sounds. The true post-punk era only really lasted a few years before fragmenting into further genres (goth, indie, alternative rock, industrial etc).
KEY ACTS: Joy Division, The Cure, Gary Numan, U2, Echo & The Bunnymen.

New Romantic

A style-oriented movement combining the individualism of punk with glam-rock's flamboyant looks. David Bowie, Chic, Kraftwerk and Roxy Music were major influences and the music was generally synthesizer rather than guitar based. The movement sprang from dedicated nights at clubs around the country (famously London's Blitz but also Birmingham's Rum Runner, Sheffield's Limit, Liverpool's Eric's, Manchester's Pips and so on) and as a result the music was generally made to be danced to.
KEY ACTS: Duran Duran, Spandau Ballet, Ultravox, Visage, Japan.

Mod

Another sprawling genre but, broadly speaking, in 1980 the term 'mod' embraces a revival of the original mod sound, as epitomised by The Who, The Kinks and The Small Faces, alongside a new generation of acts who fused the energy and attitude of punk with those original influences, or with traditional ska and reggae.
KEY ACTS: The Jam, The Specials, The Selecter, Madness, The Beat, UB40.

The Blitz Club and

The New Romantic movement starts in clubs around the country where like-minded, creative individuals can react against punk's austerity and anti-fashion stance by becoming ever more flamboyant, colourful and expressive. The keyword is glamour and the best-known and most influential club of them all is London's Blitz, whose members will famously go on to influence the worlds of fashion and music. It is a haven for style luminaries such as Melissa Caplan, Stephen Linard, John Galliano, Sue Clowes, Pam Hogg and Stephen Jones as well as for an emerging generation of musical talent, including Boy George, Spandau Ballet, Visage, Marilyn and Midge Ure.

The music is important but the club's essence also revolves around style, escapism and exhibitionism and it's a competitive world, members competing to be seen in the best, most flamboyant and most eccentric styles, which might mean Boy George in full Boadicea costume complete with helmet by Stephen Jones, or Marilyn's uncanny reincarnations of his Hollywood namesake. Inspiration is drawn from the romance of history, fiction, cinema and theatre, each with a glamorous twist.

The New Romantic look is taken to a wider audience, first by Blitz bands like Visage and Spandau Ballet and then by a new generation of style-conscious acts, including Duran Duran, Culture Club and the Human League – music-video pioneers for whom image has to be as important as the music itself, and sometimes more important! 'In retrospect I'd say the music was most important,' says Tony Hadley, 'although I would probably have said style when I was nineteen. The music certainly lives on a lot more comfortably than some of the outfits!', a sentiment echoed by OMD's Andy McCluskey who recalls 'We were very serious po-faced northern boys, The Blitz and the New Romantics was complete anathema to us - just people in poncey clothes watering down all the good work that had been done prior to them arriving on the scene!'

The Blitz Club...Up to Date

The story of the Blitz itself will go on to reach almost mythical proportions, much to the amusement of the original Blitz Kids, Tony Hadley among them: 'There has been so much written about it, and a lot of pretentious stuff as well … I think a lot of people would have you think we were all sitting there drinking coffee and reading Nietzsche where it was basically just a bunch of young girls and guys all looking the business and having a bloody good time!'. There is still a nightclub at 4 Great Queen Street in London's Covent Garden, the site of the original Blitz, for a while it was the home of the notorious 'celebrity' hangout Browns but has since gone through a flurry of name changes and renovations and is currently called The Red Rooms.

'It was all about getting away from what punk had become - the music had been great and I loved that whole period, but it had become very media manipulated, quite violent and just got a little bit nasty - so the whole Blitz scene was meant to be the antithesis of that really, with people dressing up and probably looking ridiculous!'

SPANDAU BALLET'S TONY HADLEY

the New Romantics

GAME OVER – SPACE INVADERS AND BEYOND

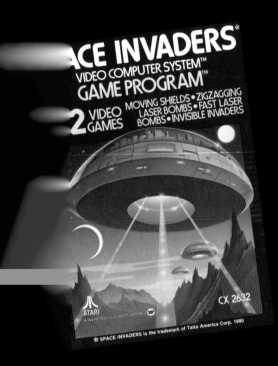

Like so many things in life, there are the 'haves' and there are the 'have-nots'. In this particular case I am a 'have-not', which makes my desire for the Atari VCS, a black-plastic box fronted with its sleek panel of simulated wood, so much more acute. Over 25 million of them will be sold around the world over the next few years and talk of high scores, tactics and tricks are the stuff of playground conversation. The World Record high score is allegedly around two and half million although my personal best hovers somewhere around the four hundred mark, hampered somewhat by a lack of access to the game to practise – only one friend has the VCS and there's a limit on how many times I can invite myself round.

'Space Invaders' is the first video game to hold me in its thrall and I'm not alone, in Japan in 1979 the arcade version of the game was so popular that it caused a coin shortage, entire arcades were turned over to the game and players were treated for 'Space Invaders' addiction. It's also the first arcade game to make the transition from arcade to home console, a move that sets the Atari company on the road to phenomenal success, selling 2 million VCS units and millions of 'Space Invader' cartridges (each one containing an incredible 112 different versions of the game, including mind-bending variations featuring invisible invaders or invisible missiles) by the time 1980 ends.

Although Atari's 'Space Invaders' is my personal video-gaming favourite – I find the bleeping aliens who scroll across the screen mesmerising and addictive – Atari have more games up their sleeve. In 1981 they release a version of the arcade game 'Asteroids' whose stark graphics briefly pull my interest away from 'Space Invaders', but again, lack of access to an Atari console results in an embarrassingly low personal best, generally achieved playing on display models in electrical shops.

'Pac-Man' – a yellow circle with a mouth who runs around a maze eating dots and bonus prizes while being chased by four ghosts called Blinky, Pinky, Inky and Clyde – is another game to make the transition from the arcades. It becomes available on the VCS in 1982, and goes on to be one of the most successful and recognisable games of all time with a range of commercial spin-offs that include a Hanna-Barbera TV series, Pac-Man shaped pasta and a Pac-Man whoopie-cushion.

By the end of 1982 there are over two hundred games available for the Atari VCS (now renamed the Atari 2600), and honourable mentions should go out to 'Defender' 'Frogger' and 'Tank Battle', but it's a game based on the film E.T. that signals the beginning of the end for Atari. Having paid $21 million for the rights to release the title Atari take just five weeks to rush release a low-quality sub-standard game that fails to sell. Urban legend states that the company produced twelve million E.T. cartridges to serve the ten million customers who owned an Atari console and were then forced to bury eleven million of them in a landfill in Alamogordo, New Mexico. More conservative sources claim that of five million cartridges produced four million were subsequently destroyed. Either way the debacle is the beginning of the end for Atari's games division, which was already fighting new systems introduced by Sega and Nintendo in 1983, as well as an emerging home-PC market.

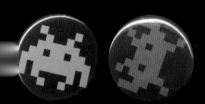

GAME OVER :
A little-known Atari 2600 trick for 'Space Invaders' is to obtain double bullets by turning the game on while holding down the game reset switch. If only we'd known that at the time!

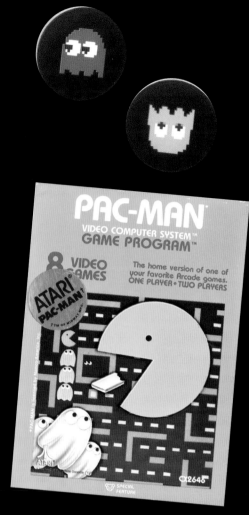

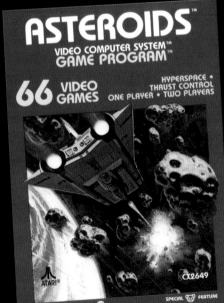

Space Invaders ... Up to Date!

I never did get an Atari VCS games system, but 'Space Invaders' has had something of a renaissance in recent years with various hand-held and online versions being made available for those of us who remember the game with wistful nostalgia and want to recapture some of that gaming excitement! It seems however that 'Pac-Man' is more popularly remembered as the ultimate gaming experience of the eighties.

WHO SHOT JR?

It's the evening of 21st March 1980 and, unlike millions of other people around the world, I'm not watching the *Dallas* series finale. I'm not specifically avoiding it, but it's a show that has never caught my attention; I don't know who any of the characters are, just that it centres around businessmen in cowboy hats, oil-wells and immaculate women with enormous hair.

By the morning of 22nd March I am in no doubt as to who at least one character is (although it seems doubtful he'll make it into the next series!) as newspapers, radio, talk at school and even the TV news are all asking the same question, 'Who shot JR?'

It's a question that will be debated endlessly for well over six months until the new series of *Dallas* hits the world's screens in November, and even then the show will run for three episodes before finally revealing the murderer's identity on 21st November. 'Who Shot JR?' and 'I Shot JR' will become the slogans of 1980, appearing on badges, T-shirts, belt buckles and even cowboy hats as merchandisers cash in on the media frenzy. Bookmakers take millions of pounds in bets on the identity of the killer, offering odds on around ten *Dallas* characters each with a sufficient grudge against JR, with odds ranging from 3-1 for the prime suspect, JR's wife Sue Ellen, through to 12-1 for the show's more gentle matriarch, Miss Ellie.

The reality is that no one knows who committed the crime, including the show's writers who, under pressure to deliver another series, deliberately included the cliffhanger as a way of buying time to work out where the show was going. Even when the scripts are written, not even the cast know the outcome, as several alternative scripts will be written and all the major characters will be filmed in the 'smoking-gun' scene.

The highest ever TV audience for a soap – an estimated 350 million people in 53 countries around the world – will tune in to watch the final revelation, and discover that the killer is in fact Kristin Sheppard (played by Mary Crosby, the daughter of film legend and singer Bing Crosby). JR will eventually recover from the assassination attempt (and JR actor Larry Hagman will use his subsequent high profile to renegotiate his contract with the show up to a cool $100,000 per episode) and spare Kristin because she is expecting his child, and *Dallas* will continue for another eleven years, raking up 356 episodes and in the process becoming known as perhaps the ultimate eighties' soap.

Dallas … Up to Date!

Larry Hagman stayed with *Dallas* until the end of the show in 1991, appearing in all but one of the show's episodes. In 1995 he underwent a liver transplant brought on by years of heavy drinking but still makes occasional TV appearances. Mary Crosby crossed over to the *Dallas* spin-off series *Knots Landing* before returning to *Dallas* in 1981 shortly before her character, Kristin Sheppard, was found drowned in the Southfork Ranch swimming pool. She has continued to appear in films and TV shows including *Star Trek: Deep Space Nine* and *Beverly Hills 90210*.

> 'Dallas and Dynasty were a must, they were the 80s!'
>
> ANN BEGGS

> 'I loved *Dallas*, it's so camp-looking now, but I got addicted to the storylines.'
>
> JAY SPEARS

'I hated all those American soaps like Dallas and Dynasty. At the time it seemed so unreal. I see them now and think 'Was I really the only person who did not know who shot J.R?"

NICK MILLS

Blue Peter's PeterDuncan

I'm not really sure when I stopped watching *Blue Peter*. I'd say that the classic line-up for me would have revolved around John Noakes, Peter Purves, Valerie Singleton and Lesley Judd, but towards the end of the seventies they had already left the show. Then there was a year or so of anxious presenter-shuffling, which culminated in 1980 when both Christopher Wenner and Tina Heath left. I don't remember Christopher at all, but I remember Tina very well; she had a particularly mischievous smile at a time when I was just starting to be susceptible to such things. Their departure led to two new presenters, Peter Duncan and Sarah Greene, joining Simon Groom on the show, a line-up so familiar to me that I must have still been watching the show fairly regularly in the early eighties, although in my defence I do have younger siblings, so it may have just been on for them!

I remember Peter Duncan best as a John Noakes action-type who caused a brief tabloid sensation when it was revealed that he had appeared in adult films. Sarah Greene I remember for being pretty and nice, but mostly for a show in which she modelled vintage corsets along with Tina Heath. Given this vivid memory it's probably a good job that it's Peter, and not Tina, I speak to in 2006 about *Blue Peter* in the eighties, asking him first about his memories of starting on the show in 1980: 'It was a bit strange because I didn't really want to be a presenter. I had actually rejected it once because I was offered it a couple of years earlier, to take over from John Noakes. I was a working actor, but there were aspects that appealed to me; the adventure, the travel … I just thought, let's do it and see what happens!' What happened was that he would be with the show, with a short break in 1984, for the next six years, going on to host his own show, *Duncan Dares*, and in the process becoming one of children's TV's most famous faces.

When we meet he is friendly, down-to-earth and reassuringly ordinary, slightly baffled that anyone would still want to talk to him about his *Blue Peter* days. I wonder if he's always been like this; whether it ever felt strange to be Peter Duncan, to be that recognisable, an early crush for so many girls? 'I suppose you kind of get used to people recognising you but I wouldn't say it was strange, you get used to it so much that I think you notice it more when you go abroad and everyone ignores you! But yes there was that crush thing, although now they're all mums … now I get these girls coming up and saying "my mum used to fancy you", which isn't nearly as flattering.'

And wasn't there once a scandalous myth that he had been a porn star? 'That is one of those media myths, but the reality is that it was just a film, an arthouse film, that wasn't pornographic at all apart from me showing my bare chest and my co-star baring her breasts and saying things like "I'm on fire …", which is a shame, I quite like the idea of being seen as a porn star!'

Peter Duncan has made a series of travel documentaries with his family, which he has released on DVD via his own company, Here's One I Made Earlier Ltd.

In 1980 Peter Duncan also appeared in the film *Flash Gordon* as 'The Young Treeman', a character who dies after just eleven seconds on screen. 'I remember trying to build my part up! I spent a lot of time walking up and down and dying, which they obviously liked because they kept it all in, and I got a good few close-ups! I didn't really know much about it at the time, it was just a week's work for me.'

Peter Duncan was elected Chief Scout in 2004 and was awarded the highest *Blue Peter* accolade, the Gold Blue Peter Badge, in 2007.

1980 ICON

▶▶ Adam & the Ants

In the late seventies the tedium of having to go shopping on a Saturday with my parents was partly offset by my fascination with the punks that used to hang around by the fountain in Chelmsford's shopping precinct. The haircuts, the clothes, the leather jackets, the attitude, everything about them resonated with me but I was far too young to participate in any real way. Then in 1979, when I started secondary school, I began listening to the radio a lot, almost indiscriminately. I found out about music of all types and started to sort out what I liked, and what I wanted to align myself with. Admittedly my early passion for heavy metal may have been misplaced but it was a starting point in my search for something that would be mine, something that could be my punk.

In 1980 Adam & The Ants' 'Antmusic' changed music for me forever. For me the song was revolutionary, a rejection of the music of the past and a call to arms for a new generation … my generation. I loved it for its pounding tribal drums, for Adam's bold theatrical glamour, for the whole package. It was new and exciting and I felt like I understood, we all did. The single, released in December 1980, made number two in the singles charts and coincided with an Adam & The Ants tour which included a show at the Chelmsford Odeon. I was only thirteen so I didn't go, but that the Ants came to Chelmsford at all felt like being touched by greatness.

Adam & The Ants had already released their epic *Kings Of The Wild Frontier* album in November, which topped the charts – there was an earlier single from the album, 'Dog Eat Dog', which made number four in the UK singles charts but passed me by entirely – and marked the beginning of an awesome run of hits. Three old Ants' singles – 'Young Parisians', 'Cartrouble' and 'Zerox' – recorded for the band's previous labels Decca and Do It were rush released to take advantage of the band's new marketability, but it is the band's next proper single, a reissue of the track 'Kings Of The Wild Frontier', in February 1981 that hit the same emotional peak for me as 'Antmusic' had back in December.

By May 1981 Adam & The Ants had moved into a new phase with 'Stand & Deliver', the first single from a new album, *Prince Charming*, which would be released in November. 'Stand & Deliver' completed the trio of singles (with 'Antmusic' and 'Kings Of The Wild Frontier') that would make the band forever mine, scoring the band their first number one single in the process. The next single, 'Prince Charming', would be another chart-topper, as

was the album of the same name, but my personal interest was on the wane by now, and as it turned out so was the band's. Adam & The Ants split up in March 1982.

Adam would have a series of solo hits between 1982 and 1984 (most notably with 'Goody Two Shoes', 'Friend Or Foe' and 'Puss N Boots') in partnership with the Ants' guitarist and co-writer Marco Pirroni, before moving to LA and turning his attention to acting. Returning to the UK Adam would go on to very publicly suffer mental health problems, before putting the record straight in his excellent 2006 autobiography, *Stand & Deliver*. Pirroni, meanwhile, would go on to collaborate as a co-writer and producer for a number of other artists, most notably for Sinead O'Connor on her *I Do Not Want What I Haven't Got* album in 1990.

Incredibly for me, whose musical view was so utterly changed by Adam & The Ants in 1980, I have interviewed Marco Pirroni twice – in 2005 to talk about the legacy of the Ants in view of their catalogue being reissued as remastered and expanded CDs, and again in 2006 when he announced the birth of a new project, The Wolfmen. What follows is a combination of both interviews.

'We were almost exactly the band I had imagined being in whilst daydreaming during maths lessons at school; Roxy Music and the Glitter Band do soundtracks to spaghetti westerns. It was as unlikely an idea in 1973 as it was in 1981 and I'm still amazed we got away with it!'

MARCO PIRRONI, ADAM & THE ANTS

'Adam embodied what would later become such an eighties' trend – style over content. The package was what became important – costume, a theme, artwork, video – almost as if the music was a by-product. But it all came together in such an exciting, vibrant way.'

ALAN FOLEY

WHEN *KINGS OF THE WILD FRONTIER* WAS RELEASED THERE WAS SIMPLY NOTHING TO TOUCH IT – THE MUSIC AND THE IMAGERY AND THE WHOLE PACKAGE WAS JUST SO NEW AND FRESH AND EXCITING … FROM YOUR VIEWPOINT INSIDE THE BAND WERE YOU AWARE OF ANY OF THE IMPACT YOU WERE MAKING?

It's a little like being in the eye of a hurricane. You also begin to live a very isolated life, you tend never to go any-where on your own, never travel on public transport, hardly ever walk any-where because ninety per cent of your time is spent working, so what free time there is you spend asleep.

ARE YOU COMFORTABLE THAT PEOPLE STILL WANT TO TALK TO YOU ABOUT THE ANTS?

It's weird … there was a period when I really didn't want to talk about it, not that I was ever ashamed or embarrassed about it, but I just didn't want to talk about it, I was just bored of talking about it. There's this weird thing now, as I get older, that it doesn't seem to be that long ago … I don't know, everything seems to co-exist in one time-frame. But no, it's fine.

YOU'VE BEEN SIFTING THROUGH VAST AMOUNTS OF OLD ANTS' MATERIAL FOR THE ALBUM REISSUES – WHAT SORT OF EMOTIONS DOES THE PROCESS OF REVISITING THE BAND'S HISTORY STIR UP FOR YOU?

It's certainly not nostalgia. One of the reasons I wanted to do this is to consign Adam & The Ants to history. I'm really proud of what we did and wouldn't change it if I could, but it's nice to gather up all the loose ends and have them in the shops.

GIVEN THAT A LOT OF THE 'NEW' TRACKS HERE ARE DEMO VERSIONS AND NEVER REALLY MADE FOR PUBLIC EARS, WAS THERE REALLY NO TEMPTATION TO POLISH THEM UP AND MAKE THEM SOUND BETTER, OR ARE THEY PRESENTED JUST AS THEY WERE?

No, they are presented the way they were at the time.

LISTENING BACK TO ALL THIS MATERIAL NOW, ARE THERE ANY FEELINGS OF 'I WISH WE'D DONE THAT DIFFERENTLY' FOR ANY OF THE TRACKS?

Yes of course, but it's ultimately useless to keep thinking that. Chris Hughes and I have been talking about doing an album of 'Ant revisited' tracks; that is new mixes and updates on old tracks. Not to supersede the old stuff but more of a 'director's cut' type of thing … but that will be down the line sometime.

ANYTHING YOU'D HAVE DONE DIFFERENTLY OUTSIDE THE MUSIC?

What? Are you kidding? Of course! Who doesn't want to go back and change the past? But I ain't Captain Kirk so there's no point in giving it much thought!

MOVING AWAY FROM THE MUSIC LEADS ME ON TO THE IMAGERY OF THE BAND … WHO WAS RESPONSIBLE FOR THAT?

Adam has to take credit or responsibility for that, depending on your point of view!

I SUPPOSE IT'S EASY TO BE JUDGEMENTAL NOW, BUT THE WHOLE IMAGERY OF ADAM & THE ANTS WAS SO IMPORTANT THERE MUST HAVE BEEN INCREDIBLE PRESSURE ON THE BAND TO KEEP REINVENTING YOURSELVES?

I never felt that because as people will tell you, I have this annoying urge to change everything every day anyway. What was more difficult was going to other countries and having to present what you did six months ago as new!

WAS THERE EVER A POINT WHERE THE STYLE OF THE BAND WAS THREATENING TO OVERTAKE THE MUSIC AND SUBSTANCE?

We never let our music get in the way of our image.

TO MY SHAME I'M NOT SURE THAT I ACTUALLY KNOW WHY ADAM & THE ANTS BROKE UP … WHAT HAPPENED?

Adam and I wanted to go back to being musicians instead of running an international corporation.

WAS IT LIBERATING FOR YOU BOTH TO BE ABLE TO WORK OUTSIDE THE GROUP WHEN YOU STARTED WORKING ON ADAM'S SOLO MATERIAL?

Absolutely. I think we made it clear to our management and label that we would no longer be attending meetings about international marketing strategy, tax planning or offshore investments, because if we were not left alone to make our music then there would be nothing for anyone to talk about.

ARE YOU STILL IN TOUCH WITH ANY OF THE OTHER ANTS? I THINK IT'S FAIRLY WELL KNOWN THAT YOU'RE STILL FRIENDS WITH ADAM, BUT WHAT ABOUT THE OTHERS?

I have been working with Chris Hughes a lot recently and it's been great, we just started where we left off twenty years ago like it was the next day. I think we've both

grown ever more eccentric in our old age and what reality there was has all but disappeared!

I CAN'T IMAGINE YOU'D EVER DO A DURAN DURAN AND REFORM THE 'CLASSIC' LINE-UP?
We all have our price, but mine is unrealistically inflated – it's unlikely that any promoter could ever meet it.

ARE YOU PROUD OF EVERYTHING ADAM & THE ANTS ACHIEVED?
We were almost exactly the band I had imagined being in whilst daydreaming during maths lessons at school; Roxy Music and the Glitter Band do soundtracks to spaghetti westerns. It was as unlikely an idea in 1973 as it was in 1981 and I'm still amazed we got away with it!

YOUR NEW PROJECT, THE WOLFMEN, IS WITH ANOTHER FORMER ANT, CHRIS CONSTANTINOU, BUT IT DOESN'T SOUND LIKE A NEW RECORD AT ALL – IT'S KIND OF A MELTING POT OF ROXY MUSIC, DAVID BOWIE, MAYBE SOME T-REX AND THINGS FROM THAT GLAM ERA.
It's all of those things – and all of those things were Adam & The Ants really. When we started working on the stuff we spent a long time trying to make it sound as old as possible and even going back to kind of a pre-seventies' sound, a kind of Motown. Not that it actually sounds like Motown but that was kind of the idea in our head, and we played to a couple of people who are our age and they said, 'No no no – you've got to remix it … it sounds too old, it doesn't sound fresh.'

I ACTUALLY THINK IT DOES SOUND FRESH, EXACTLY BECAUSE IT SOUNDS OLD, IT'S THAT WHOLE THING WHERE MUSICAL STYLES LOOP BACK AROUND.
You're right, it is that whole loop thing …

so these people are in their late forties and they are doing that kind of 'hey man you've got to be down with the kids' thing, and for a few minutes I actually bought in to all that bollocks! But then we started playing it to twenty-year-olds and they were saying 'yeah it sounds great, it sounds modern' blah blah blah, which just goes to prove that you should never, ever try to be down with the kids!

THE PICTURE THAT I CONJURE UP IN MY HEAD WHEN I LISTEN TO THE WOLFMEN IS A KIND OF TEDDYBOY IMAGE – NOT THE CARTOON TEDDYBOY LIKE SHOWADDYWADDY OR SOMETHING, BUT SOMETHING DANGEROUS AND A BIT SINISTER … VIOLENCE IN DARK ALLEYWAYS, THAT SORT OF THING!
It's funny … I don't know if all this stuff, all the things you're talking about, is deliberate but it's definitely the kind of things that I like. I always really liked teddyboys when I was growing up as a teenager, even though I grew up as a teenager in the seventies and there weren't really many teddyboys around … and then that's what attracted me to the SEX shop and the whole punk thing.

WHEN I LISTEN TO THE WOLFMEN MATERIAL, AND I MENTIONED A FEW OF THE THINGS IT REMINDS ME OF, I CAN'T REALLY FIND ANY CONTEMPORARY INFLUENCES ON THERE. DO

YOU HAVE ANY OR IS IT A CASE OF LOOKING BACK FOR INSPIRATION?
Um … yeah I do … I'm trying to think of what they are really. Yes I do, but much like you and your website I look back and have a particular period, a particular year even – I think it was 1972 – and all the music from that year and from that time is the music I love the most, and it's the music that I just can't find anything to match it today, things like 'Ziggy Stardust' and 'Transformer'. That's not to say that I live in any sort of seventies' timewarp or anything because I definitely don't, but those are my formative times, my formative albums.

WHAT WOULD YOU SAY IS THE MOTIVATION BEHIND THE PROJECT? IS IT PURELY FOR THE MUSIC? FOR FUN? FOR COMMERCIAL GAIN? OR A COMBINATION OF THOSE?
Well obviously it's for all those things. That's the whole point of doing it, I can't do anything else … but I don't make music purely for my own pleasure … it's just too much bloody work to make a record just for fun. People have to hear it and like it and I have to get something back from it, even if it is only 'you're great' … or not! I suppose the idea behind doing anything is so that people can say 'you're great' and you make a few bob out of it. I wouldn't do it purely for my own pleasure; I'd just watch TV or something.

1981

Snapshot

John Lennon's 'Imagine' is the first new number one single of the year and Adam & The Ants' *Kings Of The Wild Frontier* is the first chart-topping album (and will also end up being the year's bestselling album) ● The Church of England allow the ordination of women priests ● Police arrest Peter Sutcliffe, the Yorkshire Ripper ● On 29 July Lady Diana Spencer marries the Prince of Wales at Westminster Abbey in front of a global TV audience of more than 700 million ● Ronald Regan is inaugurated as the 40th US President ● MTV is launched in the USA ● At Wimbledon John McEnroe beats Bjorn Bjorg in the Wimbledon Men's finals and Chris Evert Lloyd beats Hana Mandlikova to take the women's trophy ● The Sony Stowaway is renamed the Sony Walkman ● The Queen is attacked by a man who fires six blank shots at her during the Trooping of the Colour ceremony in London ● Pope John Paul II and Ronald Regan both survive assassination attempts ● James Bond is Roger Moore and the new Bond film this year is *For Your Eyes Only* ● Space Shuttle Columbia is successfully launched for the first time ● Bucks Fizz win the Eurovision Song Contest with 'Making Your Mind Up' ● The first US test-tube baby is born ● France abolishes capital punishment ● Ken Livingstone becomes leader of the Greater London Council ● Bill Haley, Bob Marley and football manager Bill Shankly pass away ● The first recognised cases of AIDS are reported in the USA, and in the UK, the Social Democrat Party is created by four former Labour ministers – Roy Jenkins, Shirley Williams, William Rodgers and David Owen ● *Chariots Of Fire* wins the Oscar for Best Picture ● As the year closes the Human League are number one in the singles charts with the year's bestselling single, 'Don't You Want Me', and ABBA are top of the album chart with *The Visitors*

'We just decided to go off and do whatever we were interested in, which at that time was military tattoo drumming and religious choral sounds. We just threw it all together and that was Architecture & Morality!'

ANDY MCCLUSKEY, OMD

1981

Number One Singles

John Lennon 'Imagine', John Lennon 'Woman', Joe Dolce 'Shaddap You Face', Roxy Music 'Jealous Guy', Shakin' Stevens 'This Ole House', Bucks Fizz 'Making Your Mind Up', Adam & The Ants 'Stand & Deliver', Smokey Robinson 'Being With You', Michael Jackson 'One Day In Your Life', The Specials 'Ghost Town', Shakin' Stevens 'Green Door', Aneka 'Japanese Boy', Soft Cell 'Tainted Love', Adam & The Ants 'Prince Charming', Dave Stewart & Barbara Gaskin 'It's My Party', The Police 'Every Little Thing She Does Is Magic', Queen & David Bowie 'Under Pressure', Julio Inglesias 'Begin The Beguine', Human League 'Don't You Want Me'

Sounds like...1981

Following the death of John Lennon in December 1980 the early part of this year's charts are given over to his memory. The first new number one single of the year is a reissue of Lennon's classic 'Imagine', which is knocked off the top of the charts four weeks later by a reissue of 'Woman', which in turn – after an inexplicable three weeks of Joe Dolce – gives way to Roxy Music's version of 'Jealous Guy' (which I buy as a single without realising that it isn't actually a Roxy Music original). In the album charts Lennon's collaboration with Yoko Ono, *Double Fantasy*, knocks Adam & The Ants' *Kings Of The Wild Frontier* from the top of the charts to become the second new number one album of the year (although *Kings Of The Wild Frontier* will regain the number one position in March for a further ten weeks, to become 1981's bestselling album).

Putting Lennon aside though, it's the so-called New Romantics who are starting to dominate the charts this year, the term already broadening to include any band with a synthesizer sound and a futuristic haircut. Blitz club original Midge Ure reaches number two with 'Vienna', his debut release with a revitalised Ultravox, and his hand is also felt in two hits from Visage ('Mind Of A Toy' and 'Visage') and Phil Lynott's new *Top Of The Pops* theme 'Yellow Pearl'. Post-punk electronic pioneers the Human League narrow their original line-up down to Phil Oakey and Adrian Wright, recruit two girl singers from a Sheffield nightclub, and go on to release one of the decade's definitive albums – *Dare* – as well as the ubiquitous 'Don't You Want Me', which will become the year's bestselling single, eventually going on to be one of the decade's best selling singles with almost one and a half million UK sales. Meanwhile, in Liverpool Orchestral Manoeuvres In The Dark will release two top five singles with 'Souvenir' and 'Joan Of Arc', and the classic album *Architecture & Morality*.

Former Human League members Martyn Ware and Ian Craig Marsh recruit singer Glenn Gregory and release '(I Don't Want That) Fascist Groove Thing' as Heaven 17, which, although arguably their finest single, will only make number 45 after being banned by the BBC for its overtly political lyrical content. To my shame I miss it entirely. A song it's impossible to miss however is Leeds duo Soft Cell's debut hit 'Tainted Love', an old Northern Soul classic remade in a sleazy, seductive electro-style which will top the charts for a fortnight in September and become one of the very few records that I will always make the mistake of thinking I can

'We had no aspirations to being in a group, we were at school doing our A levels and we didn't join the group because we thought it would bring us fame and fortune, the reason we went on that first tour was because we'd get six weeks off school!'

SUSAN SULLEY, HUMAN LEAGUE

'Depeche Mode's *Speak And Spell* is my ultimate eighties' album because it carries the most typical examples of Vince Clarke's "disposable pop" – candy sweet plastic melodies and lyrics constructed into the melody, not intending to have a meaning.'

HEINER BREUER

'"Vienna" by Ultravox remains my all time favourite single. Something haunting about the video and the vocals.'

AMANDA L

dance to. Soft Cell will have another huge hit with 'Bedsitter' and a top five album with *Non-Stop Erotic Cabaret*, simultaneously turning frontman Marc Almond into an eighties' icon.

The first chapters in two of the greatest success stories of the decade are also written this year. Birmingham's Duran Duran release their first two singles, 'Planet Earth' and 'Girls On Film', plus an album, *Duran Duran*, and Basildon's Depeche Mode release their first singles ('Dreaming Of Me', 'New Life' and 'Just Can't Get Enough') and debut album *Speak And Spell*. At this stage I probably prefer Duran Duran, who seem somehow less poppy and more stylish, but given time it's Depeche Mode who will go on to become possibly my favourite artists of all time. Godfathers of the New Romantic movement, Kraftwerk, meanwhile claim their crown with 'The Model', a track originally released as the B-side to 'Computer Love' which stalls at number 36 in July, but which will make the top-spot when it's reissued – with the sides flipped over – in early 1982.

I am of course a rocker as the year begins, and although there are some notable rock successes this year (Rainbow's 'I Surrender', Motorhead & Girlschool's 'Please Don't Touch', Meat Loaf's 'Dead Ringer For Love' and Slade's 'We'll Bring The House Down') I will have firmly positioned myself in the midst of the New Wave/New Romantic explosion by the time the year draws to a close. It's a step towards a more balanced view of the music that is happening around me, but is still a step away from appreciating the impact of 2-Tone or the eighties' mod movement, which this year offers not only continued success for The Jam (their 'That's Entertainment' will chart at 21 on import sales of a German single

alone in February, and they will have top five success with both 'Funeral Pyre' and 'Absolute Beginners') and the sombrely political sounds of The Specials' finest hour 'Ghost Town' (their sole single release this year) and UB40's 'One In Ten' on the one hand, and the exuberant pop-ska of Madness' 'Shut Up' and Bad Manners' 'Can Can' on the other. 'Can Can' is also an essential part of a new experience for me, the youth-club disco, as one of the records that is played towards the end of the night which not only can we awkward, shuffling boys dance to, but which also allows us to link arms with the girls, at a time when such moments of physical contact are becoming strangely important!

Smokey Robinson's number one single 'Being With You' is the record playing when I have my first ever slow-dance, a rite of passage event which happens to me at a youth-club disco held in the hall of my school. The memory will remain with me for years and the song is destined to be a lifelong

'The ultimate single has to be "Tainted Love" by Soft Cell – I still remember seeing Marc Almond on TV and dancing to it at school discos!'

FLASH

Sounds Like 1981
The Year as a Mixtape

SIDE ONE

Adam & The Ants 'Kings Of The Wild Frontier', Tom Tom Club 'Wordy Rappinghood', Talking Heads 'Once In A Lifetime', Grace Jones 'Pull Up To The Bumper', OMD 'Joan Of Arc', Imagination 'Body Talk', Smokey Robinson 'Being With You', Ultravox 'Vienna', Godley & Creme 'Under Your Thumb', Laurie Anderson 'O Superman', UB40 'One In Ten', The Specials 'Ghost Town', The Pretenders 'I Go To Sleep', Hazel O'Connor 'Will You', Soft Cell 'Bedsitter'

SIDE TWO

Human League 'Don't You Want Me', Kraftwerk 'The Model', Depeche Mode 'Just Can't Get Enough', Duran Duran 'Girls On Film', Landscape 'Einstein A Go Go', Dollar 'Mirror Mirror', Bucks Fizz 'Making Your Mind Up', Cliff Richard 'Wired For Sound', Olivia Newton-John 'Physical', Shakin' Stevens 'This Ole House', Kim Wilde 'Kids In America', Toyah 'Thunder In The Mountains', Queen & David Bowie 'Under Pressure', XTC 'Sergeant Rock', Squeeze 'Labelled With Love'

favourite as a result, although it will take another twenty years or so before I will fully appreciate the extraordinary talent of the man behind the song. It's a sneaky nod towards soul music, which in general is a genre outside my interest, although I do quite like Linx (who release 'Intuition' and 'So This Is Romance' this year), and especially Imagination ('Flashback' and 'Body Talk'). The other key soul and funk offerings this year kind of pass me by, including Michael Jackson's fantastic number one 'One Day in Your Life'. The term disco

seems to be giving way to funk, although – as embodied in 'Can You Feel It' from The Jacksons and Kool & The Gang's 'Get Down On It' – it still sounds pretty much the same to me! There's even a brief foray into salsa-style party rhythms on Modern Romance's hits 'Ay Ay Ay Ay Moosey' and 'Everybody Salsa'. Disco isn't quite dead though, and the *Disco Daze And Disco Nights* compilation proves this point by taking the number one album spot for a week in July.

Possibly as a reaction to the futuristic electronic music that is starting to dominate the charts, old fashioned rock'n'roll makes a reappearance, with US trio the Stray Cats chalking up three hits in the shape of 'Rock This Town', 'Stray Cat Strut' and 'The Race Is On', ably supported by hits from The Jets ('Yes Tonight Josephine') and The Polecats ('John I'm Only Dancing', 'Rockabilly Guy'). But rock'n'roll's true champion this year is Welshman Michael Barrett who,

'Even now The Specials still sound like nothing else around. "Ghost Town" summed up where Thatcher's Britain was heading.'

NICK MILLS

THE HUMAN LEAGUE DARE

under the name Shakin' Stevens, leads the pack with four single hits ('This Ole House' and 'Green Door' are both number ones while 'You Drive Me Crazy' and 'It's Raining' peak at two and ten respectively) and three hit albums (*Shaky* and *This Ole House*, which reached numbers one and two respectively, and Shakin' Stevens, a reissue album of seventies' material that reached 34), and who will go on to become one of the bestselling UK artists of all time.

The New Wave will continue apace this year with The Police notching up another number one single and album ('Every Little Thing She Does Is Magic' and *Ghost In The Machine*), Elvis Costello releasing a cover of George Jones' 'A Good Year For The Roses' (which makes number six), and Grace Jones - promoting the release of her 'Pull Up To The Bumper' single and *Nightclubbing* album - who will make TV history when she slaps chat-show host Russell Harty across the face during a live interview. The line between

New Wave and post punk becomes increasingly blurred; Adam & The Ants cross firmly into the mainstream with the album success of their *Kings Of The Wild Frontier* release and its follow-up *Prince Charming* (which peaks at two in the charts), a pair of number one singles in 'Stand & Deliver' and 'Prince Charming' and two top three hits with a reissued 'Kings Of The Wild Frontier' and 'Ant Rap'.

Another artist who will combine punk style and attitude with chart-friendly material is Toyah, who will have no fewer than four singles hits this year and a platinum album, *Anthem*. Straddling a musical ground that runs from the darkly earnest Siouxsie And The Banshees (who will themselves release a compilation of their hits to date, and have new hits with the singles 'Spellbound' and 'Arabian Knights' and the album *Ju Ju* this year) to the commercial, intelligent pop of Kim Wilde (who will also have four singles hits this year with 'Kids In America', 'Chequered Love', 'Water On Glass' and

'Bucks Fizz's music was infectious, up beat and fun. It got me through many hours of homework and revision for exams. I used to take a photo of them into every exam for good luck.'

CHRIS HAILEY

'Elvis Costello is one of the ultimate eighties' artists
... edgy, edgy, edgy and never boring or repetitive.'

MARILU

'Cambodia' and a number three album *Kim Wilde*), Toyah will appeal across the board and will influence a generation. I am smitten and, although I don't yet know it, Toyah will become a recurring part of my life for many years to come.

Sharing Toyah's path by combining both singing and acting careers are Hazel O'Connor – who has a major hit this year with 'Will You' from the 1980 film *Breaking Glass* – and Clare Grogan, whose band Altered Images will come straight off a tour supporting the Banshees to rack up a pair of bubblegum-pop hits with 'Happy Birthday' and 'I Could be Happy', coinciding neatly with Grogan's appearance in the film *Gregory's Girl*. Pop is no longer a dirty word and a number of exuberant pop singles will be released this year, from the fantastically upbeat 'Favourite Shirts' – the first hit for a youthful Haircut 100 – through the polished pop of Dollar's 'Mirror Mirror' and Bucks Fizz's Eurovision winner 'Making Your Mind Up' to 'Japanese Boy', the quirky number one from Aneka.

The old wave is equally active. Cliff Richard releases his catchy ode to the personal stereo 'Wired For Sound', one of three hits this year and, astonishingly, his 83rd UK single hit

to date. I know I shouldn't really like it but I do, and the video that accompanies the release captures another early eighties' craze – albeit one in which I will never participate – roller disco! Queen will score their first number one single since 1975 with their David Bowie collaboration 'Under Pressure', and Yes singer Jon Anderson hits number six with Vangelis and their collaboration 'I'll Find My Way Home'. Godley & Creme, formerly members of 10cc, will have two top-ten singles this year with 'Under Your Thumb' and 'Wedding Bells' and will also direct the videos for both songs, as well as the controversial and rather saucy video for Duran Duran's 'Girls On Film' and 'I Want To Be Free' and 'Thunder In The Mountains' for Toyah. Genesis release their second number one album, *Abacab*, while their singer Phil Collins will kick off his career as a solo artist with three single hits ('In The Air Tonight', 'I Missed Again', 'If Leaving Me Is Easy') and a number one album in his own right, *Face Value*.

Aneka was the one-hit wonder creation of folk singer Mary Sandeman, who is still active on the Scottish traditional folk scene and regularly plays with the Scottish Fiddle Orchestra.

Joe Dolce's 'Shaddap You Face' is still the most successful pop single in Australian music history and cover versions have been recorded in more than twelve languages, including Aboriginal dialect and pidgin Papua New Guinean.

8

The Jam's 'Absolute Beginners' is named after Paul Weller's favourite book, Colin MacInnes' 1959 novel of the same name. The book was made into a film in 1986 and although David Bowie recorded the title track, Weller's The Style Council do appear on the soundtrack.

Dollar's 'Mirror Mirror' brought Trevor Horn's production skills to the attention of Sheffield's ABC, who after hearing it went on to ask Horn to produce their debut album The Lexicon Of Love.

It will also be a year with more than its fair share of novelty songs. The Tweets' 'Birdie Song' is arguably the main offender, although Joe Dolce's 'Shaddap You Face' will be forever remembered as the record that kept Ultravox's 'Vienna' off the top spot. Dutch act Star Sound are equally inescapable, with their *Stars On 45* album going to number one for five weeks and spawning a frankly terrifying three hit singles. Even TV show *Multi-Coloured Swap Shop* will release a top-twenty single, 'I Wanna Be A Winner', under the name Brown Sauce. Less novelty and more oddity is Dave Stewart & Barbara Gaskin's 'It's My Party', a cover of Lesley Gore's 1963 hit, which stays at number one for four weeks in September.

A novelty of a very different kind is the success of the minimal, hypnotic and experimental 'O Superman' from New York performance artist Laurie Anderson. This innovative, eight-minute long epic will originally be championed by John Peel, but will soon cross into the mainstream to claim a surprise number two singles hit. Elsewhere in the charts there is innovation of a very different kind in the shape of New York art-rock act Talking Heads, whose fusion of rock, pop and funk on 'Once In A Lifetime' sounds startlingly modern and will be accompanied by an equally innovative and memorable video (choreographed by Toni Basil who will go on to have a huge hit with 'Mickey' in 1982). Tom Tom Club, a side project for Talking Heads' Chris Frantz and Tina Weymouth, will also score a major chart hit this year with 'Wordy Rappinghood'.

I WANT MY MTV

It was almost instantly accused of being sexist, racist, homophobic, violent and pornographic; of dumbing-down music, delivering style over content, promoting drug use, undermining morals and promoting bad behaviour. It set out to bring us a diet of rock and roll music, imagery and attitude twenty-four hours a day, seven days a week. Little wonder then that viewers flocked to MTV from the moment of its launch, sealing the channel's success and making it one of the most influential and recognisable brands in the world. Let's face it, MTV was onto a winner from the moment it broadcast its first video and that's before they even brought us 'Beavis & Butthead', 'Jackass' or 'The Osbournes'.

The channel was launched at midnight on 1 August 1981, broadcasting to a modest 800,000 American homes, with the words 'Ladies and gentlemen, rock and roll', a montage of footage of the Apollo 11 moon landing and the airing of MTV's first ever video, The Buggles' 'Video Killed The Radio Star'. Watch MTV today and it's difficult to imagine that originally the channel played nothing but music, a kind of radio station with images - a marriage of rock and roll and television, perhaps the two most important elements of popular culture - nothing like anything we'd seen before.

Even though MTV wouldn't reach the UK and Europe until 1987 we became known as the 'MTV generation' and we rapidly began to expect glossy imagery to accompany our music, the two mediums inextricably linked from this point forward, changing the way music was presented, marketed and consumed forever while making global superstars of the early artists who were quick to deliver style with their music, among them Michael Jackson, Madonna, Prince, Duran Duran and U2.

As with all innovations MTV attracted imitators and competition as quickly as it's novelty wore off and by 1987, when the channel was purchased by media giant Viacom and was set to be launched globally, it underwent the first of several major overhauls which saw the first move away from mainstream music programming towards genre-based music shows, catering to rap, heavy metal and dance music, as well as towards more traditional programming which included game shows, cartoons and reality TV series'. Today of course you're hard pushed to find any music on the channel at all.

Further expansion saw local versions of MTV launched around the world. Dire Straits' 'Money For Nothing' was the first video to be played on MTV Europe when it launched in 1987, its almost dreamlike 'I want my MTV' line, sung by Sting, making it the perfect debut clip while helping to reinvent Dire Straits for a whole new generation of music fans. Since then MTV Europe has been further divided into a series of local versions, while the channel as a whole has been successfully launched across the globe from MTV Latino to MTV Ukraine and MTV China to MTV Arabia.

At time of writing MTV in one form or another is now available in well over 500 million homes around the world.

Peter Gabriel's 'Sledgehammer' is MTV's most played video of all time. 'Sledgehammer' won nine MTV Video Music Awards in 1987, a record it still holds today.

Michael Jackson's 'Thriller' was the first video from a black artist to be fully championed by MTV but the first to be shown on the channel was Grandmaster Flash & The Furious Five's 'The Message' which first aired in October 1982.

The first ten videos to be broadcast on MTV when it originally launched in the USA were 'Video Killed The Radio Star' The Buggles, 'You Better Run' Pat Benatar, 'She Won't Dance With Me' Rod Stewart, 'You Better You Bet' The Who, 'Little Suzi's On The Up' Ph.D., 'We Don't Talk Anymore' Cliff Richard, 'Brass In Pocket' The Pretenders, 'Time Heals' Todd Rundgren, 'Take It On The Run' REO Speedwagon and 'Rockin' The Paradise' by Styx. 'Video Killed The Radio Star' was also the one millionth video to be played.

Greenham Common

Greenham Common is a story that will go on to span two decades, but it started in September 1981 when a Welsh group, Women For Life On Earth, marched from Cardiff to Greenham Common in Berkshire to protest against the decision to site 96 NATO nuclear missiles at the site. On their arrival they delivered a letter to the Base Commander requesting the chance to debate the decision, and when that request was ignored they set up a camp of women and children just outside the airbase.

The protest was largely sidelined by the media until the women of the newly christened Greenham Common Women's Peace Camp began to adopt some of the tactics of the suffragette movement, chaining themselves to the fences, obstructing vehicles entering and leaving RAF Greenham Common and generally disrupting the running of the base. Convoys leaving the base to embark on nuclear exercises were blocked and then followed by protesters who would obstruct the exercises.

In December 1982 the Greenham Common protesters made their biggest statement to date when over 30,000 women, mostly recruited by chain letter, gathered at the base. The protesters at this 'Embrace The Base' event joined hands around the RAF site in peaceful protest and succeeded in bringing their Greenham Common protest to the attention of the world and giving media focus to the peace and feminist movements for almost twenty years.

In April 1983 CND (who weren't directly affiliated with the peace camp, but naturally shared their aims) organised a similar event, this time one that attracted over 70,000 people who joined hands and linked the nuclear bases at Greenham, Aldermaston and Burghfield. It also included several hundred protesters dressed as animals entering RAF Greenham Common and staging a protest picnic.

The last of the high profile Greenham Common events took place in December 1983, shortly after the arrival of the first Cruise Missiles at the base, when around 50,000 women encircled the camp, holding up mirrors and taking down fences. Hundreds of protesters were arrested and faced controversial court cases, fines and even imprisonment.

The peace camp would remain at Greenham Common for 19 years and would witness not only the arrival of the 95 Cruise Missiles starting in November 1983, but also the exit of the last of those weapons in 1991, following the signing of the Intermediate-Range Nuclear Forces treaty by presidents Ronald Reagan and Mikhail Gorbachev in 1987.

Greenham Common ...
Up To Date!

RAF Greenham Common no longer exists and the peace camp finally closed in September 2000. The land has been given over to a business park but it also includes a Women's Peace Camp commemorative and historic site, which is funded and managed by the women who participated in the protests and their supporters.

The Greenham Common Women's Peace Camp was made up of nine different colour-coded encampments around the perimeter of the base, including an exclusively women's camp (the others allowed male visitors during the day), an artists' camp, a New Age camp and a religious camp.

ON

New shows made this year include *Brideshead Revisited, Cagney & Lacey, DangerMouse, Dynasty, The Fall Guy, Game For A Laugh, The Hitchhiker's Guide To The Galaxy, Only Fools & Horses, Postman Pat, Tenko* and *Willo The Wisp.*

OFF

It's the end of an era for *Ask Aspel, Bergerac, Blake's 7, Charlie's Angels, The Dick Emery Show, It Ain't Half Hot Mum, Monkey* and *The Muppet Show*, all of which go out of production this year.

1981

On The Big Screen

Other new cinema releases include *Chariots Of Fire, The Empire Strikes Back, Scanners, Time Bandits, Raiders Of The Lost Ark, The Elephant Man, Clash Of The Titans, Raging Bull, The Blues Brothers, An American Werewolf In London, The Cannonball Run, Diva* and *The Shining* (which is still the single most frightening film I have ever seen!).

Gregory's Girl

In 1981 I was going through that mad gangly stage where my arms and legs seemed too long for my body, my hair utterly refused to do anything I wanted it to (certainly not anything that could be even remotely classified as 'cool'), I was rubbish at sport and, if that wasn't enough, there was suddenly girls everywhere, and I was rubbish with them too.

Gregory's Girl is about a gawky teenage boy with uncool hair who, against all odds, gets the girl. Unsurprisingly, I love it. It's a film about ordinary life at a time when I'm trying to make sense of ordinary life. It also features a character who, for reasons never explained, is always dressed as a penguin and I like that too. Who doesn't like penguins?

Look away now if you've not seen the film because here's the story. Gregory (John Gordon Sinclair) is a scruffy but amiable fifteen-year-old whose place on the school football team is taken by Dorothy (Dee Hepburn), a 'thoroughly modern girl' who runs rings around the boys both on and off the pitch. Gregory, naturally, falls for Dorothy. He awkwardly tries to get to know her better through scheduling extra football practice and taking Italian lessons. Along the line, and much to his own disbelief, he manages to get a date with Dorothy. On the night of the date he undertakes a series of journeys with a number of Dorothy's friends before meeting Susan (Clare Grogan) who turns out to be his intended date for the night. The pair agree on a 'sort of date', which turns out to be perfect; the pair connect, the conversation flows, they lie on the grass and dance to a silent version of The Police's 'Walking On The Moon' before walking home and successfully negotiating their first kiss.

It's how I want my first date to be, and Clare Grogan is the girl I want to have that date with. Unsurprisingly she isn't but, a mere 21 years later, I do interview her for RememberTheEighties.com and the ghost of *Gregory's Girl* still looms large over her career. When I ask her if she resents being remembered in this way she admits, 'There was a wee moment in time when it kind of dragged me down, and I feel slightly ashamed of that now – but it was because I couldn't escape it, no matter what I did it could never be bigger than *Gregory's Girl*. I kind of think now that I was really really privileged to have been a part of such a significant moment in so many people's lives … to have been part of something that captured the mood of a whole generation of people is an amazing thing to have been involved in and I will never, ever knock it.' I don't ask about the penguin.

Gregory's Girl ...Up To Date!

Clare Grogan continues to be involved in acting and TV presenting. She still dabbles in music and has toured sporadically under the Altered Images name since 2002. Dee Hepburn went on to appear in *Crossroads* for several years before leaving acting altogether to start a family. Apparently she now works in cosmetic sales. John Gordon Sinclair has made a number of films since *Gregory's Girl*, notably *Local Hero* (1983), *The Girl In The Picture* (1986) and a *Gregory's Girl* sequel, *Gregory's Two Girls*, in 1999.

The Royal Wedding

'Here is the stuff of which fairy tales are made – the prince and princess on their wedding day' proclaimed the Archbishop of Canterbury on 29th July 1981 after marrying Prince Charles to Lady Diana Spencer in front of an international TV audience of over 700 million people.

The Royal Wedding was the culmination of what felt like years of speculation, frenzy and excitement, but it had actually been just a few months. Charles and Diana had only been a couple since the middle of the previous year and only announced their engagement in February. Odd then that I have no recollection of the actual wedding at all. I can remember some pictures of the wedding; Diana's train shot from above as she walked up the aisle, Charles and Diana leaving the church in an open topped carriage, their kiss on the balcony. But it's possible that these aren't memories at all and I'm just remembering the images from later news footage, or from mugs, tea towels, keyrings, posters, stamps, coins or any one of the estimated 1600 different items of merchandise produced for the day. The only facts I can confidently remember are that Diana was a fan of Duran Duran and that Spike Milligan, one of my favourite comedians, was among the wedding guests.

The celebrations started in earnest the night before the wedding when, despite a third night of riots in Toxteth, over a hundred official bonfires were lit across the UK, culminating in a huge pyrotechnic display in Hyde Park. People slept on the streets along the wedding route to ensure that they got a good view the next day, when almost a million people turned out to watch the wedding procession live. A further 28 million tuned in on TV, giving the wedding the UK's second highest television audience of the eighties (second only to the Christmas Day episode of *EastEnders* in 1986 when Den presents Angie with divorce papers).

By all accounts the wedding day – a national holiday – was a perfect summer day and Lady Diana travelled to St Paul's Cathedral in a fairytale glass coach wearing a £20,000 wedding dress made by Elizabeth and David Emmanuel. The ceremony, in front of 2500 guests, went off successfully, although Diana did mix up Charles' names (calling him Philip Charles Arthur George) and Charles stumbled over his vows, and the couple emerged from the Cathedral and made their way to Buckingham Palace in a open carriage cheered by joyous crowds before appearing on the Palace balcony and sealing their marriage with a public kiss.

The Royal Wedding . . . Up To Date!

Diana went on to become one of the most famous women in the world and gave birth to Princes William (1982) and Harry (1984). The couple separated in 1992 and divorced in 1996. Diana tragically died in a road accident in Paris in 1997. The Prince of Wales went on to marry Camilla Parker Bowles in 2005.

Gambian President Sir Dawda Jawara attended the wedding only to be told on his arrival that he had been deposed by a political coup launched in his absence.

Lady Diana first met Prince Charles in 1977 when the Prince was briefly dating her elder sister, Lady Sarah Spencer.

Lady Diana's dress was made from forty yards of silk taffeta, one hundred yards of crinoline and some lace that once belonged to Queen Mary. It was covered in thousands of mother-of-pearl sequins.

Diana's stepmother was the only daughter of romantic novelist Barbara Cartland.

1981 ICON ▶▶ Toyah Willcox

Obsession is an extreme word, but in some situations it's the only word and this is one of those situations. This story rather appropriately starts on Valentine's Day 1981, the day that Toyah releases the 4-track 'Four From Toyah' EP. 'It's A Mystery', the EP's lead track, will go on to be something of an eighties' classic, and I quite like the song, but it's Toyah herself who captures my imagination. She's a colourful, charismatic, rebellious figure and I'm hooked. A trip to Parrot Records in Chelmsford (a thrillingly dark punk and rock shop) reveals that Toyah has already released three albums, including a live album *Toyah! Toyah! Toyah!* which is the one I buy, the first album I purchase with my own money.

The album is a revelation, precisely capturing the energy and potential I had hoped for, and from this point on I am a fan. I buy everything and absorb facts about Toyah, her career, her lyrics, even the catalogue numbers of her releases (I think it's a boy thing – I never set out to learn them, I just sort of picked them up as I went along!). I collect everything Toyah-related I can lay my hands on, even cutting out tiny mentions in the press. It's not particularly cool to like Toyah but I don't care. Toyah is everything to me and I spend hours making compilation tapes of B-sides and album tracks for my friends, designed to convert them to the Toyah way. It rarely works but I love making the tapes! Fortunately my best friend is also a fan and we obsess together.

Toyah releases no less than four singles in 1981 – the 'Four From Toyah' EP, 'I Want To be Free', the 'Four More From Toyah' EP (lead track 'Good Morning Universe') and 'Thunder In The Mountains' – as well as an album, *Anthem*. I loved everything, how could I not? I knew all the words to all the songs, I knew the credits on the album (years later I will still be able to reel them off: 'Produced by Nick Tauber', 'Sleeve by John Gordon', 'Hair by Keith at Smile'). Everything is a huge hit and Toyah is everywhere. *Anthem* goes platinum and is in the album charts for 46 weeks.

The holy grail of being a Toyah fan is, of course, to see her in concert and to meet her. My first Toyah concert is at London's Hammersmith Odeon in July 1982; it's the tour for her album *The Changeling* and just to be sure we're there in time we arrive at the venue before lunch, a mere eight hours before the doors open. I don't get to meet Toyah that day, but we do pass our autograph books to her bodyguard, Tom, and he gets them signed for us, and the thrill of holding that autograph is indescribable: 'To Richard,

Love Toyah' and a kiss. A kiss! The concert is incredible, not just the spectacle of the show but the almost tribal validation of being in a room with three thousand other people who obviously understand. It is also recorded and parts of it are released on her 1982 live double-album *Warrior Rock*, the ultimate souvenir and to my mind one of the best live albums ever.

I continue to follow Toyah avidly and obsessively and I finally meet her for the first time in 1983, briefly, at the stage door of the Mermaid Theatre in London - during her run in the wrestling play *Trafford Tanzi* - the first of many stage-door meetings.

By 1992 I am working for a record label in London and Toyah is looking for a new record deal, so a mutual friend introduces us backstage at the Marquee Club after her fantastic comeback show … our first meeting as equals, although it certainly doesn't feel like that to me and I blow my cool by asking to have my picture taken with her! Nothing comes of the meeting but our paths will cross a few times over the next few years, which is thrilling but strange because every time we meet I feel like a thirteen-year-old fan again and I struggle to behave normally in such strange circumstances.

When the Connoisseur label reissue the two most commercially successful Toyah albums, *Anthem* and *The Changeling*, on CD in 1999, I use my newfound familiarity to request an interview with her, for the American magazine *Lexicon*, which also becomes the first interview on my RememberTheEighties.com website when I launch it in 2002. The conversation here is mostly taken from that original interview, although I have brought it up date somewhat by including parts of a second interview I did with her for my website in 2006.

GAUMONT THEATRE
IPSWICH
Telephone 53641

Stalls   Seat No.

L   35

TOYAH

7.30 p.m.

MON., 28th NOVEMBER

Admission £4.50

Official merchandising on sale only in Theatre
Retain this portion   No cameras in Theatre

Printed by The Halesworth Press Limited

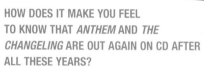

HOW DOES IT MAKE YOU FEEL TO KNOW THAT *ANTHEM* AND *THE CHANGELING* ARE OUT AGAIN ON CD AFTER ALL THESE YEARS?

I'm relieved they've come out because for years people have been asking me to put them out and nothing's been done about it. What's even better for me is that it's *The Changeling* which has been the most positively received. When we first released *The Changeling* it was such a huge departure from *Anthem* that it actually got slated in the press. It sold well – but not as well as *Anthem* – and it's actually a better album and that's bloody brilliant, I'm really chuffed about that!

ANTHEM WAS RELEASED AT A TIME WHEN YOU WERE AT YOUR MOST COMMERCIALLY SUCCESSFUL, WAS THERE PRESSURE ON YOU TO MAKE A 'HIT' ALBUM?

Well it just happened! It was a fantastic

time, I mean there was just such a buzz ... we did a tour in, I think, early 1981 – when we knew 'It's A Mystery' was coming out on the 'Four From Toyah' EP – and I was almost embarrassed about 'It's A Mystery', I just hated it, but it was so well received on tour! Then I went off to do *Tales Of The Unexpected* and the new band was put together by Nick Tauber (the producer) – I wasn't even around because I was away filming – and they went into the studio and recorded the backing tracks without me even meeting them all, and it was just fucking brilliant!

WHEN YOU WENT BACK INTO THE STUDIO TO MAKE *THE CHANGELING* WERE YOU SCARED THAT YOU WOULDN'T BE ABLE TO MATCH THE SUCCESS OF *ANTHEM*?

Well, I was quite depressed at the time. We did *Anthem*, we toured the whole year, and we finished by doing the *Old Grey Whistle Test* live on Christmas Eve, which played to 12 million people. That was such a pinnacle of a night and I never really got over it. I was expected to write an album over the winter, which is the worst time of year with me, and I was finding it incredibly difficult. The pressures were incredible because I was doing interviews all day and that's not very inspiring ... you're kind of left drained. So I found that by the time I settled down to write it I was so angry and so anxious to get away from everything that *The Changeling* came out

as quite a dark piece. I was coming into the studio in very dark moods and incredibly emotional and I cried my way through that album, but in retrospect I think that it's quite a remarkable record.

WERE YOU PUSHED BY THE RECORD COMPANY TO COME UP WITH SOMETHING TO MATCH THE COMMERCIAL SUCCESS OF *ANTHEM*?

No, they were actually the only people who would listen to me and again that had a detrimental effect because I was going through a time when I shouldn't have been listened to! I needed someone ... I needed a bit of a guru or a mentor, to tone me down because the potential was infinite. That's what really baffled me because I could have gone in any direction and I didn't really know which choices to make. I was just writing and writing and writing all day long, every day, and coming up with tons of ideas but not able to formulate them because there wasn't enough time.

IN VIEW OF ALL THE TURMOIL YOU WERE GOING THROUGH WHILE YOU WERE MAKING THE RECORD, WAS IT A RELIEF WHEN IT DIDN'T PERFORM IN THE SAME STRATOSPHERIC WAY THAT *ANTHEM* DID?

'I always remember Toyah saying on a chat show, "Dye your hair and give yourself a chance in life." And she was right!'

ANDREW

No, it was terrible! 'Creepy Room', which I think is about the best song I've ever written, 'Run Wild, Run Free' and 'Castaways' are among the most exploratory writing that I'd ever done and you can hear their influence elsewhere … they were copied in little ways and I'm incredibly proud about it because for me, OK it may not have been a huge commercial success, but people did listen to it!

IF *THE CHANGELING* WAS WRITTEN TO BE PERFORMED, WAS YOUR LIVE ALBUM *WARRIOR ROCK* A DELIBERATE FOLLOW UP, TO PRESENT THOSE SONGS IN THAT WAY?

We were really one of the best live acts around at the time and we wanted to concentrate all our work on live work, and therefore *The Changeling* had to have a certain live feel. Interestingly *Warrior Rock* was reviewed as the greatest live album ever. It got better reviews than *The Changeling* and it was as if the music had to be played in. What we had with our first few albums were tours playing the music before we recorded. *Anthem* and *The Changeling* were the first albums we recorded when we'd never played the music live, and that is terrifying because you really grow into a record when you play it live.

YOU'VE NEVER REALLY STOPPED PLAYING LIVE HAVE YOU, AND RECENTLY YOU'VE BEEN ON SOME OF THOSE BIG TOURS ALONGSIDE A LOAD OF OTHER ARTISTS, HOW DIFFERENT IS THAT?

The whole thing about being on a bill with other artists is that it's not such a strain, at least I find that! I really enjoy sharing a bill with other people because you just feel you can get on with being you, rather than being someone who has to solve all the problems, who has to deal with the ticket sales and just has to get involved with everything except just being a creative musician.

IT MUST BE REALLY NICE TO BE IN THAT BUBBLE FOR A WHILE.

It is really nice and it kind of puts me back in love with music again! For me music has become more about accountants than about music and my big problem with the music industry at the moment is that it's just not about spontaneity any more, so to kind of be with a group of like-minded people and be in that bubble is a really nice place to be, and it reminds you of just why you did it in the first place.

ARE YOU STILL WRITING?

Well there is a lot going on at the moment. I'm writing on my own and I'm writing with my band but, because I'm not solely a musician, I do have to prioritise the higher profile stuff first, but I am always writing. I'm writing to some of my husband's soundscapes and I'm also writing some stuff with my band.

YOU INFLUENCED A GENERATION OF GIRLS – AND BOYS AS WELL – TO EXPERIMENT WITH THEIR IMAGE … MANY PEOPLE HAVE CONFESSED TO ME OF HAVING PAINSTAKINGLY PAINTED BIRDS ON THEIR FACES, BUT WHAT HAS BEEN YOUR OWN FAVOURITE LOOK?

The birds. Because it's so delicate, and I was very thin at the time and the cheek-bones look great and everything was right.

HOW MUCH OF THOSE IMAGES CAME FROM YOU?

Well we used to have meetings and with 'Brave New World' we had a meeting about what I wanted to portray and I'd seen Caroline Cohen's paintings, her artwork, so I asked if she could do anything like that on my face, something more literal and delicate and she said yes so we just let her get on with it.

HOW STRONGLY DO YOU IDENTIFY WITH YOUR PAST LOOKS?

Well, they are history and I like them and I'm proud of them, but I don't really identify with it – it's history. But obviously when you see certain things you can see your own influences, and in a way I'm most proud of that.

'Toyah was, and still is, ahead of her time - her voice is so unique and her images were so bright, zany and out there. She's a true face of the eighties.'

STEVE SHAW

1982

Snapshot

UK unemployment figures exceed three million ● Laker Airways goes bust ● The European Court of Human Rights rules that teachers who physically punish children against the wishes of their parents are in breach of the Human Rights Convention ● London's Barbican Centre opens ● The Falklands War begins on 2nd April and continues for 74 days ● Canada gains full political independence from the United Kingdom ● Spurs beat QPR 1-0 to win the FA Cup ● Three-quarters of a million people attend a rally against nuclear weapons in New York's Central Park ● Prince William is born ● Roy Jenkins is elected leader of the SDP ● Michael Fagan breaks into Buckingham Palace, gains access to the Queen's bedroom and spends ten minutes chatting to the monarch ● Italy beat West Germany 3-1 to win the World Cup ● Helmut Kohl becomes Chancellor of Germany ● Barbra Streisand's *Love Songs* is the bestselling UK album of the year ● Disney World in Epcot, Florida opens ● Henry VIII's flagship the *Mary Rose* is raised after being underwater since 1545, and TV channel Channel 4 is launched in the UK (the first show broadcast is *Countdown*) ● The Soviet Union invades Afghanistan ● Israel invades Lebanon ● Dexys Midnight Runners' 'Come On Eileen' is the bestselling UK single of the year ● At Greenham Common over 30,000 women protest against the nuclear base there by forming a nine-mile human chain around the perimeter ● John Belushi, Thelonious Monk, Arthur Lowe, Grace Kelly and Ingrid Bergman pass away ● The Coca-Cola Company introduce Diet Coke ● USA Today is launched ● The term 'Voicemail' is patented by Texas Instruments ● Pope John Paul II is the first Pope since 1531 to visit Britain ● The Boeing 747 makes its first commercial flight ● The 20p coin is introduced ● Ozzy Osbourne is hospitalised after biting the head off a bat during a concert

'For me, Japan managed to do that rare thing which was to combine a slick, superficial, glamorous image with sophisticated, layered, well-crafted music that had bags of integrity. In short, they managed to marry art and artifice – no mean feat.'

LEE KYNASTON

Sounds like...1982

Any sort of credible New Romantic movement is well over by 1982, the mainstream having absorbed the influence and style to the extent that even Princess Diana is sporting pedal-pushers and ruffled shirts, and although some of the artists emerging from the scene successfully manage to reinvent themselves and remain contemporary, others are less successful. Visage will release *The Anvil*, which will reach number six in the album charts, and a pair of great singles in 'Damned Don't Cry' and 'Night Train', but it's pretty much the end of their run of success. Japan will also bow out after their most successful year in which will they release no less than six top-forty singles, among them 'Ghosts', 'I Second That Emotion' and 'Nightporter'. I will love 'I Second That Emotion' without realising that it's a cover of an old Smokey Robinson hit and when I finally hear the original I think someone is covering Japan.

Blitz Club regulars Jeremy Healy and Kate Garner will reach number eleven as Haysi Fantayzee with 'John Wayne Is Big Leggy' but their success will be overshadowed in September when Culture Club make their *Top Of The Pops* debut with 'Do You Really Want To Hurt Me?' and the club's most famous son, Boy George, provokes a massive 'is it a boy or is it a girl' debate across the media and in school playgrounds around the country. The song

will reach number one and establish Boy George as one of the decade's most striking and charismatic icons. Culture Club's second single, 'Time (Clock Of The Heart)', will go to number three in November on the back of a top five placing for their debut album *Kissing To Be Clever*. Spandau Ballet, meanwhile, will release their second album, *Diamond*, in March. The album will peak at fifteen but its third single 'Instinction', remixed by Trevor Horn, will be the band's first move away from New Romanticism, a hint of an emerging soul-sound for the band and a deliberate change of direction as the band's Gary Kemp will explain when I interview him in 2003, 'After being on *Top Of The Pops* six times there comes a moment when you realise that you can't continue being a cult group, and if we were going to continue and succeed … it had to be with a much more song orientated record'.

The Human League release a new single 'Mirror Man', which will reach number two, and a reissue of their 'Being Boiled' will become a much deserved hit when it reaches number six. Depeche Mode, picking themselves up after the departure of songwriter Vince Clarke, will still manage to release three singles and the album *A Broken Frame*; 'See You' and 'Dreaming Of Me' are very much pop

'Duran Duran's *Rio* summed up the mood of 1982 and onwards. Exotic places, champagne, living the high life. It's an album I have played and played and played.'

AMANDA L

Bucks Fizz 'The Land Of Make Believe', Shakin' Stevens 'Oh Julie', Kraftwerk 'The Model', The Jam 'Town Called Malice', Tight Fit 'The Lion Sleeps Tonight', Goombay Dance Band 'Seven Tears', Bucks Fizz 'My Camera Never Lies', Paul McCartney & Stevie Wonder 'Ebony & Ivory', Nicole 'A Little Peace', Madness 'House Of Fun', Adam Ant 'Goody Two Shoes', Charlene 'I've Never Been To Me', Captain Sensible 'Happy Talk', Irene Cara 'Fame', Dexy's Midnight Runners 'Come On Eileen', Survivor 'Eye Of The Tiger', Musical Youth 'Pass The Dutchie', Culture Club 'Do You Really Want To Hurt Me?', Eddy Grant 'I Don't Wanna Dance', The Jam 'Beat Surrender', Renee & Renato 'Save Your Love'

'"Come On Eileen" by Dexys is my ultimate eighties single. I'd just left school and it was my first clubbing experience, dancing with my arms behind my back . . . doh!'

ANDY RAVEN

'Grandmaster Flash & The Furious Five were my ultimate eighties act. I loved pop but they made me fall in love with hip hop, a music I still love today.'

SIMON

'A Flock of Seagulls' look rather detracted from the excellence of their music. Even now I judge a person by their answer to one simple question: A Flock of Seagulls - synth band or guitar band? Those in the know always say the latter.'

LEE KYNASTON

singles, but the third – 'Leave In Silence' – is a hint of the darker more serious material to come. Vince Clarke meanwhile goes on to greater success with his new project with singer Alison Moyet, Yazoo, whose first singles 'Only You' and 'Don't Go' will reach three and four on the singles chart respectively, preceding the duo's debut album *Upstairs At Eric's*, which goes to number two. Duran Duran's second album *Rio* will also peak at two when it is released in April but will remain in the UK album charts for over two years. Duran Duran will also release three top-ten singles from the album this year, with 'Hungry Like The Wolf', 'Save A Prayer' and 'Rio'. Other new acts to make major waves this year are Tears For Fears, whose debut single 'Mad World' peaks at three, and A Flock Of Seagulls, who have their only top-forty hits with 'Wishing (If I Had A Photograph Of You)' and 'Space Age Love Song', although frontman Mike Score's haircut will be forever remembered.

Soul and funk seem to make something of a comeback in 1982, Marvin Gaye will enjoy his first hit for five years in October with the classic 'Sexual Healing' and Paul McCartney & Stevie Wonder will enjoy a number one single and massive international success with 'Ebony & Ivory'. Artists previously associated with the disco scene are also updating their sound for the eighties, and this year will see disco queen Donna Summer back in the charts with 'State Of Independence', Evelyn 'Champagne' King in the top ten with 'Love Come Down' and Shalamar chalking up an impressive four hits including top tens with 'I Can Make You Feel Good', 'A Night To Remember' and 'There It Is', as well as a top ten album Friends. Shakatak will also have their highest charting single with 'Night Birds'. Not being much of a soul fan I will spend the year constantly

confusing Shakatak with Shalamar and vice versa, to the understandable derision of my funkier friends! Despite my continued neutrality towards soul it does provide a number of records which will soundtrack those 'end of the disco' slow dances this year, including Hot Chocolate's 'It Started With A Kiss', which could have been made for such an occasion, and Fat Larry's Band's hit 'Zoom', which I will go so far as to buy this year, just because it reminds me of a girl I like.

Musical Youth, a Birmingham reggae act whose members are all aged between twelve and sixteen, will have one of the year's biggest hits with their number one single 'Pass The Dutchie'. They will go on to sell over four million copies of the single around the world and spark much debate over the true meaning of the word 'dutchie'. It turns out that the song is based on the Mighty Diamonds' marijuana anthem 'Pass The Kouchie' but the words are altered to make the song more family friendly. 'Dutchie' is a cooking pot, but at

'My ultimate eighties single is "Rock the Casbah" by The Clash, because it was fun, pure rock, and definitely a social commentary – all that the eighties were about. And the Clash kick serious ass.'

ASHLEY DEAN

my school we all think it's about drugs anyway!

The year also brings a new sound to the fore which is more to my taste, a style previously hinted at in the UK with Sugarhill Gang's 1979 single 'Rapper's Delight' but which had already started to cross into the US mainstream at the start of the decade. It's the sound of urban America; a fusion of styles incorporating soul, funk and electronic elements, combined with the attitude of punk and showcasing innovative scratching and breaking DJ techniques and rapped vocals. August will see Afrika Bambaataa's Kraftwerk-sampling 'Planet Rock' reach the top sixty and Grandmaster Flash & The Furious Five's 'The Message' hit number eight. Hot on their heels is arguably the first hip-hop record from a British artist, in the form of Malcolm McLaren's 'Buffalo Girls', a collaboration with the US crew The World's Famous Supreme Team, which will reach number nine in December. For me in Essex, listening to 'The Message' and Whodini's 'Magic's Wand' is like glimpsing

an alien world – a world of ghettos, graffitti and pan-handlers, populated by DJs, MCs, rappers and crews – a long way from the America I'm used to seeing on television!

The early eighties' mod movement is to take a triple blow this year, from which it will never really recover: Terry Hall, Lynval Golding and Neville Staple will leave The Specials and form dour pop trio Fun Boy Three; The Jam will release their sixth album *The Gift* (their first number one album) and a pair of chart-topping singles, 'Town Called Malice' and 'Beat Surrender', and split up after a final UK tour; and The Beat will call it a day after a third album, *Special Beat Service*, and three singles which will fail to enter the top forty. Fun Boy Three however will release four top-twenty singles this year including 'It Ain't What You Do It's the Way That You Do It' and 'Really Saying Something', both collaborations with the then unknown Bananarama (who in turn will have their debut hit this year with 'Shy Boy'). The success of Fun Boy Three is effectively

1982

Number One Albums

Human League Dare, Barbra Streisand Love Songs, The Jam The Gift, Iron Maiden The Number Of The Beast, Status Quo 1982, Barry Manilow Barry Live In Britain, Paul McCartney Tug Of War, Madness Complete Madness, Roxy Music Avalon, ABC The Lexicon Of Love, Various Artists Fame OST, The Kids From Fame Fame, Dire Straits Love Over Gold, ABBA The Singles, John Lennon The John Lennon Collection

In 2006 Captain Sensible founded The Blah! Party, a political protest party that aims to give mainstream politics 'a kick up the jacksie'.

In December 1982 The Cure's Robert Smith joined Siouxsie & The Banshees as guitarist while continuing to work on Cure projects, and making an album as The Glove with the Banshees' Steve Severin.

Donna Summer's 'State Of Independence' was produced by the legendary Quincy Jones and featured Michael Jackson on vocals and Eric Clapton on guitar.

'I've had ABC's *The Lexicon of Love* for twenty years and still to this day every time I put it on it feels like a special occasion. There isn't one single track that I'd ever think about skipping past.'

MARK A. EVANS

the end of The Specials, who revert back to their previous name Special AKA on subsequent releases. Fortunately both Madness and Bad Manners will both go from strength to strength, Madness having a great year during which they will release four of their most loved singles – 'Cardiac Arrest', 'Driving In My Car', 'Our House' and their only number one 'House Of Fun' – while Bad Manners will release perhaps their daftest single, 'My Girl Lollipop'.

Dexys Midnight Runners, however, a band who appeared on the legendary 2-Tone tour in 1979 and who came very close to signing to the label at the start of the eighties, will firmly turn their back on any lingering mod connections by utilising Celtic and folk influences, adopting a new gypsy image and going on to have 1982's bestselling single – a number one in the UK and the US – 'Come On Eileen'. The video for the track is notable not only for featuring Bananarama's Siobhan Fahey's sister Marie, but also for launching its own dance trend, where dancers clasp their hands behind their back and step from one foot to the other in an increasingly frenzied way as the record accelerates towards its ending. It's a dance much imitated at the school discos I attend and will still be seen at parties and eighties clubs long after that.

Although my heavy metal days are well behind me I'm still enough of a rock fan to appreciate that this is another great year for rock music. Iron Maiden's seventh single, the fantastic 'Run To The Hills', will peak at number two in February and precede the band's first number one album, the classic *Number Of The Beast*. More mainstream rock hits include Joan Jett & The Blackhearts' 'I Love Rock & Roll', which will reach number four in April, Survivor's 'Eye Of The Tiger', which will hit number one in July propelled there by its

use in the soundtrack to the film Rocky III, and Laura Branigan's 'Gloria', which will peak at number six in December. The J. Geils Band will have two hits with 'Centrefold' and 'Freeze-Frame'. I will buy both of them, as well as the Steve Miller Band's 'Abracadabra', but pass on Chicago's middle of the road hit 'Hard To Say I'm Sorry' on the grounds that it's not proper rock and is really a record for girls, which you'd think would also be reason enough to stop me singing along every time it comes on the radio in the car in later life. It isn't.

Punk veterans The Clash will release their *Combat Rock* album, which reaches number two, but their singles 'Rock The Casbah' and 'Should I Stay Or Should I Go' will only reach thirteen and seventeen respectively. The Stranglers have more success and will release their two most successful chart singles – 'Golden Brown' and 'Strange Little Girl' this year. Captain Sensible will leave The Damned, reinvent himself as a cartoon pop star and promptly score a number one

single with 'Happy Talk' while Adam's original Ants, now working with teenage singer Annabella Lwin under the name Bow Wow Wow, will have their most successful year with two top-ten hits, 'Go Wild In The Country' and 'I Want Candy', and countless column-inches of controversy over nude pictures of seventeen-year-old Annabella on their record covers. Adam himself will launch his solo career in style when his debut single 'Goody Two Shoes' reaches number one, and 'Friend Or Foe' and 'Desperate But Not Serious' and an album *Friend Or Foe* follow it into the charts.

Siouxsie & The Banshees and The Cure bridge the gap between punk and what will become known as goth. The Banshees' single 'Fireworks' will peak at 22 this year and their *A Kiss In The Dreamhouse* album will reach eleven. The Cure do better in the album charts: *Pornography* will reach number eight, but their singles 'The Hanging Garden' and 'Let's Go To Bed' will only reach 34 and 44 respectively. Approaching goth from a New Romantic direction, Classix Nouveaux's 'Is It A Dream' will be their only top-forty hit, while Soft Cell follow a similar path releasing a pair of dark, epic hits, 'Torch' and 'Say Hello, Wave Goodbye'.

ABC will burst onto the music scene with an exuberant run of hits including two of the eighties' most definitive singles, 'The Look Of Love' and 'Poison Arrow', and one of the decade's greatest albums, *The Lexicon Of Love*. It's part of a new wave of intelligent pop which this year also includes The Associates, whose 'Party Fears Two' single and *Sulk* album are among the finest releases of 1982, and Talk Talk, whose singles 'Today' and 'Talk Talk' will both reach the top thirty, as will their debut album *The Party's Over*. A surprise success this year is Wah!'s 'Story Of The Blues' in December, as

singer Pete Wylie tells me when I speak to him in 2002: 'There was a big Christmas show being recorded up at Granada and Duran Duran got caught swapping their tapes or something weird and they got kicked off the show, and we were the nearest band! We got this Christmas show which was fantastic … the record went from number six hundred and twenty-two million to number twenty-four and then the week after to number six, and then to number three!'

It will also be a great year for two of the most unashamedly poppy bands of the eighties: Haircut 100, will score major hits with 'Love Plus One', 'Fantastic Day' and 'Nobody's Fool' and a number two album *Pelican West*, and Bucks Fizz, who will capitalise on their 1981 Eurovision Song Contest win with a trio of top-ten hits including a number one single 'My Camera Never Lies' and a top ten album *Are You Ready?*

As ever 1982 will have its share of one-hit wonders and oddities. Tight Fit will be on the singles charts for three months with 'The Lion Sleeps Tonight', which ends up at number one, as does Renee & Renato's 'Save My Love', the year's Christmas number one. There will also be chart-topping singles for The Goombay Dance Band with 'Seven Tears', and for German student Nicole with her Eurovision Song Contest winner 'A Little Peace'. German act Trio, meanwhile, reach number

two in July with 'Da Da Da' – apparently an exercise in Neue Deutsche Fröhlichkeit (New German Cheerfulness) techniques, which reduce complex song structures to simple forms. I buy it. Toni Basil will also take a number two position with her cheerleading anthem 'Mickey', while Toto Coelo score a number eight hit with their sole hit, the bizarre 'I Eat Cannibals'. Clannad's gorgeous 'Theme From Harry's Game' will not be their only hit (they will hit the top twenty in 1986 and 1989, both times with 'In A Lifetime', their collaboration with U2 frontman Bono) but it's by far their biggest when it peaks at five, and Monsoon's 'Ever So Lonely' will sadly be their sole chart success as the act will split shortly afterwards following tensions with their label over musical direction.

As the year ends Michael Jackson releases *Thriller,* his second solo album, which will go on to be not only the soundtrack to 1983 but also the bestselling album of all time.

E.T.
The Extra-Terrestrial

When it was first released *E.T.* rapidly became the highest grossing film of all time, and with box-office takings approaching a billion dollars, it remains in the top twenty to this day, the single most successful movie of the eighties. Not bad for a low-budget film about an alien with a glowing heart and finger whose facial characteristics were inspired in part by Albert Einstein, Ernest Hemingway and a pug dog.

E.T. is an alien botanist stranded on earth who is pursued by government agents before meeting and befriending ten-year-old Elliott (played by Henry Thomas) and his brother Michael (Robert MacNaughton) and sister Gertie (Drew Barrymore). As their friendship deepens *E.T.* and Elliott start to communicate and develop a psychic link. Elliott helps E.T. build a communication device so the alien can send a message home asking to be rescued, but E.T. quickly becomes ill and, because of their connection, Elliott suffers with him. The government agents intervene and Elliott recovers as the psychic link is severed when *E.T.* appears to die. The alien secretly revives and escapes with Elliott and his friends to rendezvous with a spaceship sent to rescue him. *E.T.* departs after a tearful farewell, leaving behind a bond of friendship that will never be broken.

The film was nominated for no less than nine Oscars when it came out, and went on to win four of them (Best Original Music Score, Sound, Sound Effects Editing and Visual Effects) as well as earning composer John Williams three Grammy Awards for the soundtrack. Michael Jackson also won a Grammy, for 'Best Recording For Children', for his spoken word version of the *E.T.* story.

I didn't see the film when it first came out because I thought it was a bit of a kids' film. In fact I didn't end up seeing it for another five years until I was a student, and yes, when I did see it I cried!

E.T.
was originally called 'A Boy's Life' and Steven Spielberg worked on the story while he filmed *Raiders Of The Lost Ark*.

The screenplay for *E.T.* was written by Harrison Ford's wife, Melissa Mathison. Ford himself was filmed for the movie, playing the part of the school principal, but his part was cut by Steven Spielberg.

British Telecom are said to have paid £120 million to license *E.T.* and the phrase 'Phone Home' for forty television adverts in the nineties.

E.T. The Extra-Terrestrial ...Up To Date!

Director Steven Spielberg produced a reworked version of E.T. to coincide with the film's twentieth anniversary in 2002, adding new scenes and special effects that were not possible in the original due to budgetary restraints or technical limitations. He has always refused to make a sequel but a novel, *E.T.: The Book Of The Green Planet*, based on a story by Spielberg, was published in 1985. Henry Thomas went on to appear in many more films but will forever be known as the boy who played Elliott, while Drew Barrymore would famously go on to be a Hollywood wild-child and a major star.

1982

On The Big Screen

Other new cinema releases include *Flashdance, Airplane II, Scarface, First Blood, Annie, Blade Runner, Diner, Cat People, Gandhi, Poltergeist, Tootsie, Tron* and *Fast Times At Ridgemont High*.

THE FALKLANDS WAR

Argentina was a troubled nation in 1982. The country's relatively new military dictatorship was rapidly losing popularity, inflation was up by over one hundred and fifty per cent and unemployment was soaring. The Argentine president, General Leopoldo Galtieri, was under pressure to do something to restore a sense of national pride to his ailing nation, and a row over an Argentine businessman flying his country's flag on the British-owned Falkland Islands gave him the excuse to try to seize the islands and bring them under Argentine rule. Indeed, the Falklands had once been part of the Spanish Empire, and the islands' control by the British had long been an affront to Argentina's pride. Galtieri, who was already plotting to invade the islands the following year, saw his chance to bring his plans forward and give his country a victory to celebrate, and a diversion from the nation's precarious affairs.

The Falkland Islands, located just 350 miles from the coast of Argentina, were invaded by an Argentine naval taskforce on 2nd April, easily overpowering the token garrison of eighty Royal Marines stationed there. General Galtieri believed that the UK would not go to war over the tiny cluster of islands – whose population of sheep and penguins far exceeded the number of people – located over 8000 miles from British shores. To his surprise and cost the British government immediately announced its intention to fight to reclaim the islands, and by 5th April British ships and troops were already on their way to the Falklands, and the United Nations was demanding the immediate withdrawal of Argentina's troops.

Diplomatic talks failed and the British went on to retake the island of South Georgia on 25th April. On 1st May the British mounted a series of air raids against Argentine positions around the Falklands' capital, Port Stanley, and on 4th May the British nuclear submarine HMS *Conqueror* sank the Argentine ship the *General Belgrano*, killing 368 men. Argentina's forces retaliated and destroyed HMS *Sheffield*, going on to sink HMS *Ardent*, *Antelope* and *Coventry*. By 20th May another round of peace talks had failed and UK troops landed on the islands, liberating the tiny settlement at Goose Green on the 28th and advancing on Port Stanley. On 8th June Argentine forces destroyed two British supply ships – the *Sir Galahad* and the *Sir Tristram* – killing around two hundred men. The British forces advanced on Port Stanley on 12th June and the Argentinians finally surrendered on the 14th.

The population of the Falklands Islands in 2006 was 2967 people, around 600,000 sheep and over six million penguins.

The financial cost to the UK of fighting the Falklands War is estimated to be over £700 million.

A total of 890 people died in the Falklands War and a further 1845 were wounded.

The Falklands War ... Up To Date!

Instead of diverting attention from the political and economic crises in Argentina, the war instead highlighted the failings of the country's military government and only served to hasten Galtieri's downfall and restore democratic leadership. In the UK, however, the wave of patriotic feeling generated by the victory was a significant factor in Margaret Thatcher's re-election in the 1983 General Election. Full diplomatic relations between Britain and Argentina weren't properly restored until 1990.

THE Sun

Tuesday, May 4, 1982   14p   TODAY'S TV: PAGE 12

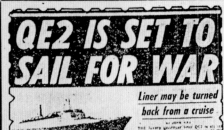

QE2 IS SET TO SAIL FOR WAR

Liner may be turned back from a cruise

We told you first

NINE days ago The Sun said that the QE2 was to be called up. Everybody denied it. Yesterday the Ministry of Defence confirmed it. If you really want to know what's going on in the war buy The Sun. We try harder. See Page 2

GOTCHA

SUNK   AN Argie patrol boat like this one was sunk by missiles from Royal Navy helicopters after first opening fire on our lads

CRIPPLED   THE Argie cruiser General Belgrano . . . put out of action by Tigerfish torpedoes from our super nuclear sub Conqueror

Our lads sink gunboat and hole cruiser

From TONY SNOW aboard HMS Invincible

THE NAVY had the Argies on their knees last night after a devastating double punch.

WALLOP: They torpedoed the 14,000-ton Argentina cruiser General Belgrano and left it a useless wreck.

WALLOP: Task Force helicopters sank one Argentine patrol boat and severely damaged another.

The Belgrano, which survived the Pearl Harbour attack when it belonged to the U.S. Navy, had been asking for trouble all day.

The cruiser, second largest in the Argy fleet, had been skirting the 200-mile war zone that Britain has set up around the Falkland Islands.

MAJOR

With its 15 six-inch guns our Navy high command were certain that it would have played a major part in any battle to retain the Falklands.

But the Belgrano and

its 1,000 crew needn't worry about the war for some time now.

For the nuclear submarine Conqueror, captained by Commander Richard Wraith, let fly with two torpedoes.

The ship was not sunk and it is not clear how many casualties there were.

HMS Conqueror was built at Cammell Laird's shipyard in Birkenhead for £35million. She was launched in 1969 and *Continued on Page Two*

UNION BOYCOTTS WAR

A UNION chief is telling seamen on two ships taken over by the Government: "Don't go to war—the union can't protect you."

The astonishing advice comes from George Cartwright the Communist leader of the National Union of Seamen at Felixstowe Port in Suffolk.

The Government has just requisitioned the Townsend Thoresen roll-on, roll-off vessels Baltic Ferry and Nordic Ferry.

'Folly'

The ferries will carry troops and battle equipment in support of the QE2.

Mr Cartwright told the 150 seamen: "Our advice is that it would be folly to go off on a dangerous adventure.

"I'm old enough to remember that one in three merchant seamen were killed in the last war.

"It is not a case of being unpatriotic. We are not at war and our advice is based on union practicalities.

"What we are saying is that if seamen put themselves under military command, they will no longer have our protection.

Question

"There is no question of politics being behind the recommendation. We were asked for our view

and gave our best advice."

He believes the majority of crew members will decide not to sail to the South Atlantic.

So far I have heard from three seamen who want to go, the rest are non-committal or against joining the task force," Mr Cartwright said.

Fame

You want fame? Well fame costs and this is where you start paying … with sweat!

> 'I loved Fame, in fact everyone I knew watched it. I think because it was a show based around kids we perceived to be our age we identified with them, everyone had their favourite character … it was escapism I suppose.'
>
> MARK FINNEGAN

The *Fame* story starts with Alan Parker's 1980 film, which made the transition to the small screen in 1982, dwarfing the success of the movie and capturing the imagination of the eighties generation. The TV series ran for six seasons – 136 episodes – generating an incredible number of spin-offs including two hit singles ('Hi-Fidelity' and 'Starmaker') and a number one album in 1982 (plus another number one album for the soundtrack of the original film and a number one single for Irene Cara with the film's title track, 'Fame'), as well as Kids From Fame tours and assorted merchandise.

The show centres around New York's High School for the Performing Arts and follows the trials and tribulations of a group of talented young dancers, singers, actors, writers and performers as they work hard towards their respective goals, although later series became more fantastic and less believable. The show only ran for two seasons in its native US but was popular enough elsewhere in the world for production to continue through to 1987.

The show – with some help from *Flashdance*, which also appeared in 1982 – was also responsible for elevating the legwarmer to such popularity that it would eventually become an icon of eighties style!

Fame … Up To Date!

Lee Curreri (Bruno) went on to become a successful musician and producer and has scored numerous TV shows including *Chicago Hope* and *Dangerous Minds*. Barry Miller (Ralph) is still a successful TV and film actor whose appearances include *Ally McBeal* and *The Practice*. Gene Anthony Ray (Leroy) sadly suffered a fatal stroke in 2003. Maureen Teefy (Doris) has retired, although she still appears in local theatre productions. Paul McCrane (Montgomery) played Dr Robert 'Rocket' Romano in *ER*. Erica Gimpel (Coco) still regularly appears on TV and has played parts in *Veronica Mars*, *Roswell* and *ER*. Carlo Imperato (Danny) now runs a skin care spa in California with his wife. Albert Hague (Mr Shorofsky) died of cancer in 2005 at the age of 81. Debbie Allen (Miss Grant) runs her own dance academy and recently hosted a reality TV show based on *Fame* for NBC.

1982
On The Small Screen

New shows made this year include *Brookside, Cheers, The Late Late Breakfast Show, Saturday Superstore, The Tube* and *Whoops Apocalypse!*

Madonna reportedly screen-tested for the *Fame* TV series but lost out to Lori Singer, who went on to play Julie Miller on the show between 1982 and 1984.

Gene Anthony Ray was himself a student at New York's High School for the Performing Arts before taking the part of Leroy Johnson. His rebellious attitude led to him being asked to leave the school before graduating.

THE YOUNG ONES

Remember the 1980 BBC2 TV show *Boom Boom … Out Go the Lights?* Actually, me neither – in fact producer Paul Jackson has since claimed that the show prompted the worst audience response the BBC Light Entertainment department had ever received. However the show was the first TV appearance for some of the leading lights of an emerging alternative comedy scene, among them Rik Mayall, Adrian Edmondson and Nigel Planer, who would go on to make perhaps the eighties' ultimate sitcom, *The Young Ones*.

The Young Ones first aired in 1982 and gathered a number of existing comedy characters together, made them students, put them in a house together and watched the results. There was Rik Pratt (a character Rik Mayall had developed in his stage routine and who also appeared in *Boom Boom …*), a socially inept, wannabe-anarchist and Cliff Richard fan; Vyvyan Basterd, a violent, fearless punk rocker (played by Edmondson and based on his existing Adrian Dangerous character) and Special Patrol Group, his equally disreputable Glaswegian hamster; Neil Pye, a suicidally depressed, vegetarian hippy (played by Planer and who first appeared in *Boom Boom …*); and Mike TheCoolPerson, a slightly shifty but basically straight character (the role was written for Peter Richardson who went on to develop *Comic Strip Presents* but was taken over by Christopher Ryan following tensions between Richardson and producer Paul Jackson). Most secondary characters seemed to be played by Alexei Sayle in the role of 'The Balowski Family', often as landlord Jerzi Balowski but variously appearing as protest singer Alexei Balowski, arms dealer Reggie Balowski and medieval Jester Balowski. I loved it and pretty much everyone I knew loved it, partly because it was new and exciting

> ## 'I loved *The Young Ones* because it was so new and my parents didn't approve.'
>
> FLASH

but, I suspect, mostly because it was rude, unpredictable, violent and anarchic and our mums didn't approve of it at all!

There were only two series of *The Young Ones* made, twelve episodes in all, but the impact of the show was phenomenal and each episode would be the main topic of conversation the next day at school. Even better, it had musical guests (I can remember Madness, Motorhead and Dexys Midnight Runners, The Damned and Amazulu!), which we simply put down to it being a very cool programme when in fact the reality was that having a band on the show elevated it to 'light entertainment' status, giving it a bigger budget than a straightforward sitcom.

Such was the success of *The Young Ones* that the cast went on the road with a stage version of the show in 1983 and had two hit records: a number one – recorded for Comic Relief in 1986 – with a version of Cliff Richard's 'Living Doll', recorded with Cliff Richard and Hank Marvin, and a number two for Nigel Planer as Neil, with a 1984 cover of Traffic's 'Hole In My Shoe'.

THE YOUNG ONES …Up To Date!

After *The Young Ones* Rik Mayall, Adrian Edmondson and Nigel Planer went on to make *Filthy Rich & Catflap* in 1986, following which the trio went their separate ways (although Mayall and Edmondson would go on to star in *Bottom* together). Rik Mayall notably went on to play *Lord Flashheart* in Blackadder, Alan B'Stard in *The New Statesman* and has made a number of movies, including the lead role in *Drop Dead Fred*. Adrian Edmondson, who married French & Saunders' Jennifer Saunders in 1985, has appeared in *Jonathan Creek* and *Holby City* among many others, and has also directed a number of pop videos, including videos for The Pogues, Zodiac Mindwarp and Squeeze. Nigel Planer has gone on to become a much respected straight actor, appearing on television and on stage in many shows including *Blackeyes* and *Shine On Harvey Moon* as well as providing voices for *Magic Roundabout* and the audiobooks of Terry Pratchett's Discworld series.

1982
Off The Small Screen

Shows that finished this year (or stopped making new episodes) include *Multi-Coloured Swap Shop*, *The Generation Game*, *The Goodies*, *Mork & Mindy*, *Not The Nine O'Clock News* and *Sapphire & Steel*.

1982 ICON

▶▶ *Boy George*

It's September 1982, a few days after my birthday, and it's *Top Of The Pops* night. I've just turned fourteen and, although *Top Of The Pops* is still essential viewing, I'm starting to adopt the cynical world-weariness that only teenagers can really pull off. Men in make-up? Seen it. So when Culture Club appear on the show with 'Do You Really Want To Hurt Me?' it's a bolt from the blue for me and, as it turns out, for the entire nation, such is the furore that their debut appearance on the show causes.

Culture Club haven't appeared on my radar at all up to this point, despite the fact that they have already released two fairly low-key singles 'White Boy' and 'I'm Afraid Of Me'. The next day however, the school playground is buzzing about the band and England purses its lips in disapproval while the media have a field day with their IS IT A GIRL? IS IT A BOY? headlines and speculation. It's exciting, and when my mum doesn't approve (although curiously my Grandma becomes something of a fan) I'm sold!

This went way beyond men in make-up, and this kind of androgeny is new to me, but it deserves to be supported and I do like the reggae-tinged single which is suddenly all over the radio on its way to becoming Culture Club's first number one. The band will appear on *Top Of The Pops* another four times with 'Do You Really Want To Hurt Me?' including a performance on the prestigious Christmas Day show. They release another single 'Time (Clock Of The Heart)', which I like even more, and an album *Kissing To Be Clever*. A third US hit – with my all time favourite Culture Club single 'I'll Tumble For Ya' – puts the band in the history books as the first band since The Beatles to have three American top ten singles from a debut album. Culture Club subsequently become one of the eighties most iconic and successful bands.

Culture Club's focus was Boy George – how could it not be? – who in addition to being a flamboyant frontman was also a colourful, charismatic character who could always be counted on by the media for an intelligent, sarcastic comment. But Culture Club was always a group and although the rest of the band were often sidelined by George it was the band as a whole – Roy Hay on guitar and keyboard, Mikey Craig on bass and Jon Moss on drums – who were responsible for their sound and their musical success.

Colour By Numbers, the follow-up to *Kissing To be Clever*, was released in 1983 and the album's four singles – 'Church Of The Poison Mind', 'Karma Chameleon', 'It's A Miracle' and 'Victims' – all made the top five of the UK singles charts: 'Karma Chameleon' going to number one with sales of over a million copies, making it 1983's bestselling single. Behind the scenes, however, all was not so good. Boy George and Jon Moss had been having a turbulent relationship that not even their bandmates were aware of (the inspiration for many of George's lyrics during his time with Culture Club), and the pressure on the band, coupled with their schedule was starting to affect their creativity.

In 1984 the band rush-released their third album, *Waking Up With The House On Fire*, to a lukewarm reception. The album still peaked at number two, as did its first single 'The War Song', but a second single, 'The Medal Song', only reached 32. Another album, *From Luxury To Heartache*, followed in 1986 but by this time George was a drug addict.

'Boy George and Culture Club were the 80s' ultimate artists without a doubt! I was 10 and a half when I first saw George on a video and I just thought, WOW! What a beautiful woman and I fell desperately in love with her. I was still in love with her after I found out she was a he!'

ERIKA JAYNE

The album peaked at ten, and the excellent 'Move Away' single managed to reach number seven but the tensions within the band, plus George's personal problems, were taking their toll and the band split after one more single; 'God Thank You Woman', only managed to reach number 32.

Boy George, still battling with heroin addiction, went on to have some solo success with 'Everything I Own', a number one single, and an album, *Sold*, before getting clean and embarking on a succession of reinventions, including Jesus Loves You and The Twin, as well as launching a successful career as a DJ. In 1995 he published the first part of his excellent autobiography *Take It Like A Man*, following it with a second volume, *Straight*, in 2005. He also wrote and produced the successful semi-autobiographical stage show *Taboo*, which ran to great critical acclaim in London's West End and on Broadway.

Boy George returned to the headlines in 2006 after a quantity of cocaine was found in his New York home. He subsequently received a $1000 fine and was ordered to do community service picking up litter on the streets of Manhattan. In November 2007 he was accused of falsely imprisoning a 28-year-old man, allegedly a male escort, who claimed he had been chained up after agreeing to visit the singer's London flat for a photo shoot...

Culture Club reformed for a successful tour in 1998 but the subsequent album, *Don't Mind If I Do*, failed to reach the top forty and the reunion dissolved. The band reunited again in 2006, this time without George or Roy Hay, and a tour – with a new singer, Sam Butcher – was scheduled and then cancelled.

I interviewed Boy George in 2003 to talk about the retrospective four-CD Culture Club box-set *Culture Club*. I'm always nervous before doing an interview but particularly this time, mindful of George's reputation for being rude and difficult. As it turns out he is neither and the interview is a pleasure to do, despite the constant distraction of the fan-voice in my head saying, 'Can you believe it … you're actually talking to BOY GEORGE!?!'

'Boy George and Culture Club helped me get through a really bad stage in my life, the lyrics just made me feel like I belonged somewhere. Boy George is after all the patron saint of all weirdos and misfits!'

DEBBIE STONE

'Boy George has trancended the 80s, survived, and reinvented himself over and over, time and time again. His talent is endless...singer, songwriter, author, dj, actor, designer...'

MICHAEL CHARLAND

HOW WEIRD WAS IT TO GO BACK THROUGH YOUR WHOLE MUSICAL HISTORY AGAIN TO DECIDE WHAT TO INCLUDE IN THE BOX-SET?
I think it was quite interesting to sort of hear myself try to find my voice – if you listen to the early demos then they're very Bow Wow Wow and that was what we wanted to do … we wanted to be hip! And then we began to find our own sound, you know?

THAT SOUND DOES SEEM TO HAVE VERY MUCH DEVELOPED IN PUBLIC AS IT WERE AS YOU WENT ALONG.
Definitely. My songwriting was originally very 'wordy' and I didn't really know about the structure of songs, and so from working with the band that's how I learnt.

WAS SORTING THROUGH THE ARCHIVES A PLEASANT EXPERIENCE?
Yeah, you know I'm a control freak, so I quite liked the idea of choosing some tracks … there was a lot of 'no not that one, no not that one …' You may have noticed that 'The War Song' wasn't on the album … although war is stupid, and people – some – are stupid but you should never tell them that!

DO YOU HAVE ANY PERSONAL FAVOURITES ACROSS THE FOUR CDS?
That's a difficult one … [long silence]

I SUPPOSE THAT GIVEN YOU'VE COMPILED IT THEN KIND OF ALL OF IT IS A FAVOURITE OF SOME SORT?
Well I like some bits more then others … I don't know really. Yeah I do like it all and I think for me that it kind of reflects what I grew up with. I mean the seventies and the very early eighties were kind of an eclectic time for music – you had reggae and you had punk, and you had disco and you had everything going on at the same time … The Goombay Dance Band and The Sex Pistols … and The Wombles!

'George came along at a time when I was coming out as a gay man. He truly eased my way out. I was just gob-smacked when I first saw him, he seemed to say all the things that I couldn't at that time.'

JOSHUA

LOOKING BACK AT CULTURE CLUB, DO YOU SEE THE CAREER TO DATE AS ONE BIG STORY OR IS IT A SERIES OF SMALLER STORIES?
I think we all have very conflicting ideas of what we want to do, and somehow we work it out – and I don't know how we do that.

ON THE FIRST CD OF THE BOX-SET THERE'S A TRACK CALLED 'SHIRLEY TEMPLE MOMENT'…
Well it's not really a track, it's an argument!

IT'S VERY ENTERTAINING!
It is isn't it? It made me laugh! I think it's important to have a sense of humour and I had heard about that tape for years and it was almost one of those urban-myth things – everyone kept saying there was this tape going round of Culture Club rowing, and when I heard it I thought it was hysterical! I thought it was hysterical that we were trying to perform this beautiful song and it was all 'you're a cunt!' and 'you fat bastard!' What came out of it was just so funny, but that was always the way – you fought all the time and then something really magical would happen!

SO WAS THAT A FAIRLY TYPICAL CULTURE CLUB MOMENT?
Oh my god, that was the least of it! It's kind of like going home for Christmas being in a band – it all starts with what you're going to watch on the TV, the Queen's speech or *Top Of The Pops* … in my house growing up was volatile to say the least, especially at Christmas!

I SUPPOSE CONFLICT CAN HAVE VERY POSITIVE AND VERY NEGATIVE EFFECTS.
Exactly, when we started the band Bow Wow Wow were our obsession and we had to sound like Bow Wow Wow, and then sort of gradually and as we found the right people to be in the band it gradually began to form its own sound and it did pretty well!

HOW COMFORTABLE ARE YOU BEING BOY GEORGE THESE DAYS? YOU SEEM TO BE A VERY DIFFERENT PERSON TO WHO YOU WERE IN THE HEADY DAYS OF CULTURE CLUB.
Well I'm older, and more lived in! I don't know really, I think you have to make a choice to change, if you know what I mean – you can be sixty and be a retard, or be two years old and be a genius, and I think that kids have that knocked out of them when they're growing up. In my case my father was always telling me to shut up so now I'm making up for lost time!

LOOKING BACK AT EVERYTHING YOU'VE ACHIEVED, IS THERE ANYTHING YOU'RE PARTICULARLY PROUD OF?
Um … yes there're a few songs I think are great. 'Unfinished Business' – I like that, 'If I Could Fly', 'Il Adore', 'Bow Down Mister' … I mean you have to write one happy song in your life!

YOU MUST HAVE WRITTEN MORE THAN ONE!
Have I? Name three …

WELL 'KARMA CHAMELEON'S QUITE CHIRPY ISN'T IT?
Yes, on the surface … we're talking about the undercurrent here which I think was always the irony of the band anyway. We had this kind of very brightly, shiny, colourful surface, but underneath there's this sort of dark melancholy – which I like! But you know, people just don't listen to words which really shocks me – I have the whole of Bowie's catalogue in my head and he forgets the words!

DO YOU FEEL THAT CULTURE CLUB EVER REALLY GOT THE RESPECT DUE TO THEM?
Difficult question to answer really, the media sort of disrespected us, but the people who bought the music – the fans – they loved it and there are faces that have been around for twenty years that I still see at gigs.

YOUR FANBASE IS CERTAINLY VERY DEDICATED.
There are some really quite amazing people, but I wonder sometimes where they get their money from … when I was into Bowie when I was growing up, the option of flying to America to see him play was just unthinkable, so when I see fans in Brazil or Singapore it's like 'My god, it's Dawn and Julie!'

WHAT DO YOU THINK WAS THE APPEAL OF CULTURE CLUB, BECAUSE IT WAS SO BROAD…
Me [laughs]! I think we wrote good songs, I think we looked good, and I think that a lot of misfits connected with us and there were a lot of them out there, gay, straight, overweight, with braces, whatever.

MY GRANDMA LOVED YOU … 'THAT LOVELY BOY GEORGE …'
I know! I don't know what my appeal was for old ladies – how little they knew! But you know, people of all ages come to see *Taboo* and it's quite a racy show – I would have made it more racy – but people don't seem to be that offended. We've had a couple of people walk out … a few uptight grannies going 'They're walking around in underpants! What are they wearing!' In fact there was one lady who went up to the manager of the theatre and said, 'I've been cheated! Boy George isn't in this show!' and he said 'Yes he is – he's the lead!' And I found her in the audience and said, 'It is me you know!' and she said, 'I know – and you're spoiling yourself!'

1983

Snapshot

Bjorn Borg retires from tennis ● Seatbelts become compulsory for UK drivers and front seat passengers ● Swatch start selling their first watches ● Bob Hawke is elected Prime Minister of Australia ● Astronauts Story Musgrave and Donald H. Peterson complete the first Space Shuttle spacewalk ● Ronald Regan makes his initial Strategic Defense Initiative 'Star Wars' proposals ● *Gandhi* wins eight Oscars ● Disneyland Tokyo opens – the first Disneyland outside the USA ● The 'Hitler Diaries' are published ● London police start using wheel clamps ● Margaret Thatcher is re-elected as Prime Minister in a landslide victory ● Michael Jackson's *Thriller* is the UK's bestselling album ● The Nintendo Entertainment System goes on sale in Japan ● Neil Kinnock is elected leader of the Labour Party ● Microsoft debut their Word software and Lotus release their first spreadsheet package ● £26 million of gold bars are stolen in the Brinks Mat robbery ● Brunei becomes independent from the UK ● McDonald's introduce the McNugget ● Karen Carpenter, Billy Fury, David Niven, John Le Mesurier and Tupperware inventor Earl S. Tupper die ● Roger Moore is James Bond in *Octopussy* ● Race horse Shergar is kidnapped and will never be found ● Ibuprofen becomes a non-prescription drug ● Nancy Regan launches the 'Just Say No' anti-drugs campaign ● Culture Club's 'Karma Chameleon' is the UK's bestselling single of the year ● The first regular mobile phone service is introduced in Chicago for $3,000 plus $150 per month service charge ● Terry Pratchett's first Discworld novel, *The Colour Of Magic*, is published ● John McEnroe wins the men's singles at Wimbledon and Martina Navratilova wins the women's title ● The first Cabbage Patch Dolls go on sale ● Apple's Lisa computer is the first to use a mouse and incorporate pull-down menus ● The first *Now That's What I Call Music* compilation is released in the UK ● The US invades Grenada after a military coup in the country ● Crack cocaine is developed in the Bahamas ● Brighton play Manchester United twice in the FA Cup Final – the first game is a 2-2 draw after extra time but Manchester United win the replay 4-0 ● Toto

'The ultimate eighties' artist? David Bowie. Please, it's Bowie. What else is there to say?'

MARILU

Sounds like. . .1983

Later in my life when I come to look back on 1983, I will remember it as year that seemed perpetually set in summertime, a never-ending school holiday and my first real summer of independence. Which is entirely appropriate because it's a year of buoyant, exuberant, optimistic pop music, the first of the golden years of eighties' pop and the commercial peak of some of the most important bands and artists of the decade. Culture Club, Duran Duran, Michael Jackson, David Bowie, Billy Joel and The Police will all enjoy their most successful year ever and a number of important artists will have their first real tastes of fame, including U2, Wham!, the Eurythmics, the Thompson Twins, Howard Jones, Paul Young and The Smiths.

The first new number one single of the year, setting a frenetic pop pace, is Phil Collins with his first chart-topping hit, a cover of a 1966 Supremes' song 'You Can't Hurry Love'. It is Collins' only solo hit this year, although with Genesis he will also have two huge singles – 'Mama' and 'That's All' – as well as a number one album *Genesis*. Men At Work will be next to top the singles charts with 'Down Under', a song destined to become an international eighties' classic with additional number one placings in the USA and the band's native Australia. An album, *Business As Usual*, will also top the charts

in those countries, although further singles 'Overkill' and 'It's A Mistake' won't fare quite so well. Another successful band this year – who will often be confused with Men At Work and will even more frequently find themselves described as Australian when they are in fact Canadian – is Men Without Hats, who will score a quirky hit with 'The Safety Dance' in October.

If 1982 was conspicuous for being a year of new artists, then this year sees the return of the old guard. Elton John will have four singles hits, most notably with 'I Guess That's Why They Call It The Blues' and 'I'm Still Standing', which will both make the top five, and a top ten album *Too Low For Zero*. Rod Stewart will have a number one single with 'Baby Jane', a second massive hit – 'What Am I Gonna Do (I'm So In Love With You)' – and an album, *Body Wishes*, will go top five. Bonnie Tyler will have number ones in both the singles and albums charts with 'Total Eclipse Of The Heart' and *Faster Than The Speed Of Light* respectively. But it's David Bowie who best adapts to survive (again!) in this new environment; his number one album *Let's Dance* will become the biggest album of Bowie's career, spending well over a year in the charts and launching a series of massive singles including 'Let's Dance' (which will go to the top of the singles charts), 'China Girl' and 'Modern

'The Style Council brought sincerity and emotion to a pop music world that had been lacking in both for quite some time.'

KEVIN

Love' (both of which will go to number two).

Michael Jackson's *Thriller* is the bestselling album of the year and will top the album charts twice in 1983, once in March for a week on the back of a number one single for the epic 'Billie Jean', and then again in May for a further five weeks on the back of 'Beat It', which reaches number three in April. Michael Jackson's success will continue through the year with a series of top ten singles, including 'Wanna Be Starting Something' and 'Thriller' as well as 'Say Say Say', a duet with Paul McCartney from the former Beatle's solo album *Pipes Of Peace*, and a second number one album with *18 Greatest Hits* – a compilation of solo and Jackson Five hits.

Jackson's friend, the former Commodores mainman and fellow Motown artist, Lionel Richie will also have a successful year in the charts with a number one album, *Can't Slow Down*, and a pair of top ten singles, 'All Night Long (All Night)' and 'Running With The Night', but with the exception of another US chart veteran, Billy Joel (who has a number one and number four hit respectively with 'Uptown Girl' and 'Tell Her About It' from his *An Innocent Man* album), this is a year when British talent truly dominates the UK charts.

Duran Duran, Spandau Ballet and Culture Club will have all shed any lingering New Romantic trappings and will all enjoy massive mainstream success this year, each act scoring a number one single and album apiece. Their trio of albums – *Seven And The Ragged Tiger*, *True* and *Colour By Numbers* respectively – will go on to become classics of the decade and,

in the case of Spandau Ballet and Culture Club, arguably their definitive albums. The combined trio will also enjoy ninety weeks in the singles charts, Duran Duran's 'Is There Something I Should Know' debuting at number one, Culture Club's 'Karma Chameleon' becoming the year's bestselling single and Spandau Ballet's back-to-back hits with 'True' and 'Gold' marking their most successful year.

Following the demise of The Jam, Paul Weller will also reinvent himself in a more accessible and chart-friendly way with his new project The Style Council, who will release four hit singles this year with 'Speak Like A Child', 'Money Go Round', 'Long Hot Summer' and 'A Solid Bond In Your Heart' (a song originally intended to be The Jam's last single) and a number two album, *Cafe Bleu*.

Another new act, the Eurythmics, will dominate the charts in 1983, releasing two albums: *Sweet Dreams (Are Made Of This)* which will reach number two in February and *Touch* which will top the charts in November. The duo will also have four singles hits, two from each album ('Sweet Dreams (Are Made Of This)' and *'Love Is A Stranger' from Sweet Dreams (Are Made Of This)* and 'Who's That Girl?' and 'Right by Your Side' from *Touch*). Heaven 17 will finally move into the mainstream with a trio of hits this year, including their best-known single 'Temptation', which will narrowly miss the number one spot in April, and a landmark album *The Luxury Gap*, while debut electronic artist Howard Jones' first two singles, 'New Song' and 'What Is Love?' will reach numbers three and two respectively.

'"Relax" . . . that was a real revelation at the time, almost as shocking to the Mary Whitehouse brigade as 'God Save The Queen'. Great use of video, and one of the first really great 12" mixes I'd heard that was an almost entirely different track.'

SHAUN

The Thompson Twins, now a three-piece, will release a third album, *Quick Step & Side Kick*, in February, which along with a flurry of great singles including 'Love On Your Side' and 'We Are Detective' will establish the band as a major act in the UK and around the world. The trio will end the year with 'Hold Me Now', the first single from a brand new album *Into The Gap*, which will not be released until early 1984 but is destined to become a true eighties' classic.

Kajagoogoo's debut single 'Too Shy' will be a number one in January, propelled by the fact that the record's producer is Duran Duran's Nick Rhodes. It will be followed by a pair of top fifteen hits – 'Ooh To Be Ah' and 'Hang On Now' – and a top five album, *White Feathers*. Fellow popsters Wham! will follow up their late 1982 hit 'Young Guns (Go For It)' with a run of top ten singles – 'Wham Rap! (Enjoy What You Do)', 'Bad Boys' and 'Club Tropicana' – which will establish George Michael and Andrew Ridgeley as one of the biggest pop acts of the year. A Christmas megamix of tracks from the duo's debut album *Fantastic* will reach number fifteen in the singles charts in December, testament to the loyalty of their fanbase. The album *Fantastic* will reach number one, and a 115-week chart run will make it the most successful of what will be a short but stellar career.

Tears For Fears will more than fulfil the potential they showed on their 1982 debut single 'Mad World' and will notch up two more top five singles by the end of April, with 'Change' and 'Pale Shelter', as well as a March number one for their debut album *The Hurting*. Following the demise of his band the Q-Tips in 1982, Paul Young's third solo single will give him his first chart action since 1976 (when he charted with Streetband's novelty record 'Toast') when

New Order and Frankie Goes To Hollywood will release perhaps the most important singles of the year. New Order's groundbreaking 'Blue Monday' reaching number nine and becoming the bestselling 12" single of all time, while Frankie Goes To Hollywood's epic 'Relax' - banned by the BBC after Radio 1 DJ Mike Read refuses to play it on the grounds of its explicit sleeve and lyrics - will still go on to reach number one in early 1984.

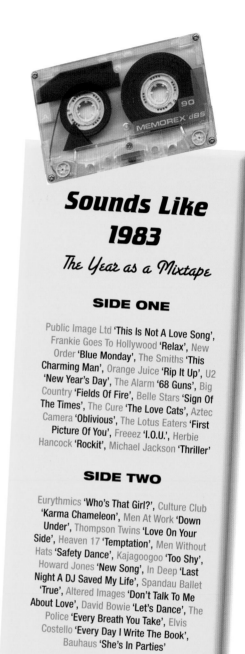

Sounds Like 1983

The Year as a Mixtape

SIDE ONE

Public Image Ltd 'This Is Not A Love Song', Frankie Goes To Hollywood 'Relax', New Order 'Blue Monday', The Smiths 'This Charming Man', Orange Juice 'Rip It Up', U2 'New Year's Day', The Alarm '68 Guns', Big Country 'Fields Of Fire', Belle Stars 'Sign Of The Times', The Cure 'The Love Cats', Aztec Camera 'Oblivious', The Lotus Eaters 'First Picture Of You', Freeez 'I.O.U.', Herbie Hancock 'Rockit', Michael Jackson 'Thriller'

SIDE TWO

Eurythmics 'Who's That Girl?', Culture Club 'Karma Chameleon', Men At Work 'Down Under', Thompson Twins 'Love On Your Side', Heaven 17 'Temptation', Men Without Hats 'Safety Dance', Kajagoogoo 'Too Shy', Howard Jones 'New Song', In Deep 'Last Night A DJ Saved My Life', Spandau Ballet 'True', Altered Images 'Don't Talk To Me About Love', David Bowie 'Let's Dance', The Police 'Every Breath You Take', Elvis Costello 'Every Day I Write The Book', Bauhaus 'She's In Parties'

'For me Wham! just epitomised the mid-80s . . . sun-kissed, good-time, tongue-in-cheek fun, wrapped up in designer-branded, pastel-coloured clothing and trying hard not to think about having to grow up too quickly.'

MICHAEL NEIDUS

'Big Country's The Crossing is the ultimate album because at the time, the music didn't sound like anything else on the radio, and I loved the images that their songs brought to my mind – it was how Scotland should sound.'

JEFF

his version of Marvin Gaye's 'Wherever I Lay My Hat (That's My Home)' peaks at number one, as does his album *No Parlez*. Two more singles this year, 'Come Back And Stay' and 'Love Of The Common People', will also reach the top five, the start of a run of success that will see the singer dominate the charts for the next couple of years.

Irish rock band U2 are a relatively unknown act at the start of 1983 but by the end of the year – after the release of two top-twenty singles, 'New Year's Day' and 'Two Hearts Beat As One', and their third album, *War*, which tops the charts – they are on the brink of becoming one of the biggest and most important bands in the world. But they are not the only band this year to be ploughing this particular post-punk furrow of anthemic Celtic-tinged rock and chiming guitars. Welsh act The Alarm will release their best known single '68 Guns' this year while Scotland's Big Country will score three hits with 'Fields Of Fire (400 Miles)', 'In A Big Country' and 'Chance' as well as a number three chart position for their debut album *The Crossing*. Big Country also kindle an overwhelming desire in young men across the country to wear checked shirts, which is as much of an eighties' fashion statement as many of them will make.

The Police will release perhaps their finest, certainly their most successful, single 'Every Breath You Take', taken from their equally successful album *Synchronicity*, their final studio album. Both will go to number one (in the US the album would be number one for seventeen weeks!). A second single, 'Wrapped Around Your Finger', will peak at number seven, and the band will embark on a massive world tour which I will spend the next 25 years regretting I

missed (although the album is a firm Walkman favourite on my paper round!).

'This Charming Man', the debut release from The Smiths, is the start of a whole new musical chapter in my life this year, an obsession that will go on to see The Smiths become one of my favourite bands of all time. 'This Charming Man' will only peak at 25 in November but the release will consolidate the year's emerging eighties' indie scene into which I will throw myself with enthusiasm. If London was the spiritual home of the New Romantics two years earlier, the UK indie movement, which will truly gather momentum this year, comes from further north. Manchester's The Smiths and New Order of course, but also Liverpool's Echo And The Bunnymen who will release 'The Cutter', the Icicle Works with 'Love Is A Wonderful Colour' and the Lotus Eaters who release the gorgeous 'First Picture Of You', and as far north as Scotland in the case of 'Rip it Up' and 'Oblivious', wonderful records from Orange Juice and Aztec Camera respectively. It's intelligent pop music and it immediately finds an audience among the sensitive. It helps create an environment

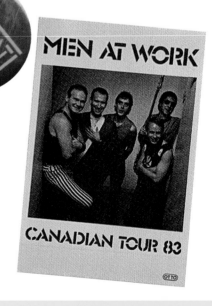

where a number of more experimental and sometimes fragile songs are allowed to bloom, among them This Mortal Coil's epic 'Song To The Siren', David Sylvian's beautifully stark collaboration with Riuchi Sakamoto, 'Forbidden Colours', and the Cocteau Twins' debut album *Head Over Heels*.

These intelligent, arty and often pretentious records will also overlap into goth, another movement to emerge from a splintering post-punk scene, which will continue to gather momentum this year. It builds on the 1982 emergence of bands like Bauhaus, Southern Death Cult and the Birthday Party on the one hand, and the continued popularity of The Cure and Siouxsie & The Banshees on the other. Bauhaus will release perhaps their greatest single this year, 'She's In Parties', while The Cure will become the year's most unlikely popstars when 'The Walk' gets to number twelve in the UK singles charts, 'The Love Cats' peaks at seven and the first Cure compilation, *Japanese Whispers*, makes 26 in the albums charts. Siouxsie & The Banshees will enjoy their biggest ever singles success with a dark, swirling version of The Beatles' 'Dear Prudence' and the band's Siouxsie Sioux and Budgie's spin-off project The Creatures will have two hit singles and a hit album with 'Miss The Girl', 'Right Now' and *Feast* respectively. If The Creatures' metallic, percussive sounds are a startling alternative to the shiny, commercial pop that makes up a lot of the charts this year, then it will be Public Image Ltd's 'This Is Not A Love Song', which peaks at number five two days before my sixteenth birthday in September, which is the true brutal

antithesis of all that is pop this year.

But for every dark gothic anthem that I will love this year there is a flurry of more mainstream hits, some of which I will publicly like (Freeez's brilliant 'I.O.U.', which goes to number two in June; Herbie Hancock's superb 'Rockit'; Yes' 'Owner Of A Lonely Heart'), some that I will privately like but which are far too poppy and commercial to admit to liking (Rocksteady Crew's '(Hey You) The Rocksteady Crew', In Deep's 'Last Night A DJ Saved My Life', Galaxy's 'Dancing Tight' and Irene Cara's 'Flashdance'), and some which I will really dislike. For example, I will never meet anyone who likes Ryan Paris's irritatingly catchy 'La Dolce Vita' but it will still make number five in the charts. Thankfully it remains a one-hit wonder!

Ryan Paris of course is just one of the usual selection of novelty hits and one-hit wonders that will fill the charts this year. Black Lace will just make the top ten with 'Superman' in September (their first hit, but a true taste of things to come) and Roland Rat will have his biggest single hit in November with 'Rat Rapping (Brilliant Isn't It)', which reaches number fourteen. The balance will be redressed somewhat with a bunch of great one-hit wonders this year, including JoBoxers' 'Boxerbeat', Mezzforte's 'Garden Party', Flash And The Pan's 'Waiting For A Train' and Icehouse's 'Hey Little Girl'. New Edition's 'Candy Girl' is a few steps away from being a novelty record, as is the Flying Pickets' a capella version of 'Only You', but this doesn't make them any less irritating, especially as they will both end up as number one records; 1983 in fact will close with the Flying Pickets in the top spot.

Goth

Another wide and sprawling genre but, broadly speaking, goth is an offshoot of post-punk and is known as much for its style (black clothes, make-up and hair with fashion influenced by everything from the Edwardians to punk) as for its music. It's still a popular genre today although it now consists of many sub-genres covering various styles, clothes and sounds.
KEY ACTS: Siouxsie & The Banshees, The Cure, Bauhaus, Sisters Of Mercy, The Mission, Fields Of The Nephilim

Michael Jackson

At noon on 14th April 1982 Michael Jackson and Paul McCartney went into Westlake Studios in Los Angeles to record a duet, 'The Girl Is Mine', a new track written by Jackson and the first to be recorded for his second solo album, which then had the working title of 'Starlight'. Final mixing was completed on 8th November and the resultant album, renamed *Thriller*, was released in December 1982.

Thriller was America's number one album for 37 weeks and went platinum eleven times in the UK alone on its way to become the world's bestselling album of all time – a record it still holds 25 years later with accumulated sales well in excess of a hundred million copies. Seven of the album's nine tracks will become hit singles and the fourteen-minute video for its title track – originally given the working title 'Give Me Starlight' – will be hailed the greatest video of all time and is still the only music video ever to be classified as a film by America's National Film Registry.

The album marked Michael Jackson's elevation to the mainstream – amazingly he was the first black artist to be playlisted on MTV when the video to 'Billie Jean' was released in 1983 – and confirmed his superstar status, crossing genres from the soul-funk of 'Wanna be Starting Something' (written during the *Off The Wall* album sessions), through the saccharine pop of 'The Girl Is Mine' to 'Thriller's blistering rock guitar courtesy of Eddie Van Halen.

Michael Jackson holds eight Guinness World Records: Most Successful Entertainer of All Time, Youngest Vocalist to Top the US Singles Charts (at the age of eleven as part of the Jackson Five), First Vocalist to Enter the US Singles Chart at Number One (for 'You Are Not Alone'), First Entertainer to Earn More Than $100 Million in a Year, Highest Paid Entertainer of All Time ($125 million in 1989), First Entertainer to Sell More Than 100 Million Albums Outside the US, Most Weeks at the Top of the US Albums Chart (for the album *Thriller*) and Most Successful Music Video (for the music video 'Thriller').

Jackson's music, combined with his dazzling dancing (including the debut of his trademark 'moonwalk' performing 'Billie Jean' at a Motown anniversary concert) and endearing eccentricity, turned him into one of the biggest stars the world had ever seen. In 1984 *Thriller* won seven Grammy Awards, setting a new record for the most awards won by one artist in a single year, and Michael Jackson became known as the King of Pop.

Jackson reunited with his brothers for the *Victory* album and tour in 1984 and wrote the song 'We Are The World' with Lionel Richie in 1985 before starting work on a new album, *Bad*, which would be released to enormous success in 1987 and spawn another seven hit singles, including 'I Just Can't Stop Loving You', 'Bad', 'The Way You Make Me Feel', 'Man In The Mirror' and 'Dirty Diana'. In September Michael Jackson embarked on a sixteen-month tour to promote the album, his first tour as a solo artist, and played 123 concerts to almost four and a half million fans worldwide.

More albums were to follow with varying levels of success, but by the end of eighties Michael Jackson's music was starting to take a backseat to numerous speculations, allegations and controversies that would threaten to overshadow his musical accomplishments. They included rumours that he had undergone multiple cosmetic procedures to alter his appearance and that he had been bleaching his skin to make his skin paler, allegations that he had molested a child who had stayed with him at his Neverland ranch (the case was settled out of court, and when similar allegations were made against him again in 2003 he was found not guilty), and controversies surrounding his marriages to Lisa Marie Presley and Deborah Jeanne Rowe, the paternity of his children and his precarious financial situation.

Michael Jackson ...Up To Date!

Following a 'financial restructuring' of his business affairs in 2006, Michael Jackson released an expanded edition of *Thriller* - featuring a number of contemporary re-workings of the album's classic singles - in 2008 to mark the album's 25th anniversary, and is thought to be working on new material for a full comeback.

MARGARET THATCHER

Born in Grantham, Lincolnshire in October 1925 Margaret Hilda Roberts was just 25 when she first ran as a Conservative candidate in Dartford. She took her first seat in the House of Commons in 1958, by which time she had married businessman Denis Thatcher, qualified as a barrister and given birth to twins, Carol and Mark. She was rapidly promoted through the Conservative Party and joined the Shadow Cabinet under Edward Heath in 1967. The Conservatives came to power in 1970 and Mrs Thatcher became Secretary of State for Education, and was immediately propelled into the public consciousness when she abolished free milk in schools the same year. That is my first memory of her, and if anything I was happy with her decision - the free milk at my school was always warm, and always tasted horrible!

When the Conservatives lost the 1974 election Mrs Thatcher successfully challenged Edward Heath's leadership and took over the party in February 1975. She capitalised on the Labour government's escalating difficulties with industrial disputes, strikes, high unemployment and collapsing public services by positioning the Conservatives as the only alternative to such miseries. She led the Conservatives to victory in the 1979 General Election and I can still remember walking to school the next morning with friends, talking about the momentous political event the night before which had seen her become the country's first female Prime Minister, and echoing our fathers by tut-tutting that we were to be governed by a woman. I was eleven then, and I don't think anyone could have predicted that Margaret Thatcher would still be Prime Minister when I graduated from university over ten years later.

Margaret Thatcher's first term as Prime Minister is most notable for soaring unemployment and deepening recession, but the wave of national pride and optimism that swept the country after her uncompromising handling of the Falklands War in 1982 played a major part in ensuring that the Conservatives still won a landslide victory in the 1983 General Election and gained a second term in office. Mrs Thatcher used this time to gradually reduce the power of the trade unions despite widespread strikes – most notably the 1984–85 miners' strike – while encouraging the privatisation, free market and entrepreneurialism that are symbolic of the eighties in general and synonymous with what became known as Thatcherism.

I was a student in 1987, the year of the first General Election that I could vote in, and such was the anti-Conservative feeling around me that I was confident that the election would signal the end of Conservatives. Instead, with inflation down, a booming economy and weak Labour opposition, they were re-elected with a 102-seat majority, making Margaret Thatcher the longest continually serving Prime Minister since 1827. However, the writing was on the wall for the Conservatives and a series of deeply unpopular policies, including the introduction of the Poll Tax, led to a massive backlash against Mrs Thatcher and her policies from both inside and outside her own party, and a motion of no confidence in her leadership led to her resignation as Prime Minister in 1990.

'That woman single-handedly ruined this country and put us in a place from which we may never recover.'

MARK FELL

'I hated the woman with an absolute passion. I grew up thinking I'd never have a job. My grandfather used to spit at the TV if she came on!'

LEE KYNASTON

After graduating from Oxford University with a degree in Chemistry, one of Margaret Thatcher's first jobs was for the Lyons food company where she helped develop methods for freezing ice-cream.

In South Africa there is a nectarine named Margaret Thatcher in honour of the former Prime Minister.

Margaret Thatcher ...Up To Date!

Margaret Thatcher retired from the House of Commons in 1992 at the age of 66. In 1993 she was hired by the tobacco giant Philip Morris as a 'geopolitical consultant'. She has written two volumes of memoirs and was awarded The Order of the Garter, Britain's highest order of chivalry, in 1995. Her husband, Denis, died in 2003 and since then Mrs Thatcher has kept a low profile while battling problems with her physical health as well as her short-term memory.

'I had a Commodore 64. Me and my mates used to play games every Saturday afternoon while listening to The Blue Nile, Billy Bragg, David Sylvian and The Cure.'

JOHN B

'I had a ZX Spectrum which I loved! Linking it up to a tape player and TV, waiting for the funny noises and then the games would appear on the TV!'

KARLA SKINGSLEY

'I remember getting a Spectrum 16k and playing Jet Pack and Football Manager. The games had to be loaded via a cassette player and it took forever. My mate had the much more advanced Commodore 64!'

MARK SHEEN

The Home Computer Wars

VHS or Betamax? Agnetha or Frida? Space Invaders or Pac-Man? Duran Duran or Spandau Ballet? Sinclair Spectrum or Commodore 64? These were a few of the important issues for debate that I remember from 1983, although hindsight has now allowed us to put some of them to rest. Put aside the relative merits of Duran Duran versus Spandau Ballet (let's not go there!) and given the obvious answers to others (VHS, Frida and Space Invaders!) the one the jury is still out on is the Sinclair Spectrum versus the Commodore 64, and in some of the slightly scarier retro-computing communities on the internet it's a debate that is still going on today.

In April 1982 Clive Sinclair launched the Sinclair ZX Spectrum home computer (originally called the ZX82 – in line with 1980's ZX80 and 1981's ZX81 – until the company renamed it to highlight the machine's colour display capabilities). Boasting up to 48k of RAM memory, rubber keys and an integral loudspeaker, the Spectrum was housed in a sleek black case that could be connected to a domestic television and load data and programs from cassettes in domestic cassette recorders. Selling for under £100 the Spectrum was the first home computer to truly corner the home computing market, selling almost a quarter of a million units in the UK in it's first year by mail order alone. Once the model was made available on the high street, sales increased to a staggering 15,000 units a week. My best friend had a Spectrum and I would go to his house and watch in awe as he loaded cutting-edge games from cassette in as little as twenty minutes.

The Commodore 64 was developed under the name VIC-40, the follow-up to Commodore's popular entry-level VIC-20, but was renamed to fit the company's new policy of naming their business products with a letter and the unit's memory size, becoming the C64. The unit came with a proper keyboard, advanced sound capabilities and 64k of RAM, loading data from not only cassettes but also from cartridges and even from floppy discs using a separate drive. However, the less programmable C64 retailed for twice the cost of the Spectrum. The C64 was launched in the UK in 1983 and would go on to become the bestselling personal computer model of all time, a title it still holds today despite its finally going out of production in 1994.

Which is better? Well the Spectrum was always the cheaper of the two, which was perhaps the main factor in its popularity, but it also had a faster processing speed (which made it much better for playing games) than the C64, and from a programming point of view it had graphics commands as standard which the Commodore didn't have, although I won't pretend to understand what that means. The Commodore 64 on the other hand could handle graphics better, and was vastly superior in terms of sound as it used a three-channel synthesizer where Spectrum could only manage simple beeps. Which is better? I have no idea, and if the level of ongoing online arguments is to be believed, nor does anyone else. Like Duran Duran versus Spandau Ballet, let's not go there!

THE COMPACT DISC

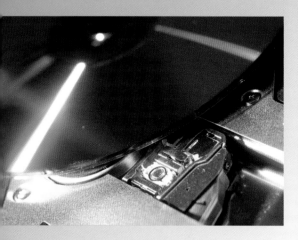

A 1981 episode of the TV technology show *Tomorrow's World* became the stuff of legend when Kieran Prendeville presented the CD as a miracle in audio-technology, and demonstrated its near indestructibility by throwing it around the studio and, more bizarrely, smothering it in jam. The technology behind CDs was adapted in part from techniques adopted in Philips' development of the video disc in the late seventies, the idea being that a laser would read a pitted pattern embedded into the disc. This would make a physical connection between the disc and the player redundant, in turn eliminating the various pops, crackles and rumbles produced by vinyl records and offering a far better reproduction of sound. I saw the show and, along with its usual promises of domestic jet-packs and collapsible personal hovercrafts, dismissed it as a sci-fi fantasy.

Then Sony, CBS, Philips and Polygram issued a statement that they had jointly developed the world's first domestic CD system, which was to go on sale first in Japan in 1982 and then in the rest of the world the following year. By 1983 however, the future of the CD wasn't quite as assured. As with most new technology the early CD players came with a hefty price-tag – around US $1,000 – and there was only a very limited number of titles available on CD (although you were OK if you were a fan of Pink Floyd's *Wish You Were Here*, Michael Jackson's *Thriller*, Billy Joel's *The Stranger* or Toto's *Toto IV*, which, along with a selection of classical and jazz titles, made up the first dozen titles released outside Japan). Sales were slow and just 30,000 CD players were sold in the US in 1983, their first year of availability, and the media gleefully started to predict that the CD revolution might not happen at all. In actual fact falling prices for CD players and a rapidly expanding catalogue of available titles meant the opposite, and by the end of 1985 over 20 million CDs had been sold in the US alone.

I didn't actually know anyone with a CD player until I was at university in 1986 and one of my friends bought one, along with a small selection of CDs (among them the almost obligatory Dire Straits title *Brothers In Arms*). Obviously anything that used laser technology back then was to be admired, and 'Money For Nothing' did sound brilliant, but I wasn't convinced that it was really the future of music. It just didn't feel 'right' somehow and, technophobe that I am, it was another five years before I bought my first CD player (incidentally the first CD I bought was Scritti Politti's *Cupid & Psyche '85* and it did sound brilliant!), by which time CDs had overwhelmingly taken over the market as the main audio format.

CDs ...Up To Date!

An estimated 20 billion CDs were sold worldwide in 2006, but for the first time in over twenty years the format was under threat from the next miracle in audio-technology, digital downloads, sales of which are estimated at around 2 billion.

The first CD player, a 1978 demonstration model, was named 'Pinkeltje' after a friendly gnome in a Dutch children's story.

The first CD ever manufactured for sale to the public was Billy Joel's *52nd Street*.

The size of a standard CD was decided by Sony Vice-President Norio Ogha, who insisted that the format should be able to contain an entire performance of Beethoven's Ninth Symphony on one disc. The longest known recording lasted 74 minutes, which dictated that a CD would need to be 12 cm.

1983 ICON

▶▶ *Spandau Ballet*

I'm not sure I can properly describe the impact, for me at least, of Spandau Ballet appearing on *Top Of The Pops* for the first time in 1981. 'To Cut A Long Story Short' was the first New Romantic hit, reaching number five in the UK, and consequently the first time that a lot of people, myself included, had a proper glimpse of this new movement. Spandau Ballet – Tony Hadley, Gary Kemp, Martin Kemp, Steve Norman and John Keeble – appeared in kilts and tartan and the combination of their image and their music, a quite stark but danceable fusion of guitars and synthesizers was very genuinely new and exciting.

Spandau Ballet was everywhere that year with more hit singles – 'The Freeze', 'Musclebound' and 'Chant No 1 (I Don't Need This Pressure On)' – plus a top five album, *Journeys To Glory*. I liked the singles and I liked *Journeys To Glory*. At the time the band truly sounded like the future, but for some reason they never became 'my' band, and when their popularity dipped slightly around the release of their second album *Diamond* I lost sight of them, only to rediscover them (along with pretty much the entire world!), when they released their next album *True*.

With the release of *True* in 1983 Spandau Ballet was everywhere again, and had pretty much entirely reinvented itself as a blue-eyed soul group; guitarist Steve Norman had switched instruments and had taken up the saxophone and the band's New Romantic image had been shed in favour of vintage-style suits. The *True* album launched four singles, all of which were major UK hits – 'Lifeline', 'Communication', 'Gold' and 'True' – the latter two becoming major international hits and perhaps the band's trademark songs; 'True' went on to become one of the most popular and successful songs of the eighties and beyond. One of my sisters was a huge fan of this new Spandau Ballet and consequently I continued to follow their career vicariously through her. I really liked the *True* album (although that wasn't something to be widely advertised at the time: the band, alongside their arch-rivals Duran Duran, were now pin-ups for the teen-pop market and therefore too 'girly' for me to admit liking at the time!) and unlike many of the records from that era it still sounds great today.

The band released a fourth album, *Parade*, in 1984 and enjoyed more success, the album peaking at number two in the album chart and launching another four singles. For me however it was the next album, 1986's *Through The Barricades*, where they moved away from soul towards a more guitar-focused sound, that saw them regain the form that made True so special, and I consider the title track in particular to be one of the highlights of their career. I even took my sister to see them at Wembley Arena on the *Through The Barricades* tour, her first concert and my first experience of screaming pop hysteria. A final album, *Heart Like A Sky*, was released in 1989 but none of the four singles from the release broke into the top forty and the album itself peaked at 31.

Spandau Ballet subsequently split and spent much of the nineties locked in legal battles between Tony Hadley, John Keeble and Steve Norman on one side and Gary and Martin Kemp on the other over the division of songwriting royalties. Rumours that the band will reform circulate periodically but as the band's singer Tony Hadley tells me in an interview in 2007, such an event sounds unlikely: 'I can't see it to be honest, I really can't … I think it all went too far and it got very personal and very nasty. It's a shame but there are just too many issues to be resolved.'

Tony Hadley continues to make albums and tour and his drummer on those tours is usually John Keeble who has also been involved in a number of other musical projects, the most recent of which is I Play Rock who released their debut album in 2006. Tony Hadley made a swing album, *Passing Strangers*, in 2006, which led to his starring in the West End production of the musical *Chicago*. Martin and Gary Kemp went on to star as the Kray twins in the 1990 film *The Krays* and both have continued to make acting appearances on television, in films and on stage, although Martin Kemp's role as the evil Steve Owen in *EastEnders* between 1998 and 2002 is probably the most well known. Gary Kemp released a solo album, *Little Bruises*, in 1995 and continues to write for other artists, and Steve Norman went on to produce, arrange and write songs for a variety of dance artists and fronts the ambient electronica band Cloudfish with former Bucks Fizz singer Shelley Preston.

Spandau Ballet released a twentieth-anniversary edition of the *True* album in 2003 featuring bonus video material and pictures and sleeve-notes from the band's guitarist and songwriter Gary Kemp, whom I interviewed about the project at the time. The interview here is taken from that conversation.

CAN YOU BELIEVE THAT IT'S BEEN TWENTY YEARS SINCE YOU FIRST RELEASED THE *TRUE* ALBUM?

It still feels quite modern, I mean it still feels … current is probably the word to use. I think that in the eighties a certain production sound was discovered which was very landscape and very three-dimensional and that in a way hasn't been bettered, and because there's been a fashion over the last fifteen years to have very retro sixties' and seventies' sounding production, which sounds quite flat and two-dimensional, a lot of the tracks still sound like a modern record. Also a lot of it is constantly on the radio, and you hear tracks from the album on commercials or in films, and even young black hip-hop groups in America are using bits of it.

THERE'S A VERY MARKED TRANSITION BETWEEN THE FIRST TWO ALBUMS AND *TRUE*, WHICH HAS A VERY DIFFERENT SOUND.

It's much more melodic and song-orientated, and I think the main reason was that we were very much a cult group, a group that had grown out of the club culture of London. That's how we saw ourselves – very much as part of that world and representing that world, but after being on *Top Of The Pops* six times there comes a moment when you realise that you can't continue being a cult group! If we were going to continue and succeed – and I certainly wanted to sell records in the rest of the world – it had to be a much more song-orientated record. I think that once we'd discovered that particular sound, it became the sort of sound that we ended up playing for the next seven years, a cleaner sound, but more song orientated, whereas the first two albums were very much about four-on-the-floor dance beats, on the first album with a rather European-sounding synthesizer backdrop, and on the second playing around more with traditional funk grooves.

HOW DID SPANDAU BALLET GO ABOUT WRITING A SONG? DOES THE SENTIMENT COME FIRST, OR THE LYRICS, OR THE MUSIC?

In those days the inspiration to write songs was slightly different, the inspiration to write a song was to try and write a great song and to be as good as other people who I thought wrote great songs. It was to write songs that would be hits for Spandau Ballet rather than it being a need to get something out of my system because of any personal reason. Having said that, I have to draw on the personal and the *True* album is very much the first album where I had written about love and about unrequited passion – which is what a lot of the album is about – I was actually suffering from the pangs of that at the time.

HOW FAR DO YOU IDENTIFY NOW WITH THE GARY KEMP OF TWENTY YEARS AGO?

It's not me now … I don't really identify with it. In fact it's an interesting moment in our lives because the Spandau Ballet that everyone knows didn't even exist at that moment because we were literally a cult group selling records in the UK alone and we'd just had a moment where it had dipped a bit – 'She Loved Like Diamond' didn't even make the top forty …

So I look back and it's quite interesting because we were on the cusp of a lot of success and a huge life-change … I think that at that moment in time, in 1982, I was 22 and I was still living at home with my mum and dad! I suppose I also envy myself as well – I envy the all-encompassing passion to have success with the group, where I was 24/7 just living and working for Spandau Ballet.

THE 'TRUE' SINGLE WAS A PHENOMENAL SUCCESS AND A TRUE MARKING POINT IN SPANDAU BALLET'S HISTORY. HOW DO YOU FEEL ABOUT THE IMPACT IT MADE? PROUD I IMAGINE, BUT IS THERE ANYTHING ELSE?

More than proud … sometimes fearful – certainly in the early days there was a kind of fear of it because it became kind of monolithic later on in our career. I wouldn't say it became our worst enemy but it gave us a lot to live up to and I think in many ways there were other songs later that sat alongside it very comfortably. 'Only When You Leave' and 'Through The Barricades' probably did, but to write one classic in a life is more than enough! I don't know what it is about the song that has captured people's imagination for so long … but it definitely became the school disco number one in 1983 and it got under people's skin, which makes it special for people. I remember the first time I danced in a disco with a girl – to 'Betcha By Golly Wow' – and to this day when I hear it I get goose-bumps and I get nostalgic for that time!

YOU MENTIONED THAT THE TRUE ALBUM WAS WRITTEN VERY MUCH WITH AN EYE ON WIDENING YOUR INTERNATIONAL APPEAL, WHICH YOU ACHIEVED, BUT WHEN YOU HAD IT WAS IT EVERYTHING YOU HOPED IT WOULD BE?

During the successes of *Parade* and *True*, when things were going very well for us, then of course it was – it was always a fantastic ride, but I do think that we struggled with a certain amount of longevity, in America in particular. We had successful albums and then when we moved to Sony we had a situation where *Parade* was never released in the US, there was this kind of blindness to the band from Sony US that has always frustrated me. It was ironic because one of the reasons that we left Chrysalis and went to Sony was because we felt that we weren't really being sold as well as we should have been in the States!

TO HAVE HAD THE AMERICAN SUCCESS YOU DID ACHIEVE, AND TO BE A WHITE GROUP BREAKING OUT OF THE BLACK MUSIC AND SOUL MUSIC COMMUNITIES, MUST HAVE BEEN A VERY GRATIFYING EXPERIENCE FOR YOU, PARTICULARLY GIVEN YOUR OWN SOUL INFLUENCES.

I think that is something I'm most proud of, because as a working-class kid dancing to black music – and black music was hated by the British music press at the time, unmentionable at a time when music wasn't supposed to be aspirational. Punk was the opposite of that, but I liked both … I liked punk and I liked Bowie and I liked disco – not the most glamorous word for it but it wasn't called dance music then! We recently picked up an airplay award for three million plays of 'True' in the US, the same as a Beatles' track, I think it was 'I

Wanna Hold Your Hand', and you think, God, that's been out for years longer, but it's because we get played on white and black radio and The Beatles don't.

YOU SEEM TO HAVE BECOME A KIND OF CURATOR FOR SPANDAU BALLET. THE ATTENTION TO DETAIL AND THE WORK THAT YOU'VE OBVIOUSLY PUT IN ON THIS RELEASE OF *TRUE* AND ALSO ON LAST YEAR'S 'REFORMATION' PACKAGE IS STAGGERING.
You know, I'm very honoured that you said it that way, rather than looking on it in a cynical way. For me, after the court case it was very important to reclaim what we had destroyed … I thought we had besmirched our own name, pissed on our own doorstep and I wanted to reclaim that.

The other reason is that, although it's beyond my control that EMI will put out packages of Spandau Ballet's old stuff, I wanted to make sure that if they did do that then they did it well and they did it right, so I have been involved in it, just trying to keep all of the stuff that is released good and worth buying, and in a few years time when people listen back they will have a genuine idea of what the band were.

OF ALL THE SONGS YOU'VE WRITTEN DO YOU HAVE ANY PERSONAL FAVOURITES?
I'd have to say 'True', I'd have to say 'Through The Barricades', and there's a really great song on *True* that I still get a buzz from when I listen to it called 'Heaven Is A Secret' … probably those. Another song on the last album called 'Empty Spaces' I'm really pleased with, lyrically in particular, and that's about the break-up of a relationship I'd had that was at the great storm in 1987 and is about me taking a walk with her while all these trees were lying on the ground, and finishing that relationship.

YOU MADE A SOLO ALBUM LITTLE BRUISES IN 1996 DIDN'T YOU? WILL YOU DO ANY MORE MUSIC AS A SOLO ARTIST?
I don't know. I am thinking about making an album, but I had such a huge inspiration to make the first one – huge changes in my personal life; a divorce, a reassessment of myself, a lot of things that I wanted to say

and needed to get out, and music was the way to do that. It was also an opportunity to make music and work with musicians who I couldn't have worked with in the band, and make the kind of music that I couldn't have made in the band. That kind of got it all off my chest in a way and at the moment I'm not sure.

DO YOU MISS PERFORMING AS A MUSICIAN?
Yep! I miss the big stage certainly, but I enjoyed doing a bit of theatre when I did *Art* and that kind of gave me the same sort of adrenaline buzz, and I really love that feeling.

AND FINALLY, A GOOD WAY TO FINISH … WHAT IS YOUR MOST MEMORABLE SPANDAU BALLET MOMENT?
They all fall into my head at once … probably running into Tony Hadley's hotel room at about nine o'clock in the morning and telling him that we'd gone to number one with 'True' and all of us just jumping up and down on his bed!

'My favourite band would be Spandau Ballet. From the first time I heard 'To Cut A Long Story Short' I was hooked really. I loved the newness of it, something I hadn't heard before. In my opinion Spandau's output and ability to experiment and reinvent themselves from record to record is something they just do not get enough credit for and it's the reason why I still love listening to them. It's a joy to put on one of their albums and still be able to enjoy it like I was hearing it for the first time.'

MARK FINNEGAN

1984

Snapshot

The first Apple Macintosh personal computer goes on sale ● Michael Jackson is seriously burnt while filming a TV advert for Pepsi ● The Winter Olympics take place in Sarajevo and the Summer Olympics in Los Angeles ● *Miami Vice* is aired in the US for the first time ● Marvin Gaye, Eric Morecambe, Tommy Cooper, Jackie Wilson, John Betjeman, J.B. Priestley and Richard Burton all pass away ● The miners' strike begins on 6 March ● The Australian one-dollar coin is introduced ● *Starlight Express* opens in London ● Band Aid's 'Do They Know It's Christmas?' is the year's bestselling UK single ● O Levels and CSEs are replaced by GCSEs ● Virgin Atlantic makes its first flight ● France win the European Cup when they beat Spain 2-0 ● The first MTV Video Music Awards takes place in New York ● The IRA bomb the Grand Hotel in Brighton during the Conservative Party Conference ● Indian Prime Minister Indira Gandhi is assassinated ● British Telecom is privatised ● Ronald Regan is re-elected as American President ● Colin Baker takes over from Peter Davidson as Doctor Who ● The world's population is estimated at 4.769 billion people ● TV satire show *Spitting Image* is shown for the first time ● Prince Henry is born on 15 September but will always be known as Harry ● The Detroit Tigers win the World Series ● 'Trivial Pursuit' is the year's most successful game, selling over 20 million sets ● L'Oreal introduce 'Free Hold', the first hair mousse, and predict the end to hair-gel ● John McEnroe beats Jimmy Connors in the men's competition at Wimbledon and Martina Navratilova beats Chris Evert-Lloyd in the women's ● Budweiser beer is sold in the UK for the first time ● The half-pence coin and the one-pound note are withdrawn from UK circulation ● Moon boots are a winter fashion essential ● Lionel Richie's *Can't Slow Down* is the UK's bestselling album ● The first baby born from a frozen embryo is born in Sydney, Australia ● William Gibson and Jay McInerney's first novels, *Neuromancer* and *Bright Lights Big City*, are published

'Ultimate artist has to be Frankie Goes To Hollywood – they ignited my love for music and I have never looked back!'

JUSTIN CAMPBELL

1984
Number One Singles

Paul McCartney 'Pipes Of Peace', Frankie Goes To Hollywood 'Relax', Nena '99 Red Balloons', Lionel Richie 'Hello', Duran Duran 'The Reflex', Wham! 'Wake Me Up Before You Go Go', Frankie Goes To Hollywood 'Two Tribes', George Michael 'Careless Whisper', Stevie Wonder 'I Just Called To Say I Love You', Wham! 'Freedom', Chaka Khan 'I Feel For You', Jim Diamond 'I Should Have Known Better', Frankie Goes To Hollywood 'The Power Of Love', Band Aid 'Do They Know It's Christmas?'

Sounds Like 1984

The bestselling single of this year is also the start of one of the biggest humanitarian stories I will ever witness. Band Aid's single 'Do They Know It's Christmas?' will be number one as the year ends, staying at number one for five weeks, knocking Frankie Goes To Hollywood's 'The Power Of Love' from the top and then keeping Wham!'s 'Last Christmas' at number two (giving George Michael and Andrew Ridgeley the frustrating honour of having the bestselling single ever to fail to reach the top of the singles charts). The success of Band Aid, however, does little to diminish the triumphs this year of either band, each of which will have the most commercially successful year of their careers, and who together will make Katharine Hamnett slogan T-shirts the year's essential fashion item – Wham! popularising such slogans as 'Choose Life' and 'Go Go' while Frankie go to the other extreme with 'Frankie Say Relax', 'Frankie Say War Hide Yourself' and 'Frankie Say Arm The Unemployed'.

Frankie Goes To Hollywood will enter the record books in 1984 as the first band to reach number one in the singles charts with their first three singles releases since Gerry And The Pacemakers in 1963. The band's controversial debut 'Relax' will go to number one in January (subsequently going down the charts before climbing again and reaching a second peak at number two in July), 'Two Tribes' in June and 'The Power Of Love' in December. Their debut album, *Welcome To The Pleasuredome*, will also peak at number one in November, going on to spend over a year on the album charts.

Wham! will do almost as well with two magnificently exuberant number one singles, 'Wake Me Up Before You Go Go' and 'Freedom', plus 'Last Christmas' and a number one album *Make It Big*, which will stay in the UK charts for a year and a half. Frontman George Michael will also have a number one single in the summer with 'Careless Whisper', released under his own name, which is confusing to say the least because the song also appears on Wham!'s *Make It Big* album, is co-written by Andrew Ridgeley and is credited as being a Wham! song on the American single. Either way it will be enough to spark a tide of speculation over the future of the duo.

'Careless Whisper' is one of a trio of epic ballads this year and, with Lionel Richie's 'Hello' and Stevie Wonder's 'I Just Called To Say I Love You', will go on to become a genuine eighties' classic and an essential end-of-the-night school disco slow-song. The other two songs will be number one singles for six weeks each this year, and on the back of the success of

'George Michael's "Careless Whisper" is my favourite eighties' single – good memories of my first love!'

VINNY

'As a teen at the time Footloose seemed so edgy! But the music was great!'

CAROLINE

'Hello', Lionel Richie's 1983 album *Can't Slow Down* will return to the number one position in the UK charts on its way to becoming the bestselling album of the year. Two more singles will also be taken from the album – 'Stuck On You' and 'Penny Lover' – both of which will become top twenty UK hits (and bring the number of singles taken from the eight-song album to five). Stevie Wonder's 'I Just Called To Say I Love You', from the soundtrack to the film *The Woman In Red*, will be his first UK solo number one single and will also top the US charts and earn an Oscar for Best Original Song.

The year is a good year for film soundtrack music generally. The soundtrack album to Kevin Bacon's *Footloose* will peak at number seven and launch two hit singles: the title track by Kenny Loggins, which will reach number six, and Deniece Williams' upbeat and poppy hit 'Let's Hear It For The Boy', which will be held off the top spot only by Lionel Richie's 'Hello'. Ray Parker Junior's *Ghostbusters* theme will also narrowly miss the number one position in August, and the Human League's Phil Oakey's collaboration with Giorgio Moroder, 'Together In Electric Dreams', for the film *Electric Dreams*, will reach number three in September.

The Human League will return this year with a long overdue new album, *Hysteria*, and a trio of singles, 'The Lebanon', 'Life On Your Own' and 'Louise'. The album will reach number three in May but none of the singles will quite make the top ten. Duran Duran will also release three singles, 'New Moon On Monday' and 'The Reflex' from their *Seven And The Ragged Tiger* album ('The Reflex' reaching number one in the UK and the USA and becoming the band's most commercially successful single ever), and a number two single with 'The Wild Boys', released in conjunction with a live album *Arena*, which will make

'One of the best 80s songs has to be Prince's 'When Doves Cry'. It has this multi-layered richness and this deep emotional centre. It was with this song that his legacy was born and cemented.'

JOHN CARDONA

number six in November. Personally however, my allegiance has now switched to Depeche Mode who will also release their fourth album this year, the darker, more experimental *Some Great Reward*, which reaches number five, plus a trio of singles – 'People Are People', 'Master & Servant' and 'Somebody/Blasphemous Rumours' – which will reach four, nine and sixteen respectively.

Ultravox, who have been steadily releasing a succession of excellent hit albums and singles since the pinnacle of 'Vienna', will come close to repeating that success this year when their brilliant 'Dancing With Tears In My Eyes' peaks at number three. The band have further success with the album *Lament*, which reaches number eight in April. The success of *Lament* will then be eclipsed by the success of the first Ultravox compilation album, *The Collection*, which will reach number two in November and will spend over a year in the albums charts.

When it comes to ballads I think I'm a fairly typical male in that I will admit to having no interest in them whatsoever while actually having a small selection of secret favourites. This year Depeche Mode's 'Somebody' will be close to the top of my list of guilty pleasures, as will Cyndi Lauper's 'Time After Time', a number three single for her in June. I like Cyndi Lauper for her colourful individuality and personality and 'Time After Time' will be one of four singles released by her this year to varying degrees of success ('Girls Just Want To Have Fun' will reach number two while 'All Through The Night' will peak at just 64) from her hugely successful *She's So Unusual* album.

Another ballad on the guilty list this year is Sade's 'Your Love Is King', which will be a number six hit in February – her highest ever singles chart position – and her debut album *Diamond Life*, which

features another equally sultry single, 'Smooth Operator', and will go to number two. I like Sade too, but for very different reasons to why I like Cyndi Lauper. The brother of someone I know slightly is the keyboard player in her live band – enough to make a meeting very tenuously feasible, although going as far as to hope that Sade is on the look-out for a sixteen-year-old Smiths' fan with rubbish hair will, perhaps, be stretching the point.

Tina Turner will launch her solo career in spectacular style with her *Private Dancer* album this year. The record will peak at two in the UK and three in the US and will go on to become one of the most successful albums of the decade, selling well over 20 million copies and featuring a succession of hit singles including 'What's Love Got To Do With It?', 'Let's Stay Together' and 'Private Dancer', and establishing Turner as one of the most successful female artists of all time.

Stevie Wonder will feature on a second number one hit this year when he plays harmonica on Chaka Khan's hit 'I Feel For You', which also features rapping from Melle Mel who will also enjoy success in the line-up of Grandmaster Flash & The Furious Five's epic hit 'White Lines', which will peak at seven in February. 'I Feel For You' is a cover of a song written by a relatively new American artist, Prince, who is starting to enjoy significant chart success in his own right in 1984. Prince, who had already scraped the UK top thirty in

'I loved Madonna's early image . . . kinda punky, gothy, poppy – and damned sexy.'

SHAUN

1983 with the anthemic '1999', will also have a pair of top-ten singles hits under his own name this year, with 'When Doves Cry' and 'Purple Rain', as well as album success with his *Purple Rain* soundtrack which reaches number seven in July, re-igniting interest in his 1983 album *1999*, which will finally chart amid the considerable interest and excitement surrounding this new star.

Another US artist to taste UK success for the first time this year is Madonna whose debut singles 'Holiday' and 'Lucky Star' will make six and fourteen in the singles charts, but a third single – the first release of 'Borderline' – will peak at 56 and her self-titled debut album will only just scrape into the top forty. Salvation will come in the form of the mildly controversial 'Like A Virgin' single, which will reach number three in November, and the *Like A Virgin* album, which will go on to be a multi-platinum number one record around the world establishing Madonna as one of the ultimate artists of the era.

The Smiths are already a very public part of my life when they release their debut album, *The Smiths*, this year, which will reach number two in the albums charts; I view this as a huge triumph seeing that no one else I know had bought it or even cared about the band. They will also release a trio of classic singles: 'What Difference Does It Make', the band's first top ten single 'Heaven Knows I'm Miserable Now', and 'William It Was Really Nothing'. The Smiths now have a place alongside the hundreds of Toyah pictures on my wall, although at this point in time there are a few of other artists that are there not entirely for reasons to do with their music. The fact that Altered Images have split up doesn't seem reason to take down my pictures of Clare Grogan, and

Bananarama will actually release my favourite single from them this year when they put out 'Robert De Niro's Waiting' in March, their most successful single to date when it peaks at number three.

A picture of Hazell Dean also seems justified because she went to my school and I deliver her parents' weekly free paper and, although I'm not entirely sure which house they live in, I know they will be very proud when Hazell has two hits in succession with 'Searching' and 'Whatever I Do (Wherever I Go)' this year. Both are among the early work from a new production team, Stock, Aitken & Waterman, whose first collaboration will be an unlikely hit this year for Harris Glenn Milstead – working under the stage name Divine – when his 'You Think You're A Man' reaches number sixteen. Liverpool's Dead Or Alive will enjoy some success this year with their debut album *Sophisticated Boom Boom* and a single, 'That's The Way (I Like It)', but it's when they make the decision to work with Stock, Aitken & Waterman later this year that their fortunes truly change. Dead Or Alive will release a new single, the first from their SAW-

'The Smiths were the ultimate eighties' band, seeing them on TOTP as a teenager really was an epiphany. It was time for change, for someone to take it all one step further into doubt, androgyny, intellect, vulnerability and that glorious guitar sound. They were an eighties band, every bit as much as Spandau Ballet or Haysi Fantayzee were. They summed up the era as well as anyone could have done.'

DARREN BEACH

> **'Scritti Politti is my ultimate eighties' act … utter genius, fabulous productions, great songs, great videos.'**
>
> JUSTIN BINDLEY

produced second album, in December, although the effect of 'You Spin Me Round (Like A Record)' won't be felt until next year.

Intelligent pop is also very much at the fore this year and both Howard Jones and Nik Kershaw will have astonishingly successful years. Howard Jones' debut album Humans Lib will go to number one, preceded by the brilliantly atmospheric single 'Hide & Seek' and followed by the more upbeat and catchy 'Pearl In The Shell'. As much as I like it, Humans Lib will be eclipsed for me by the release of an album of fantastic 12-inch mixes and extended versions, *The 12" Album*, in December, my first real introduction to remix culture. Nik Kershaw is arguably one of the most successful artists of this year, releasing five top-twenty singles from two top-ten studio albums – *Human Racing* and *The Riddle* – which will establish him as one of the great British pop writers. Scritti Politti will also have two gorgeous pop hits this year with 'Wood Beez (Pray Like Aretha Franklin)' and 'Absolute'.

U2 will release their fourth studio album in October, their second number one album *The Unforgettable Fire* which they will precede with perhaps their greatest ever single, 'Pride (In The Name Of Love)', in September. These releases will mark a brand new chapter in the U2 story, as global superstars. This year they will suddenly stop being 'my' band and will truly join the mainstream and – putting the gloriously anthemic 'Pride' to one side – even the music is different, Bono at the time describing the sound perfectly as 'blurred and out of focus'. Big Country's *Steeltown*, on the other hand, is less of a disappointment to me and will deservedly become a number one album in October, preceded by an equally worthy hit single 'East Of Eden'. Queen will also return to their rock roots and will have a great year,

with an album (*The Works*), four hit singles ('Radio Ga Ga', 'I Want To break Free', 'It's A Hard Life' and 'Hammer To Fall'), each supported by a memorable and inventive video – including an all-time classic in their *Coronation Street* spoof for 'I Want To Break Free' – and re-establishing the band as a truly contemporary force.

There will be some great songs in the one-hit wonder category this year and one of the weirdest is one of my favourites, Malcolm McLaren's hip-hop, electro-opera version of 'Madame Butterfly', the closest I will ever come to liking opera. Nena's '99 Red Balloons', an English reworking of a German hit '99 Luftballons', will be another favourite, although I will always, rather pretentiously, claim to prefer the original. Another German act, Alphaville, will also have a major hit this year with 'Big In Japan'. Strawberry Switchblade will enjoy a brief moment in the spotlight, when 'Since Yesterday' becomes their sole hit in November, although their polka-dot-goth styling will go on to have far greater impact in alternative clubs across the country. The Weather Girls will have a similarly stellar career; 'It's Raining Men' reaching number two in August. Meanwhile, Michael and Jermaine Jackson's backing vocals on 'Somebody's Watching Me' will help ensure a number six hit for Rockwell in February.

When it comes to novelty records, 1984 will be the year forever associated with Black Lace's 'Agadoo', which peaked at number two and stayed in the charts for almost a year, becoming the irritating party hit of the eighties, a record that will be played unmercifully at every works do, wedding or office party from this point on. Forever.

Sounds Like 1984
The Year as a Mixtape

SIDE ONE

Grandmaster Flash 'White Lines', Prince 'When Doves Cry', Chaka Khan 'I Feel For You', Miami Sound Machine 'Dr Beat', Break Machine 'Street Dance', Pointer Sisters 'Automatic', Shannon 'Let The Music Play', Deniece Williams 'Let's Hear It For The Boy', Bananarama 'Robert De Niro's Waiting', Madonna 'Like A Virgin', The Weather Girls 'It's Raining Men', Wham! 'Wake Me Up Before You Go Go', Lionel Richie 'Hello', George Michael 'Careless Whisper', Tina Turner 'Private Dancer'

SIDE TWO

U2 'Pride (In The Name Of Love)', Queen 'Radio Ga Ga', Ultravox 'Dancing With Tears In My Eyes', The Smiths 'Heaven Knows I'm Miserable Now', Nena '99 Red Balloons', John Waite 'Missing You', Bronski Beat 'Smalltown Boy', Kane Gang 'Closest Thing To Heaven', Strawberry Switchblade 'Since Yesterday', Nik Kershaw 'The Riddle', Duran Duran 'Wild Boys', Depeche Mode 'Master & Servant', ZZ Top 'Sharp Dressed Man', Special AKA 'Free Nelson Mandela', Band Aid 'Do They Know It's Christmas?'

Trivial Pursuit

The four original partners are still friends and now own two golf courses, a number of racehorses and a junior hockey team.

The author of a number of trivia books sued Trivial Pursuit in 1984 when a deliberate wrong answer, which the author had included in his books in an attempt to catch people violating his copyright, turned up on a Trivial Pursuit card. A judge went on to rule that facts were not protected by copyright. The question was 'What was Lieutenant Columbo's first name?' and the false answer was Philip (the answer is actually Frank!).

It's only a game. It's supposed to be fun – a gentle test of general knowledge to be played with friends and family – but how many hearts sink and competitive hackles rise on sight of the distinctive blue and gold box being pulled out on holidays, at family gatherings and at parties?

If you're one of the people with a sinking heart then you have to feel sorry for the Canadians, because they've had the game the longest. Trivial Pursuit was invented in Canada and the game first went on sale there in 1981, the result of a friendly argument between sports writer Scott Abbott and photo editor Chris Haney in 1979 over who was the better game player.

Trivial Pursuit was duly invented as a game that would settle the issue once and for all, and the pair formed a business company, Horn Abbot, with Chris's brother John and his friend Ed Werner. They produced the first thousand prototype sets, which they sold in Canada for $15 despite each set costing them around five times that amount. They then took Trivial Pursuit to the American International Toy Fair in New York in 1982 with high expectations but sold just a few hundred copies. However repeat orders started to trickle in, the media started to pick up on the game and Horn Abbott signed distribution deals in Canada in 1982 and the USA and Europe in 1983.

In 1984 the game was launched in the UK during its most successful year, when it sold more than 20 million copies in the US alone. Over the next twenty years or so it would go on to achieve sales of almost one hundred million in seventeen languages across thirty-three countries, making it the most successful board game of all time.

The original 'Genus' edition of Trivial Pursuit contained 6000 questions divided into six categories – Geography, Science & Nature, Sports & Leisure, History, Entertainment and Arts & Literature – on a thousand cards, although more sets of questions were quickly introduced and the range now includes question sets for children and specialist sets on Star Wars, cinema, The Lord Of The Rings, books, the 80s and the 90s.

Trivial Pursuit ... Up To Date!

It is now possible to play Trivial Pursuit online, on DVD, via mobile phones and using a handheld electronic version of the game. There have also been a number of TV shows based on the game produced around the world. In 1998 a light-hearted TV movie was made entitled *Breaking All The Rules – The Creation of Trivial Pursuit*. It wasn't a hit.

THE FORMAT WARS –
VHS VERSUS BETAMAX

I escaped the whole 'VHS versus beta' debate that raged in the mid-eighties simply because my family didn't own a video recorder until long after I had left home and, aside from being part of a small, nerdy team of boys whose responsibility it was to use my school's technological pride and joy – a giant early video camera – to document school events, I think my own first video experience was at university when I borrowed my hall of residence's player when all my friends were away and watched *2001: A Space Odyssey* over and over again for an entire weekend.

By then video players and recorders were fairly commonplace, the format was set to VHS and you'd be hard-pushed to find a Betamax player if you wanted to play old beta tapes. Looking back it's easy to remember the Betamax format as a well-meaning but ineffectual technological innovation, but at the start of 1984 Betamax was the most popular home video system in the UK and accounted for well over a third of the market.

Betamax was the first format to be developed and was introduced by Sony in 1975, the company hoping to present the system to their competitors so compellingly that they would all back Sony and avoid a costly and confusing format battle. A number of the other manufacturers, however, were reluctant to allow Sony to corner the market in this way, and when VHS was introduced by rival electronics giant JVC in 1976 the result was divisive. Sony, Toshiba, Sanyo, NEC, Aiwa and Pioneer favoured Betamax and JVC, Panasonic, Hitachi, Mitsubishi, Sharp and Akai aligned themselves with VHS. A format war then ensued that lasted for well over a decade.

The first Betamax machine was the SL-6300, which was twice the size of a television set, had its own integrated TV screen, cost the same as a small car and used tapes that were just 60 minutes long – crucially too short to contain a full-length film or a televised football game. Betamax was marketed as the superior quality format, offering a slightly higher-resolution image and less tape noise than VHS, but the machines were more complicated, costly and time-consuming to build. The format was also hampered by Sony's apparent reluctance to sign the licensing agreements with film companies that would allow Betamax versions of their films to be made available to rent or buy. Sony also opposed the use of Betamax tapes for pornographic films, a decision said to have more effect on driving the market towards VHS than any other.

VHS on the other hand was marketed as the cheaper format, the machines were simpler to build and manufacturers were able to keep ahead of demand. The first VHS tapes could last for two hours, and although both formats improved their running times VHS would continue to stay ahead on tape time. Crucially,

VHS was the format choice of the UK high street rental companies, who would account for 70 per cent of all VCRs in UK homes in the early eighties, and the range of films available to rent and buy on VHS was vastly superior.

The Format Wars – Up To Date!

The tide turned overwhelmingly towards VHS by 1985 and even Sony themselves started manufacturing VHS machines in 1988, although they nominally continued to support the Betamax format until its eventual demise in the early nineties. In 2003 DVD sales exceeded VHS sales for the first time and now even VHS is virtually redundant as a format.

'Betamaxed' has become business slang for situations where apparently superior technology loses out to an inferior solution which is more well-known in the marketplace.

Betamax got its name from a combination of 'beta', meaning quality and 'max' meaning maximum. VHS stands for Vertical Helical Scan.

Feed the World: THE STORY OF BAND AID

On 23rd October 1984 TV journalist Michael Buerk appeared on the evening news reporting from the Ethiopian famine. Millions of people watched that harrowing report but one man in particular decided that the situation was simply unacceptable and made a decision to do something about it. That man was Bob Geldof, then the singer with the Boomtown Rats, who decided to make a charity record to raise money for famine relief and turned to Ultravox singer Midge Ure, for help writing a song.

The next step was to draw up a list of the UK's biggest music stars and then persuade, cajole and bully them into taking part, the result being that on 25th November a stellar cast of musical talents assembled at a London recording studio to record 'Do They Know It's Christmas?' – a song they hadn't even heard at that point, as Midge Ure will remind me when I speak to him about that day in 2004: 'All those people who turned up that wet Sunday morning had never heard the song – it could have been the biggest piece of crap ever! But they came along, and they sang the song, and they put their names and their characters and their power behind the record to make the record happen.'

Midge Ure had the unenviable task of recording and mixing all the vocals for the record, as well as Phil Collins' drum part, in just 24 hours, a tall order by anyone's standards: 'I was trying to make it all work, just trying to glue it all together!' he will tell me later. Spandau Ballet's Tony

'There was just such a feeling of belonging during that particular era. Everyone thought they were changing the world and their favourite bands were on their side.'

CHAD FROM TENNESSEE

Hadley was the first to record his part and Culture Club's Boy George was the last, after being woken in New York by a telephone call from Bob Geldof telling him to get straight onto a Concorde. The other main vocal parts were taken by Paul Young, George Michael, Simon Le Bon, Sting, Bono, Paul Weller, Glen Gregory, Marilyn, Rick Parfitt and Francis Rossi, and the musical parts were provided by John Taylor and Adam Clayton on bass, Phil Collins on drums and Midge Ure on keyboards.

Over a million people bought Band Aid's 'Do they Know It's Christmas?' in the first week of the record's release on 3rd December 1984, and more than two million more people bought it over the next few weeks, ensuring that the record stayed at number one for five weeks and became the bestselling UK single ever – a title it held for over thirteen years until Elton John's 1997 tribute to Princess Diana, 'Candle In The Wind', would sell almost five million copies.

Band Aid ... Up To Date!

This original version of 'Do They Know It's Christmas?' was re-released for Christmas 1985, reaching number three in the singles charts, and returned to number one in 1989 after being re-recorded in December 1989 by some of the major stars of the day (including Kylie Minogue, Jason Donovan, Bananarama, Cliff Richard, Wet Wet Wet and Bros) and released as Band Aid II. A third version, Band Aid 20, was recorded by a new set of artists (including Bono, Coldplay, Travis and Robbie Williams) in 2004 to coincide with the twentieth anniversary of the original release and also went to number one. 'Do They Know It's Christmas?' alone has raised over £10 million for famine relief.

Who was on the original Band Aid single?

Adam Clayton, Bono (U2); Phil Collins; Bob Geldof, Johnnie Fingers, Gerry Cott, Simon Crowe (Boomtown Rats); Midge Ure, Chris Cross (Ultravox); Tony Hadley, John Keeble, Gary Kemp, Martin Kemp, Steve Norman (Spandau Ballet); Simon Le Bon, Nick Rhodes, Andy Taylor, John Taylor, Roger Taylor (Duran Duran); Paul Young; Glenn Gregory, Martyn Ware (Heaven 17); Siobhan Fahey, Sara Dallin, Keren Woodward (Bananarama); Paul Weller; Robert Bell, Dennis Thomas, James Taylor (Kool and the Gang); George Michael; Marilyn; Jodi Watley; Boy George, Jon Moss (Culture Club); Sting; Rick Parfitt, Francis Rossi (Status Quo). The B-side featured messages of support from other artists who were unable to attend, including David Bowie, Paul McCartney, Big Country and Frankie Goes To Hollywood's Holly Johnson.

Torvill And Dean

It was on 14th February 1984 that British ice-dance champions Jayne Torvill (a former insurance clerk) and Christopher Dean (a former policeman) skated their way to an Olympic gold medal in Sarajevo, Yugoslavia, cheered all the way by a home TV audience of over 24 million people. That they won was probably no great surprise – 1984 had already seen them win the European Championships for the third time and the World Championships for the fourth time – but in doing it they set a new Olympic record and became the first couple to earn maximum points for their now legendary free dance performance to Ravel's *Bolero*.

Ravel had his first top-ten single hit as a result – a version of *Bolero* by the Michael Reed Orchestra was released in February – and Torvill and Dean were hailed as national heroes. But no one was as proud as the people of their home town Nottingham, among them my Grandma who would later proudly take me around the city pointing out the National Ice Centre where the duo trained and the police station

where Christopher Dean had worked until his Olympic success. Nottingham not only sponsored the pair in the run-up to the Olympics but also went on to name a number of streets after the duo in celebration of their success.

The victory was the stuff of fairy tales. That Jayne Torvill and Christopher Dean were real people who had worked hard for their success, and who had made many sacrifices along the way, was story enough, but the fact that it happened on St Valentine's Day just added to the romanticism of the tale. The big question, the media decided, was to what extent did the duo's relationship continue

away from the ice?

It was an issue that was continually confused by apparently innocent answers from both of them. Directly after their famous Olympic performance they were asked when they were getting married, to which Christopher Dean answered 'not this week', and Jayne Torvill went on to fuel the fire when she said that they were truly in love for the four minutes they were on the ice. The papers went into overdrive, sparking instant speculation that a wedding was indeed on the cards, and a hysterical media went on to surmise that there was no better date for such an event than Valentine's Day 1985, the first anniversary of their Olympic triumph.

The date of course came and went and a disappointed media turned on the couple, speculating that Christopher was gay and Jayne was secretly seeing a Russian skater, although both stories were proved to be false. It would be another five years before wedding bells were heard when Jayne married Phil Christensen in 1990, Christopher marrying Isabelle Duchesnay a year later.

Torvill and Dean toured the world with a succession of shows until 1998 when they announced their retirement. The duo were awarded OBEs in 1999.

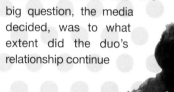

Torvill And Dean ... Up To Date!

In 1996 Torvill and Dean published a joint autobiography, *Facing The Music*, and then returned to public attention again in 2006 with the launch of the TV reality show Dancing On Ice, in which they train celebrities, paired with professional ice dancers, in the art of ice dancing. The show was an instant hit, becoming the third highest rated UK TV show in it's first year, attracting up to 13 million viewers every week.

1984 ICON

▶▶ *Nik Kershaw*

I have found that people don't just like Nik Kershaw, they *really* like Nik Kershaw and will talk of his talents in slightly hushed and awed tones. It's not just his fans who hold him in such respect either, it's also his peers who hold him in high regard as a fine guitarist and one of the great British songwriters; in fact Midge Ure, Howard Jones, Tony Hadley and Nick Beggs have all mentioned him in glowing terms in interviews for my website.

It's testament to this great respect that in the course of his career to date Nik has written and collaborated with a vast number of artists including Elton John, Bonnie Tyler, Genesis' Tony Banks, Cliff Richard, Gary Barlow, Imogen Heap and Les Rhythmes Digitale (the side-project of Madonna producer and collaborator Jacques Lu Cont). During the nineties Nik also wrote 'The One And Only' for Chesney Hawkes – a number one single – and three successive hit singles for the boyband Let Loose.

Despite these successes, it's for his work as a solo artist in the mid-eighties that Nik Kershaw is best known. In 1984 he dominated the UK charts, releasing two top-ten albums – *Human Racing* and *The Riddle* – and five hit singles – 'Dancing Girls', 'Human Racing' and 'The Riddle' as well the future eighties' classics 'I Won't Let The Sun Go Down On Me' and 'Wouldn't It Be Good'.

Nik Kershaw's domination of the charts continued into 1985 with more hit singles from *The Riddle*, 'Wide Boy' and 'Don Quixote', and with 'When A Heart Beats', the first single from his 1986 album *Radio Musicola*. He also played a four-song set at Live Aid, playing 'Wide Boy', 'Don Quixote', 'The Riddle' and 'Wouldn't It Be Good'. History also has him marked down as the man solely responsible for the mid-eighties craze for snoods and fingerless gloves.

A final major-label album followed in 1989 – *The Works* – after which Nik stopped making records under his own name. Instead he spent the next decade writing for and with other artists. In 1999 he returned to work as a solo artist and released a critically acclaimed album *15 Minutes*, which he followed with the equally well-praised *Too Be Frank* in 2001.

It would be another five years before he released his next album, the excellent *You've Got To Laugh* in 2006, on his own Short House label and I was fortunate enough to interview him about the release in December of that year. He was friendly and funny, and I managed not to mention snoods once …

YOU'RE TOTALLY INDEPENDENT AS AN ARTIST NOW, AREN'T YOU? RELEASING YOUR NEW MATERIAL ON YOUR OWN LABEL AND CUTTING OUT THE MIDDLE MAN … SO MANY OF THE ARTISTS I TALK TO ARE IN SIMILAR SITUATIONS NOW - IT'S ALMOST LIKE EVERYONE HAS BEEN UNBURDENED AND IS IN A POSITION WHERE THEY CAN ACTUALLY MAKE THE MUSIC THEY WANT TO MAKE.

Yeah it's great. There are still people out there that even after all these years still want to be seen at all the right parties and still want to be in that space up there. The way that they feel about themselves is so determined by it that they can't let that part of it go, but I think a lot of us can let it go – we're not on the telly all the time but it doesn't matter, and it doesn't matter that

we don't get attention all the time and that is a huge liberation, it really is.

SO HOW HAS IT BEEN NOT HAVING A LABEL BEHIND YOU?

The only real problem with me is that I do need someone to give me a kick up the arse every now and again … I'm not one of life's most motivated people and I do need the occasional kick! When you're with a record company and you've got schedules in place – promotion dates and marketing and all those things – then you have to get on with it, you're part of that machine. But when you're doing it yourself you're running the machine so it goes at the speed you do, which is not always very fast!

SO IF YOU HAD BEEN ON A MAJOR LABEL FOR *YOU'VE GOT TO LAUGH*, WOULD IT HAVE COME OUT A LOT EARLIER?

It would have been out … well, five years ago. That's how long I've been making it!

IS THERE EVER A PROBLEM WITH DOING IT YOURSELF IN THAT YOU CAN'T QUITE BRING YOURSELF TO CALL IT FINISHED?

Yeah, that's always a problem, particularly when you're producing your own record, which I've done on this one – and which I've done pretty much since *Radio Musicola*. You're kind of done when you haven't got any new tracks left, but even that theory doesn't really work because you can just make more tracks, so you have to sort of sit back and think, does this stand on its own or does it really need some extra wobble-board?

EVEN WHEN YOU ARE FINISHED IT MUST STILL BE TEMPTING TO JUST GO BACK AND PUT IN A BIT OF EXTRA WOBBLE-BOARD OR SOMETHING HERE AND THERE …

The thing is that it can always be different,

there's so many different ways of skinning the cat. You commit to one way of doing something when you start recording a track and you can get to the end of it and look back and go 'instead of turning left back there I should have turned right', so it is tempting to sort of dismantle it sometimes, and fix bits and pieces … which I do, I must admit! But what I try to do is to recognise when I'm at that stage – of picking things to pieces – then I just forget about it and go and sit on a mountain or whatever for two weeks and then come back and have another listen, and it's like listening to someone else somehow and quite often that does the trick.

DO YOU HAVE ANY PARTICULAR EXPECTATIONS FOR YOUR NEW MATERIAL?

No I don't … I really don't … it's just kind of out there now and it's available, kind of because there's no reason for it not to be. It really is as simple as that. I've made the record – that's what I do – and there it is, so if someone wants to listen to it that's great. I'm not expecting anything. It would be nice to make it a financially viable thing to do but I'm in a very fortunate position in that my back catalogue – writing-wise, not recording-wise – is very, very healthy and I have the luxury of being able to do this.

THERE WAS A PERIOD FROM THE EARLY NINETIES FOR ABOUT TEN YEARS WHEN YOU WERE WORKING WITH OTHER PEOPLE WHEN YOU PRETTY MUCH STEPPED RIGHT OUT OF THE SPOTLIGHT, SO WHAT WAS IT THAT MADE YOU COME BACK AND START WORKING UNDER YOUR OWN NAME AGAIN?

Frustration I think, more than anything else … it was becoming increasingly difficult to get heard. I was writing with loads of people, I was doing a lot of work ninety-nine per cent of which never got heard, and I began to start projects almost with that fatalistic resignation and just kind of going through the motions because no one was going to hear it. For various reasons,

'I loved Nik Kershaw! I even bought the trousers with the braces on and had my hair with blonde streaks in and full of hairspray to add volume!'

LISA

politics whatever, artists you've worked a year with get dumped before the record comes out, things like that … plus when you're writing for other people you're never really following it through, you're never really totally expressing yourself. You sort of half write a song and give it to someone else and just kind of wave goodbye to it, and that was frustrating. Plus there were certain things in my head, certain songs that just no one else could sing, they weren't commercial and they were very specific in what they were – so I thought either I ignore these songs or I record them, so I recorded them and once you've done that what do you do with them? My former manager persuaded me that I should sign with Eagle Records and make an album with them, which is what I did.

THEN THERE WAS THE 'HERE & NOW' TOUR WASN'T THERE? WHAT MADE YOU DECIDE TO DO THAT? UP TO THAT POINT IT HAD BEEN A VERY LONG TIME SINCE YOU'D TOURED HADN'T IT?

Yeah, I was dragged kicking and screaming! It kind of got to the stage that I'd turned it down so many times – and turned down equivalent things so many times – that in the end I just kind of ran out of reasons not to do it, you know? The final reason – apart from the fact that the money was bloody good – was that it turned out to be a good laugh! Sometimes that's all you need, to have a good laugh, and I needed one!

I INTERVIEWED MIDGE URE AROUND THAT TIME …

Yeah? And he wasn't too sure about doing it either was he? Meeting him at the press conference to announce the tour we both looked at each other and he said 'I'm only doing this because they said you were doing it' and I said, 'Well I'm only doing it because they said you were doing it!' But it was a good laugh. It was a pretty eclectic line-up but it was good, even just sitting in the bar with everyone afterwards … 'Do you remember the time when so-and-so did such-and-such?'

WAS IT GOOD TO GET OUT AND PLAY THOSE OLD SONGS TO SUCH BIG AUDIENCES?

Yeah it was, it was great to hear the old guitar bashing back off the back-wall and to play places that size again, because you don't get the same experience in working men's clubs or wherever … so that was a bit of a treat and for twenty minutes you could actually pretend they were there to see you!

DO YOU THINK THAT HISTORY HAS BEEN KIND TO THE NIK KERSHAW STORY?

[laughs] Ummmm … to give you an answer to that would indicate that I care! But I guess I do care … I don't care as much as I used to. I used to feel that I was hugely misrepresented and hugely misunderstood, which funnily enough is what everyone says! Part of it was my own fault because I didn't really pay attention to how I was perceived, so I take the blame for some of that, but in the end it doesn't matter you know? All that really matters is whether you were good to your mates and are your kids still talking to you? It's a comforting thought that your work is probably going to be remembered longer than you are, so that's really the legacy to think about.

ARE THERE ANY PARTICULAR THINGS THAT STAND OUT FOR YOU? ANYTHING THAT YOU'D LIKE TO BE AMONG THOSE THINGS THAT PEOPLE REMEMBER YOU FOR?

You know, that's why I keep going … because I haven't done it yet! I keep thinking that I have to carry on with this because I still haven't got it quite right, so you just keep on going … I suppose the next question is if there's anything I wish I hadn't done?

ACTUALLY IT WASN'T, BUT SEEING AS YOU BROUGHT IT UP …

Well I think that donning certain items of clothing … I don't really want that on my tombstone. I think it would be a bit of a shame if my whole life was summed up by that!

1985

Snapshot

British Telecom starts to phase out the classic red telephone box ● Mikhai Gorbachev becomes leader of the Soviet Union ● Comedian Ernie Wise makes the UK's first cellphone call ● Cyndi Lauper wins the Grammy for Best New Artist ● 'New York New York' is made the official anthem of New York City ● Mohammed A Fayed buys Harrods ● Coca Cola changes its formula and launches New Coke: the innovation lasts 77 days before customer pressure forces the company to revert to the original recipe ● Michael Jackson buys the publishing rights for most of The Beatles songs ● South Africa lifts its ban on interracial marriages ● The wreck of the *Titanic* is discovered in the North Atlantic ● Martina Navratilova beats Chris Evert Lloyd in the final of the Wimbledon women's competition and Boris Becker defeats Kevin Curren in the men's tournament ● Route 66 in the USA is officially decommissioned ● *Back To The Future* is the year's highest-grossing US movie ● The Greenpeace ship *Rainbow Warrior* is sunk off Auckland by the French ● The Live Aid concerts take place in London and Philadelphia ● Over 9000 people are killed and 95,000 made homeless when an earthquake strikes Mexico City ● Dire Straits' *Brothers In Arms* is the UK's bestselling album ● Ronald Reagan and Mikhail Gorbachev meet for their first Cold War summit in Geneva ● Roger Moore is James Bond in *A View To A Kill* ● The average UK house price is £34,169 ● David Lee Roth leaves Van Halen for a solo career ● San Francisco win the Superbowl, beating Miami 38-16 ● Rock Hudson, Marc Chagall and Louise Brooks pass away ● Bret Easton Ellis publishes his first book *Less Than Zero* ● Simon Le Bon's boat *Drum* capsizes during a race ● Margaret Thatcher appoints a ministerial group to tackle the problems of football hooliganism ● Steve Cram sets a new world record of 3 minutes 46.31 seconds for running the mile ● Jennifer Rush's 'The Power Of Love' is the UK's bestselling single ● Garry Kasparov beats Anatoly Karpov to become World Chess Master ● British scientists discover a hole in the ozone layer above the Antarctic ● Clive Sinclair launches his electric three-wheeler, the Sinclair C5 ● Billy Joel marries Christie Brinkley

'My ultimate eighties' album is Propaganda's 1985 record *A Secret Wish*. When I heard this album for the first time - which wasn't until the late 90s - I felt I had uncovered a lost eighties' gem! With *A Secret Wish* I get lost in the music like no other record. It is dramatic, icily haunting and deeply affecting.'

JAMES

Sounds like. . .1985

I never know what to say when people ask me what my favourite album of all time is because it changes all the time. I will eventually work out a kind of shortlist of three good answers for such situations. One of them – Depeche Mode's *Violator* – isn't released until 1990 but the other two are both released this year: Prefab Sprout's *Steve McQueen* and Propaganda's *A Secret Wish*, a pair of brilliant but very different albums.

I will first hear Prefab Sprout at a concert, 'Faron Young' playing over the PA before whatever band came on, and it blew me away on that very first listen. It turns out there's an album, *Steve McQueen*, which includes the single and I buy it, take it home and fall in love with it. It's a collection of brilliantly crafted, melodic pop songs and I feel like I have single-handedly discovered the next big thing. That it's from a pretty much unknown band is even better. I will gleefully drop their name as often as I can, almost disappointed when Prefab Sprout have their first single hit in November with the gorgeous 'When Love Breaks Down' and are thrust into the public domain!

Propaganda are almost the opposite side of the coin; where Prefab Sprout's songs are gentle, lilting and sensitive Propaganda's are punishing, uncompromising and glacial, but what links both bands is an ability to write great pop songs. Propaganda are a more obvious choice of band to become one of my favourites; I'm already becoming interested in the more experimental and industrial forms of electronic music and Propaganda's singles this year, 'Duel' and 'P:Machinery', tick all those boxes. A *Secret Wish* will get to number sixteen in July and will be followed by an album of remixes, *Wishful Thinking*, another favourite, in November.

So as the year begins my preferences are set, on the one hand electronic music, and on the other intelligent-indie and a touch of goth! – although I will also reserve the right to like a lot of stuff in between! Dead Or Alive are perhaps the ultimate 'in between' band of the year, their definitive single 'You Spin Me Round (Like A Record)' will bridge the gaps between pretty much every genre going and will make number one. The band will go on to have a further three single hits this year as well as a top-ten album, *Youthquake*. Similarly able to straddle musical genres this year is Prince, who will release five singles and although 'Pop Life' will only make number 60 in October, a reissue of 'Little Red Corvette' will peak at two in January, followed by a top-ten position for 'Let's Go Crazy' in February. Prince will enjoy further hits with

'The ultimate eighties' artist must be Propaganda. The teutonic, dark, but also (electro)poppy sound of the band, combined with this very compelling, very specific, German-accented singing voice really got my full attention as a 15-year-old when I heard them on Dutch radio. Propaganda really fed my teenage years (and I was hungry!) and stood at the base of me discovering music, literature, art and architecture. One Big Package Deal For Life!'

MARIE-JEANNE

1985

Number One Singles

Foreigner 'I Want To Know What Love Is', Barbara Dickson & Elaine Paige 'I Knew Him So Well', Dead Or Alive 'You Spin Me Round (Like A Record)', Philip Bailey & Phil Collins 'Easy Lover', Various Artists 'We Are The World', USA For Africa', Phyllis Nelson 'Move Closer', Paul Hardcastle '19', The Crowd 'You'll Never Walk Alone', Sister Sledge 'Frankie', Eurythmics 'There Must Be An Angel (Playing With My Heart)', Madonna 'Into the Groove', UB40 with Chrissie Hynde 'I Got You Babe', David Bowie & Mick Jagger 'Dancing In The Street', Midge Ure 'If I Was', Jennifer Rush 'The Power Of Love', Feargal Sharkey 'A Good Heart', Wham! 'I'm Your Man', Whitney Houston 'Saving All My Love For You', Shakin' Stevens 'Merry Christmas Everyone'

'Killing Joke's *Night Time* is the ultimate album, I first heard 'Love Like Blood' and I was hooked!'

SHARON MEADEN

'The ultimate eighties' single is "You Spin Me Round (Like A Record)" by Dead Or Alive. Perfect song. I still cannot tire of hearing it, seeing the video or listening to the many remixes of it to this day.

NOJARAMA

'Paisley Park' and 'Raspberry Beret' and an album, *Around The World In A Day*, will also make the top five. Completely unconnected, other than in name, this is also the year when Princess will have her biggest hit with 'Say I'm Your Number One'!

On the intelligent-indie front it will be a bumper year. The Smiths will enjoy their first number one album – *Meat Is Murder* – and four hit singles, including two classics: 'How Soon Is Now?' and 'The Boy With The Thorn In His Side'. The eighties indie floodgates will open wide, however, and 1985 will feature brilliant hits for Lloyd Cole & The Commotions with 'Lost Weekend', the Dream Academy with 'Life In A Northern Town' and 'The Love Parade', the Waterboys with 'The Whole Of The Moon', China Crisis' 'Black Man Ray', Kirsty MacColl's 'A New England' and the

new project from Terry Hall (previously of The Specials and Fun Boy Three), the Colourfield, with 'Thinking Of You'.

It's an equally impressive year in the world of goth, and Siouxsie & The Banshees will release one of their finest singles, 'Cities In Dust', in October, as well as the equally impressive *Tinderbox* album, and Killing Joke will release the astonishingly dark and atmospheric single 'Love Like Blood'. Treading a more commercial path, The Damned will release *Phantasmagoria*, the most commercially successful album of their career which will narrowly miss the top ten but will feature two of the band's best known post-punk singles, 'Grimly Fiendish' and 'The Shadow Of Love'. The Cure will also release their bestselling album to date this year, *The Head On The Door*, which reaches number seven and features two of the band's most definitive singles – 'In Between Days' and 'Close To Me'. I will have *The Head On The Door* recorded on one side of a C90 cassette and The Smiths' 1984 compilation *Hatful Of Hollow* on the other, a tape I will listen to tirelessly on my Walkman until it eventually wears out.

On the periphery of goth, rock, pop and alternative this year are a number of acts that won't comfortably quite fit in any one category but will drift between them all. Most significantly for me this year this includes The Cult who will release an album, *Love*, plus a pair of singles that will forever become rock club classics, 'She Sells Sanctuary' and 'Rain'. The album will be a favourite in my sixth-form common room, one of an eclectic selection which also includes this year's chart topping albums from Marillion (*Misplaced Childhood*, featuring their biggest hit 'Kayleigh') and Bryan

> 'My ultimate single is a bit off the wall, but I'd have to vote for Lloyd Cole & the Commotions' "Perfect Skin" – it's just such a great amalgam of melody, songwriting, delivery and texture. Everything that the good eighties was ever about!'
>
> KRIS FERNANDEZ-EVERETT

Ferry (*Boys & Girls*, featuring 'Slave To Love' and 'Don't Stop The Dance'), as well as Talking Heads' *Little Creatures*, which will launch their eccentric single hit 'Road To Nowhere' this year.

The album that never seems to be off the communal stereo, however, is Dire Straits' *Brothers In Arms*, the UK's bestselling album of the eighties. It's a phenomenon, the album becoming the first CD to sell a million copies and in 1985 is said to have somehow sold more copies on CD this year than there are CD players to play it on! I start off disliking it for being a bit too 'twiddly' and for the number of headbands involved; then I start to accept it based simply on the number of times I have to listen to it. I will later dislike it again because it's everywhere – it's impossible to get away from it, in particular the epic single 'Money For Nothing'. I will never buy the album, which perhaps on its own makes me unique, but I will come around to liking some of the singles much later, in particular the title song 'Brothers In Arms', but my heart will always sink on hearing the opening notes of 'Money For Nothing'!

As sixth formers of course we cannot possibly admit to liking anything remotely 'poppy' or too mainstream, which is a shame as there's some great pop records this year, led perhaps by the one-family hit machine that is Five Star who have three unashamed pop hits with their first three singles from their debut album *Luxury Of Life*. Equally irrepressible is David Grant and Jaki Graham's top five hit 'Could It Be I'm Falling In Love' and Dutch trio Mai Tai's catchy 'History'. For some reason, perhaps because of their credible roots (the band was born from the ashes of Blitz Club regulars Blue Rondo A La Turk), the equally poppy Matt Bianco is deemed acceptable listening while we study for our A-levels and their *Whose Side Are You On?* album will become a central part of my revision soundtrack, as will Katrina & The Waves' gloriously upbeat 'Walking On Sunshine'. For some reason, although I won't be able to confess this to anyone this year for fear of damage to my 'credibility', I will

> 'I would have to say that Prince had the best look of the eighties. The lace and the make-up had the gender-bending qualities of the time but he had such sass that he really made it masculine at the same time.'
>
> DANA DETRICK-CLARK

'Five Star were the ultimate eighties act without a doubt . . . they summed the eighties up for me! Apart from the excellent music, the costumes and the dance routines, they were the same age as me in the eighties, that's why I felt some affinity to them. Really I thought I was the sixth member!'

NORMAN WHITTAKER

'I loved Madonna when she did 'Like A Virgin' – the lace gloves and tatty hair!'

RUTH

also like the Rah Band's rather bizarre, and almost psychedelic, single 'Clouds Across The Moon'.

Pop rock is emerging as a more important genre as the year begins, some artists dipping in and out of the genre on a song-by-song basis, notably Simple Minds who release their best-known single 'Don't You Forget About Me' this year, their highest singles charts position when it peaks at number seven, and others who work pretty much exclusively inside it, including King who will score their biggest hit early this year with 'Love & Pride', pop rock with a nod to goth and indie, and Go West who add soul to their pop-rock formula and will enjoy four singles hits this year, their best-known UK song, 'We Close Our Eyes', reaching number five and their debut album *Go West* peaking at eight. Undisputedly a rock artist, Pat Benatar will release two of her poppiest singles this year, 'We Belong' and 'Love Is A Battlefield', which will become her first two UK hits. Another rock artist to bring a new pop edge to his music this year is Billy Idol, whose best-known singles 'White Wedding' and 'Rebel Yell' will both peak at six on the singles charts.

But when it comes to pop this year there is one clear winner. Madonna will have an astonishing seven consecutive top-five singles – including her first UK number one single 'Into The Groove' – her first UK number one album *Like A Virgin*, and a top-ten entry for her 1984 debut album *Madonna*, repackaged as *Madonna – The First Album*. Personally, Madonna's

achievements this year will be eclipsed by those of another female solo artist, who releases her first album for three years: Kate Bush with *Hounds Of Love*, an album which will be a revelation for me, my first real introduction to one of music's most important artists. *Hounds Of Love* will reach number one in October, a beautiful and cohesive album which will feature two fantastic singles, 'Running Up That Hill' and 'Cloudbusting'.

Duran Duran will release their Bond theme 'A View To A Kill', which will reach number two, but will use a post-Live Aid career-break to form two side-projects, Arcadia and The Power Station, both of which will have some success this year (Arcadia with a hit single 'Election Day' and an album *So Red The Rose*, and The Power Station with two hit singles, 'Some Like It Hot' and 'Get It On', and an eponymous album), but electronic pop in general will have a great year, largely led by a pair of significant new acts in A-Ha and the Pet Shop Boys. Norway's A-Ha will be the first to chalk up their debut hit single when a reissue of their 'Take On Me' single – complete with its cutting-edge part-animated video – reaches number two in October, closely followed by a number one single with 'The Sun Always Shines On TV', which will be released in December and will go on to knock UK duo the Pet Shop Boys first hit 'West End Girls' (also released in December) from the top of the charts in January 1986. A-Ha will also release a debut album, *Hunting High And Low*, which will reach the number two spot.

'The ultimate album is *Like A Virgin* by Madonna. It still stands the test of time as a completely artist-defining piece of work. Everything she's done since has been a result of that record.'

DANA DETRICK-CLARK

'"Don't You (Forget About Me)" by Simple Minds is my favourite eighties' single. It just sums up my entire High School experience.'

JEFF

Scritti Politti will release their bestselling album and single when *Cupid & Psyche '85* peaks at number five and its associated single 'The Word Girl' reaches number six. Tears For Fears will also achieve their highest singles charts position when their 'Everybody Wants To Rule The World' single and *Songs From The Big Chair* album both reach number two. Eurythmics meanwhile will move away from the pure synthesizer sounds that dominated their early albums when they release their star-studded, number three album *Be Yourself Tonight*, which features appearances from Elvis Costello, Aretha Franklin and Stevie Wonder (who will provide harmonica on the duo's only number one single 'There Must Be An Angel (Playing With My Heart)').

There will also be a lot of rather epic ballads released. Jennifer Rush's 'The Power Of Love' will become the year's bestselling single, reaching number one in October and spending six months in the charts, a triumph threatened only by Whitney Houston's debut hit 'Saving All My Love For You', which also topped the charts, as did Phyllis Nelson's only hit 'Move Closer'. More genuinely affecting, however, is a reissue of The Cars' 'Drive' after it is used as the soundtrack to Live Aid's deeply moving film of scenes from the famine in Ethiopia. 'Drive' will reach number four, the band's biggest hit of the eighties. David Bowie and Mick Jagger's collaboration, 'Dancing In The Street', will be another hit on the back of Live Aid, going to number one in September, as will Midge Ure's solo single 'If I Was', deservedly benefiting from his increased profile after the event.

The most irritating record of the year will undoubtedly be Baltimora's 'Tarzan Boy' alongside a couple of singles I will actually quite like, Paul Hardcastle's '19' (which will start to grate after the first couple of hundred hearings), and Aled Jones' 'Walking In The Air' which will tread a fine line between novelty and quirky! Animotion will be responsible for one of the best one-hit wonders this year, 'Obsession' making number five in the singles charts, seven places higher than The Eagles' frontman Don Henley, whose celebratory 'The Boys Of Summer' will peak at twelve beating Belouis Some's sole hit 'Imagination' by five places.

'My ultimate eighties' single has to be "We Close Our Eyes" by Go West. Apart from being my ultimate eighties' group, it was one of the first tunes I really took as 'my' tune, my soundtrack to 1985. I was gutted when they weren't at Live Aid. The video helped launch the band and the tune, but even to this day, when I'm DJing, I sometimes drop "We Close Our Eyes" and it still gets everyone dancing and singing! Love it.'

JAMES WATSON

'I can't say it was the ultimate eighties album for me, but it's iconic and whenever I see it, it screams the eighties, and that's *Brothers in Arms* by Dire Straits. I bought it at the time because everyone had it. I even replaced my vinyl with the CD version at some point, but now, while downsizing the collection, I quietly let it slip away to some charity shop where no one knows me.'

MARK FELL

the brat pack

'A group of my friends went to see *The Breakfast Club* the weekend it was released, and I remember we were all blown away at how someone had captured our humour and angst on the screen. It represented something to me that I couldn't put into words.'

JEF BLOCKER

'My favourite film was *Pretty In Pink* with Molly Ringwald – I just loved the way she didn't follow fashion and had her own style just like I did.'

SUE SKILLCORN

1985

On The Big Screen

Other new cinema releases this year include *Back To The Future, Desperately Seeking Susan, The Goonies, Legend, Mad Max - Beyond The Thunderdome, Return Of The Living Dead, St Elmo's Fire, Witness, Fletch, Brewster's Millions, Girls Just Want To Have Fun* and *The Color Purple*.

If you were to ask me to list my ten favourite films on two different days then I'd come up with two different lists, but both lists would almost certainly include at least two of three films that I have always loved – *The Breakfast Club, Pretty In Pink* and *Ferris Bueller's Day Off* – all of which were made by the same man, the American film-maker John Hughes.

The Breakfast Club, often considered John Hughes' definitive teen film, was released in 1985 and follows the experiences of five very different teenagers in Saturday detention, stripping away the layers of their own preconceptions and finishing with them as equals, friends and even couples. As Brian Johnson (Anthony Michael Hall, the brain) writes in the group's detention essay for Mr Vernon: 'You see us as you want to see us … in the simplest terms and the most convenient definitions. You see us as a brain, an athlete, a basket case, a princess and a criminal. Correct? That's the way we saw each other at seven o'clock this morning. We were brainwashed.' The film also starred Molly Ringwald (the princess), Ally Sheedy (the basket case), Emilio Estevez (the athlete) and Judd Nelson (the criminal) and gave everyone a character to identify with and a character to be attracted to – in my case two characters in Molly Ringwald and Ally Sheedy!

Pretty In Pink is my favourite John Hughes movie (Molly Ringwald again!) and was originally released in 1986. It's a kind of Cinderella story and treads a similar route to *The Breakfast Club*, dismantling the barriers between social position and school cliques when Andie (Ringwald) – who is cool and quirkily stylish but from a poor part of town – starts dating rich kid Blane (Andrew McCarthy) who is nice but bland, much to the disgust of her best friend, the unique, eccentric Duckie (Jon Cryer), who is desperately in love with Andie himself. The film follows the odd couple as they try and fail to have their relationship accepted in their very different social worlds and leaves them both adrift until prom night, when they both attend the event alone and finally reunite, with even Duckie giving his blessing to the mismatched pair. I love it; my crush on Molly Ringwald deepens and I set great store by the whole 'uninteresting but ultimately nice boy gets the fab, cool, beautiful girl' plot!

Ferris Bueller's Day Off also came out in 1986 and follows a day in the life of Ferris Bueller (Matthew Broderick) who decides to skip school with his girlfriend Sloane Peterson (Mia Sara) and best friend Cameron Frye (Alan Ruck) for a celebratory day of hedonism before the trio permanently split up to go on to college and real life. The friends 'borrow', and wreck, a vintage Ferrari, spend the day in Chicago and narrowly avoid being caught by their school principal, Mr Rooney (Jeffrey Jones), Ferris' sister Jeanie (Jennifer Gray) and his father Tom (Lyman Ward) by all sorts of ingenious means. They also talk openly and honestly about their lives, their parents and their position in the world. It's also very funny, Hughes' trademark Brat Pack teen-angst replaced in this film by a gleeful anarchy and an exuberant delight in being young.

These are not John Hughes' only films; they are preceded, notably, by *Sixteen Candles* and *Weird Science* and are followed by the excellent but underrated *Some Kind Of Wonderful* during Hughes' so-called Brat Pack years. But they are probably the three that are the best remembered and most loved, certainly they are the three that made me want to trade in my Essex comprehensive school for an American High School and my school disco experiences for a prom night!

Alan Ruck was 29 when he played 17-year-old Cameron in *Ferris Bueller's Day Off*. He went on to play Stuart Bondek in *Spin City* and Captain John Harriman in *Star Trek: Generations*.

The original ending to *Pretty In Pink* had Andie ending up with Duckie, but this was changed after much deliberation and by the time they shot the new ending Andrew McCarthy had shaved his head for his next role and ended up wearing a wig when he shot those final scenes.

the brat pack . . . up to date!

John Hughes continues to make films and his credits include *Planes, Trains and Automobiles*, *Home Alone*, *Uncle Buck*, *Flubber* and *Maid In Manhattan*. Molly Ringwald has continued to take occasional acting roles on TV, in films and in the theatre. Ally Sheedy has followed a similar career and has battled bulimia and addiction to sleeping pills but was recently reunited with Anthony Michael Hall in TV's *The Dead Zone*. Emilio Estevez was briefly married to Paula Abdul and now directs for TV and film, his credits include *Cold Case*, *CSI* and *Bobby*. Matthew Broderick continues to act on Broadway and in occasional films and is married to actress Sarah Jessica Parker. Judd Nelson has appeared in a succession of low-budget movies and was briefly engaged to Shannen Doherty.

EastEnders

The first episode started with the immortal line 'Stinks in 'ere!' and it went on to become one of Britain's best-loved soap operas, and perhaps the most consistently depressing show to hit our screens, with storylines dealing with murder, rape, homosexuality, incest, cot-death, drug addiction, prostitution, unemployment, racial abuse, one-parent families, teenage pregnancy, abortion, sexism, euthanasia, shoplifting, violence, health problems, muggings, arson, fraud, immigration, adoption, AIDS, agoraphobia, illiteracy, mental health, Down's syndrome and sexual abuse, not to mention the usual soap-opera fare of births, deaths, weddings, affairs, squabbles, successes, failures, divorces and gossip. It can only be *EastEnders*.

Premiering to an audience of 17 million viewers on 19th February 1985, *EastEnders* – set around the daily lives of the people who live and work in Albert Square in the London Borough of Walford – has continued to this day, and still consistently appears among the BBC's highest-rated TV programmes. In fact *EastEnders* gained one of the highest UK TV audiences of all time when it attracted a staggering 30.15 million viewers on Christmas Day 1986 (when Den told Angie he wanted a divorce).

EastEnders has won five BAFTA awards, eight National Television Awards and is responsible for three hit singles to date: 'Anyone Can Fall In Love', a version of the *EastEnders* theme tune set to lyrics and sung by Anita Dobson, 'Every Loser Wins' sung by Nick Berry and 'Something Outta Nothing' sung by Letitia Dean and Paul J. Medford. Mary Whitehouse meanwhile slammed the show as a 'violation of family viewing time' in reaction to the nature of some of the storylines and to the strong language used in the show.

Robbie Williams has made a cameo appearance – appearing on the telephone in the Queen Vic – one of a number of celebrities to do so. A pre-Spice Girls Emma Bunton was briefly cast as a troubled teenager, Spandau Ballet's Martin Kemp played the evil Steve Owen for four years and Altered Images' Clare Grogan played private detective Ros Blackwell, who briefly became a love interest for Ian Beale, much to the continued disapproval of the nation as Clare will tell me in a 2002 interview: 'Men in white vans still come up next to me in the car, roll down their windows and shout "Clare! How could you?"'

Eastenders . . . Up To Date!

EastEnders is still running today, although only one original member has remained in the cast since 1985 – Adam Woodyatt, who has played Ian Beale continuously since the show first went on air. At time of writing thirty-four characters have died since the show began, sixteen babies have been born, and there have been twenty-nine weddings (including three each for Ian Beale, Mark Fowler and Phil Mitchell).

Early names for the show included 'Square Dance', 'Round the Square', 'Round the Houses' and 'London Pride', but 'East 8', the Walford postcode (actually the postcode for Hackney in London), was used during the early months of the show's development before being dropped in favour of *EastEnders* when the producers decided to use a fictitious postcode (E20) for Albert Square.

The first 24 *EastEnders* characters were the Fowlers (Arthur, Pauline, Mark and Michelle), the Beales (Lou, Pete, Kathy and Ian), the Watts (Den, Angie and Sharon), Ali and Sue Osman, Kelvin and Tony Carpenter, Saeed and Naima Jeffery, Lofty Holloway, Mary Smith, Ethel Skinner, Nick Cotton, Dr Harold Legg, Andy O'Brien and Debbie Wilkins.

1985

On and Off

the Small Screen

ON

New shows made this year include *Blind Date*, *Max Headroom*, *The Colbys*, and *Moonlighting*.

OFF

It's the end of an era for *The Dukes Of Hazzard* and *Are You being Served?* which go out of production by the end of 1985.

THE GLOBAL JUKEBOX LIVE AID

'My initial thoughts are what a fantastic atmosphere there was backstage. I mean you've got all the top stars, the people you grew up listening to, and it was just, "wow, there's Paul McCartney, there's David Bowie, there's Roger Daltrey . . ." all these fantastic artists, the elder statesmen of rock, and then the young whippersnappers like us. But everyone was so friendly. There were no egos, it was just a lovely day and all the big artists were just fantastic. I grew up seeing David Bowie and Queen in concert and then suddenly there they are going "alright Tony" . . . that was fantastic!'

TONY HADLEY,
SPANDAU BALLET

Performing from London were Status Quo, Style Council, Boomtown Rats, Adam Ant, Ultravox, Spandau Ballet, Elvis Costello, Nik Kershaw, Sade, Phil Collins, Sting, Howard Jones, Bryan Ferry, Paul Young, Alison Moyet, U2, Dire Straits, Queen, David Bowie, The Who, Elton John, Kiki Dee, Wham!, Paul McCartney and Cliff Richard. Performing from Philadelphia were Joan Baez, The Hooters, The Four Tops, Billy Ocean, Black Sabbath, Run DMC, Rick Springfield, REO Speedwagon, Crosby Stills & Nash, Judas Priest, Bryan Adams, The Beach Boys, George Thorogood & The Destroyers, Simple Minds, The Pretenders, Santana, Pat Metheny, Ashford & Simpson, Kool & The Gang, Madonna, The Thompson Twins, Tom Petty & The Heartbreakers, Kenny Loggins, The Cars, Neil Young, The Power Station, Eric Clapton, Phil Collins, Plant Page & Jones, Duran Duran, Patti LaBelle, Hall & Oates, Eddie Kendricks, David Ruffin, Mick Jagger, Tina Turner, Bob Dylan, Ron Wood, Keith Richards. There were also broadcasts from Australia, Japan, Austria, the Netherlands, Yugoslavia, Russia, Germany and Norway.

'Part of the fear of going on was that you were hanging out with all these amazing people, all on the same bill, so you didn't want to make an idiot of yourself . . . not just because a hundred million people were watching, but also because Sting was!'

NIK KERSHAW

Saturday 13th July 1985. Live Aid. The biggest live concert the world has ever known, broadcast from multiple venues around the world to one and a half billion viewers in more than a hundred different countries in aid of Ethiopian famine relief.

The original idea was to put on a concert that would be an extension of Bob Geldof and Midge Ure's 1984 Band Aid project (and the ensuing We Are The World project in the USA), a concert that would raise a million pounds for famine relief. The idea snowballed and became two concerts, one in London and one in Philadelphia. More countries then became involved, building a network of satellite concerts around the world, a truly global jukebox.

Live Aid went on to raise around £3,150 million and I believe it's the one day that almost everyone of my generation will remember. I remember it as a beautifully hot summer's day, I was working as the car park attendant at a big department store in Chelmsford, and spent the day listening to the radio in the little attendant's hut as well as hearing it on all the car radios as customers went in and out all day, then later being at home and watching whatever bits I could on TV when the rest of the family didn't want to watch anything else, while listening to the rest on the radio in my room. I remember U2 and Queen being particularly amazing, but more than the music I remember the rush of the feeling of being connected to something huge and important and real. Was it just me who thought this way? I asked the people who read my website, RememberThe Eighties.com, what they remembered about the day ...

'I stayed at my friend's house on the Friday and was due to stay the Saturday as we were going out on the town. We put the TV on at 12 – Status Quo "Rockin' All Over The World" – cracked open her parents' drinks cabinet and just stayed in and watched the full show.'

CAROLINE

'I was thirteen years old and it was a hot summer in 1985. Nearly all the children of my age were playing outside or going to the swimming pool. My parents thought I was ill from the heat when I asked them to allow me to watch TV all day and night! I think I'll remember that day for my whole life!'

OLIVER OSLISLOK

'You are right, I know exactly where I was. I had been invited to stay at my best mate's house that night. I started to watch it at my house, and I remember the start when the Quo came on stage and the goosebumps came up on my arms. I watched the lot, didn't want to miss a thing, not even to go the toilet. I was alone at the time watching it when Sir Bob swore, and felt grown up like I was part of history in the making. When Phil Collins was landing in the USA, I was on my commando bike, cycling down to my friend's to watch the USA part. We stayed up right to the end, watching the rest of the show. It was a great day.'

JAMES WATSON

'It was a beautiful hot summer's day. I spent the day on the side of a cricket pitch as my husband was playing cricket. I pitched my sunbed next to the car so I could have the radio on all day – I was also videoing the whole of the show at home on our Betamax video – and we had to jump-start the car to go home because I'd drained the battery!'

HELEN WILLIAMS

'During Live Aid I was lost on a mountain in Northern Wales on a joint forces mountain training exercise. We had to do a 10-mile solo hike across forest and mountains overnight. I forgot to pack my utensils so while the world was gawping at Madonna's crazy doll-like make-up and punching the air with Freddie, I was trying to open a tin of pork rations with a stick while getting bitten to death by midges. Luckily my parents videoed it for me – until the tape ran out!'

STUART 'PASH' ELLERSHAW

'Time stood still but would Phil Collins make it to the States in time? How did everyone get along? Hunger would end because of it, wouldn't it? Being 15 and believing that all these famous people really believed in the cause was amazing. It was a beautiful summer day – it had to be – the world stopped and watched. I refused to let my parents take me anywhere unless it was during an act I really didn't care for and the place we were going had to have a TV!'

DENISE FROM LODI BUT NOT IN LODI

'I was at home, glued to the television, watching every moment. Wincing in pain as Simon Le Bon missed that note in "A View To A Kill". It's no wonder that one's been left off the DVD set! Anyway, a fantastic day, and an important cause that we unfortunately still need to help today.'

LORI ALLISON

'I can remember exactly. I was at a lake in the northern part of Wisconsin with my friend's family, vacationing. My friend was a huge Duran Duran fan at the time, and I was a Culture Club fanatic. Instead of swimming and water-skiing, we sat by the radio and listened – it reminded me of kids in the 30s and 40s just sitting around a radio listening to their favorite shows.'

PETER BALISTRIERI

"I was 16 and remember sitting in front of the TV all day – I watched it from start to finish. All of the bands were amazing but Queen blew me away and I wasn't even a Queen fan. U2 were amazing as well.'

TRACEY

'I had received a letter on the morning of Live Aid telling me I had got on to an art and design course and I was so excited. I also had a hot date that day with a cool girl who was a violinist who loved Depeche Mode!'

DAVE WATERS

'I grew up in Texas, and was driving to a neighbor's house to feed his horses. Live Aid was on the radio, and I remember hearing Paul Young singing "Everytime You Go Away". I had heard it many times before but never paid attention to it. After that moment, I appreciated the song because it reminded me of that moment.'

JEF BLOCKER

'I can remember being at work in the local fruit shop. I was at the back making fruit baskets for the airlines at Heathrow. The radio was blaring, then it started, the sadly missed Tommy Vance, the first voice of Live Aid introducing the only song and band that could have started a gig of that magnitude, Status Quo and "Rocking All Over The World". What a day! It was hot hot hot, the Merrydown was flowing, and the whole world joined as one BIG happy family! It was just the best!'

JASON RICE

'I was sitting in my basement the whole day editing out everything but the performances on my Betamax. I still have the original tapes today. I also remember making my first charitable donation and that spirit of charity still sticks with me.'

KEVIN GUEST

'I was sitting on my sofa from the moment it started, then snuggling up in my sleeping bag way after my parents had gone to bed to watch the very end. I hardly moved to eat or go to the loo! I remember being moved to tears when the scenes from Africa were shown to the sounds of "Drive" by the Cars. Compelling viewing.'

CAROLINE

'I was watching TV at our house, being amazed at how cool it was that this event was taking place, that someone had thought to plan it and that it was going on across the world. It really WAS the greatest show on earth.'

ILUVNOAH IN WILMETTE

'It was one of the first times since my childhood that my family sat and watched TV together. With no arguing over what we're gonna watch or me going to my room to listen to records.'

THE CADMAN

'I was there! It was an incredible day. Bryan Ferry was the highlight for me. Oh, and the Quo.'

DIANE

'It was the last day my then girlfriend and I spent together as she was moving away to a new job the next day. It was my best mate from school's 18th birthday party that night as well - I just seemed to cram so much into one day! Hats off to Geldof and Ure.'

SHAUN TRANTER

'I was actually in London with my parents on holiday! The closest I got though was watching snippets on TV at a restaurant and hearing Ultravox on the radio.'

JOHN

'I was in a council flat on an estate in Tunbridge Wells, with my punk mates, ripped on cheap speed and cheap cider.'

CLIVE

'I watched on TV in awe, and desperately wanted to be there and escape my monotonous life. It did make me think as it was supposed to, but it also was fab music!'

ANNETTE

'I feel that this was one day in history that the whole world came together for a common cause. No politics, no sides taken, just helping the less fortunate people, for the first time.'

MARK MATTERN

'I remember it like it was yesterday. I remember feeling that I was part of something that was changing the world. It was like the torch was being passed to a new generation. It's hard to believe that we were able to look outside our own environment, even in 1985, because in this part of the world we were still in the grip of huge unemployment and there was a lot of people struggling on our own doorstep, but we stood together despite all that and said this must stop and we reached out. I like to think that on that day humanity came together like never before to make the world a better place for our children, and I am sure we succeeded.'

MARK FINNEGAN

'I was parked in front of the TV, barely able to get decent reception for MTV. Through the static, I managed to tape record (not videotape, but audiotape with my poor little recorder up against the tv speaker) my favourite performances!'

DANA DETRICK-CLARK

'I am lucky because I was there. It was like a New Year celebration, everyone kissing and hugging each other, the world was coming together for one purpose. There was magic in the air, everyone hoping to accomplish the same goal to help fight the need.'

NIK BRASIER

'I had my 15th birthday party the night before Live Aid. It was a slumber party so we could all stay up and watch it when it started. Most of us fell asleep, but we had

the TV on so we would hear when a band was introduced that we wanted to see. My dad gave me $20 so I could donate it, which I did, of course. That day remains one of the best days of my childhood.'

MISSIE MCKAY

'I now wish I had watched it all but I was out playing with my friend Kirsty. I think we were on rollerboots. At 12 I don't think you realise when it's history in the making.'

SALLY MIDDLER

'A bunch of friends gathered at a friend's house the night before so we could get up to watch the Australian concert start up (we could NOT miss INXS). I actually took photographs of the screen, like in Nick Rhodes' Interference book, and yes, I still have them!'

LINDA PARETS-MOSKOWITZ

'I remember sitting up until the wee hours, patiently waiting for Power Station and Duran Duran. Queen's performance absolutely stunned me. To see Freddie Mercury take the audience and hold them in the palm of his hand was a thing of beauty and wonder. I can still remember Mel Smith and Griff Rhys Jones' introduction: "We've had a bit of a complaint about the noise. From a woman in Belgium . . .".'

TISHA

'Everyone was waiting for the day to arrive, and what a day! I bought the Radio Times and that week's Smash Hits (even though I was twenty!) to have the souvenirs. I still have

both in perfect condition today. What a day and what memories, I was never a Queen fan but I remember saying to anyone who would listen that their performance would be talked about for years . . . and guess what, it was!'

MICKY JOCK

'I remember looking forward to it in the same way I always looked forward to the new issue of Smash Hits – only this was like getting an entire year's worth of issues in one day! I sat and watched the entire thing from beginning to end – with my parents' indulgence – I think my dad went to the football and my mum cleaned the cupboards as ways of escape!'

LEE KYNASTON

'I dutifully camped out in the living room the night before in a sleeping bag, worried that the early start (I was living in Florida at that point) would get the better of me if I was in my comfy bed. My biggest surprise watching it back on DVD is that anyone who had hair had a mullet. I had no idea it was THAT big a fashion statement.'

HAYDEN

'I was at home making love for the first time . . . well you did ask!'

PETE FM

'I remember this day cause it was the first time I ever got high. Right about the same time Duran Duran took the stage . . . what a day!'

AARON

1985 ICON

▶▶ *Simple Minds*

My first introduction to Simple Minds was through the track 'Sweat In Bullet', which was on a compilation album I bought in 1981 called *Hits Hits Hits*. Although I didn't know it at the time 'Sweat In Bullet' was Simple Minds' eighth singles release (their ninth if you count their 1977 debut 'Saints & Sinners', which was released under the name Johnny And The Self Abusers) and was featured on their 1981 album *Sons & Fascination*, which narrowly missed the top ten when it peaked at eleven in 1981. At this point Simple Minds hadn't had a hit single and I seized upon the track as something cutting-edge to like, a cool name to drop into musical conversations.

I got to know someone who was a Simple Minds fan and she made a compilation tape of the band's earlier tracks, a jumble of bits and pieces from the albums *Life In A Day*, *Real To Real Cacophony* and *Empires & Dance*, which just served to confuse me. The tape sounded like a bunch of different bands and the tracks, taped in no particular chronological order, jumped around from punk to electronic to almost progressive. If I'm honest I wasn't even sure that I liked it.

Fortunately the next Simple Minds single was 1982's 'Promised You A Miracle' which for me consolidated their sound, combined the rock and electronic elements that drew me to them in the first place, added an accessible pop edge and became their first hit. Sitting somewhere between the New Romantics and U2, it was Simple Minds' first real step towards becoming one of the biggest bands in the world. More hit singles followed – 'Glittering Prize' and 'Someone Somewhere (In Summertime)' – and an album *New Gold Dream (81,82,83,84)*, which reached number three. The band were on *Top Of The Pops* and in *Smash Hits*. Simple Minds had arrived. The next album, *Sparkle In The Rain*, launched more hit singles in 'Waterfront', 'Speed Your Love To Me'

and 'Up On The Catwalk' and became the band's first number one album in 1984.

Simple Minds' best-known single was to follow in 1985 when 'Don't You (Forget About Me)' was released to coincide with the release of the film *The Breakfast Club*. Crucially it went to number one in the USA and, with the release of their most commercial album to date, *Once Upon A Time*, broke Simple Minds around the world. *Once Upon A Time* didn't include 'Don't You (Forget About Me)' but it did contain four equally anthemic singles in 'Alive & Kicking', 'Sanctify Yourself', 'Ghostdancing' and 'All The Things You Said'. Simple Minds' years as a world class stadium band had begun.

As a celebration of their success, and playing to their strengths as a live act, the next Simple Minds' album, *Live In The City of Light*, was essentially a double-album of their hits played live, becoming their second UK number one album in 1987. It would be another two years before the band's next studio album appeared in May 1989, their third number one album in the UK, preceded by their sole UK chart-topping single, the 'Ballad Of The Streets' EP featuring the lead track 'Belfast Child'. The *Real Life* album followed in 1991, peaking at number two in the UK, followed by the band's fourth number one album, a hits compilation *Glittering Prize*, in 1992.

Good News From The Next World, a final album for Virgin in 1995, made number two and marked the start of a period of reinvention for Simple Minds, which included 1998's Kraftwerk-inspired electronic album *Neapolis* and 2002's critically acclaimed *Cry*. I was fortunate enough to do this interview with frontman Jim Kerr in 2005 during the promotion for their excellent *Black & White 050505*, which was released that year.

'Simple Minds are the ultimate eighties band. They worked their way up from a cult following to become a massive stadium band, they worked to get to where they got, not like today's manufactured bands. If you want a top night out go and see Simple Minds; the energy is electric!'

SHAUN TRANTER

'Ultimate band? Simple Minds. Their music lifted me and transported me to another place. Their sound was always so big and expansive and I actually 'saw' pictures in my mind when I listened to them. I was finishing high school and was about to start at art school in the early eighties and their image and sound suited where I was at that stage of my life. They remain probably my fave ever band.'

SHELLY

I THINK THERE'S A MASSIVE PERCEPTION THAT SIMPLE MINDS ARE THIS HUGE STADIUM ROCK BAND, BUT ACTUALLY FOR ME THEY AREN'T THAT AT ALL … PERSONALLY, 'MY' SIMPLE MINDS IS AN EXPERIMENTAL AND FAIRLY ELECTRONIC BAND. IS IT FRUSTRATING FOR YOU TO BE PIGEONHOLED AS THIS STADIUM ROCK MONSTER WHEN PEOPLE IGNORE OR ARE SIMPLY UNAWARE OF THE JOURNEY IT'S TAKEN YOU TO GET HERE?

I have to say that it is frustrating, but also kind of understandable in as much as you rightly say, before we achieved big success we were one of the biggest cult bands around – we had four or five albums out before we achieved any sort of commercial success and they were pretty eclectic even if I say so myself; they ranged from the avant-garde and they were pretty cutting edge stuff and I think the album titles say it all … *Real To Real Cacophony, Empires & Dance, Sons & Fascination* … I mean hardly mainstream, and certainly not 'Don't You (Forget About Me)'! Then in the middle of the eighties Simple Minds both took part in Live Aid and the Nelson Mandela Concert and we did a couple of tunes that became big iconic worldwide tunes, and those images, those worldwide images – apart from our cult following – would have been the only time most people had seen Simple Minds … playing to thousands of people and me with my arms outstretched!

IT'S ALMOST LIKE DIFFERENT BANDS, YOU'VE GONE THROUGH DIFFERENT STYLES SO COMPLETELY …

That's true, and when people ask me about the music of Simple Minds I do have to say 'But which Simple Minds are you talking about?' because I think it's fair to say of the descriptions of the work of Simple Minds – where we began as this kind of art-rock thing, then we certainly had a very electronic dance thing, we had a period of being in with bands like Echo & the Bunnymen, New Order, Joy Division. We had a period doing the pop side of Simple Minds with 'New Gold Dream' and 'Promised You A Miracle', and then coming up to the sort of stadium side in America with 'Don't You (Forget About Me)' and 'Once Upon A Time' and then there was the, I don't know if it would be political or social songs: 'Mandela', 'Belfast Child' and so on, and then there's the nineties' obscurity … what the hell [laughs].

YOUR NEW MATERIAL IS DISTINCTIVELY SIMPLE MINDS BUT IT'S ALSO UP TO DATE AND CONTEMPORARY, IT HAS THAT SOUND.

Well I'm really glad you say that because what we wanted to do was to conjure up some of our previous sounds, some of those classic trademarks, but somehow for it to feel as though it has an energy from now. You very rarely get the album you want – you go in with these things and then something else comes out – and sometimes you're happy and sometimes not. We had one or two false starts where it wasn't working, but once the hair on the back of the neck was starting to stand we knew that this is what we wanted.

WHEN DO YOU FEEL YOU LAST ACHIEVED THAT ON AN ALBUM?

A long, long time ago … I think that when I listen to the albums from the past ten years there are a lot of things about them that impress me, but I can hear how we were mired in self-doubt, or perhaps we had great ideas but couldn't finish them off, or perhaps we just didn't know where we were in the greater scheme of things, or perhaps we were drowning with the weight of the past on our backs. It's been a long time I think since it has actually 'worked', but you know what? This is it!

IT'S BEEN QUITE A JOURNEY FOR YOU, ARE YOU PROUD OF WHAT YOU HAVE ACHIEVED?

Well … I don't think 'pride' is a word we use a lot. I think there will be a day when we will sit around and that is exactly how we will feel, but yeah … we really like our band! We love our band and that includes the U-turns and the mistakes and the fuck-ups. I was saying to someone yesterday that in a sense to make the good albums you have to make the bad, to write the good songs you've almost got to write the bad ones, it's all part of the process and we've loved our journey.

DO YOU FEEL THAT SIMPLE MINDS STILL HAS SOMETHING TO PROVE?

I think you have something to prove every time you sit down to write a song, because although everything has changed within our lives and everything has changed within the world of music, with technology and the relevance of music and your own perspective and so on … the one thing that has not changed, is that when you sit down to write a song – which in a sense you're carrying within you but don't quite know how to get it across – there's a need

to prove that we can still do it to ourselves. That still exists. Every time we go on stage we have to prove that we're not just some sad old things playing songs just to pay the electricity bill … we need to do things that make people say 'god, that was ten times better than what I thought it was going to be'. So yes, there's a ton to prove!

SO IF YOU'RE SETTING YOURSELVES THOSE KINDS OF GOALS THEN ACTUALLY EVERYTHING IS GETTING MORE DIFFICULT EVERY TIME YOU DO IT?

Well, it's more difficult if you're not on form, and you're not always on form you know? There're things that go on and life is just not like that, but if you're on form then things just seem to click into place.

WHICH SEEMS TO HAVE HAPPENED FOR YOU THIS TIME, NOW THAT YOU'RE AT THIS POINT – TALKING ABOUT THE RECORD, SETTING UP TOURING, THE WHOLE BUSINESS MACHINE COMING TO LIFE AGAIN – HOW DO YOU FEEL?

Yesterday I started doing interviews at nine in the morning and went through to six o'clock in the evening and then to get to where I am today I had to travel for five hours … well, [sarcastically] poor me! I called the producer on the phone and he said 'man, how do you do it – I feel so guilty sitting here by the pool', but this is my gig – his is to work on some tedious 'big sound' for twelve hours while I'm on the beach … everyone has their gig and this is mine. You've already done all this work on the record and if you want people to know it exists then you've got to be pragmatic!

IS PLAYING LIVE STILL THE THRILL IT ONCE WAS?

It is. I think what it is, is that it's managed a lot better, that thrill … I mean when I was younger I would probably think about the gig for the whole day leading up to the gig and then by the time the gig came I would be exhausted! Now it's almost the opposite and I don't feel anything until about ten minutes before we go on and then I can almost switch on and instantly feel the adrenaline, what's expected of me and the importance of the gig. If Simple Minds have a reputation as a live band it's because we have always appreciated that every gig is crucial. We don't just say, 'Oh it's alright, it's only Cambridge' … because the people there that night don't care if you were in Amsterdam yesterday and New York tomorrow; tonight's their night, they've bought the tickets and they've been looking forward to it for weeks.

GIVEN THE CATALOGUE YOU HAVE BEHIND YOU NOW, HOW ON EARTH DO YOU DECIDE WHAT YOU'RE GOING TO PLAY?

Certainly the last few times we've played, what we do is we've got about eight or ten

songs that are the icons and we play them every night … it might sound strong to say we're obliged to play them, but you've kind of got to play your greatest hits – maybe ten songs which are always there. Then for the other ten or fifteen songs you pull things from the catalogue and the new album, but we chop and change those around, which not only keeps it fresh for us but a lot of our audience comes to see us more than once and that way they get a different show and you really get to show your body of work.

Simple Minds' Jim Kerr and Derek Forbes are credited, along with David Bowie, for providing backing vocals on Iggy Pop's album *Soldier*. The whole band are also credited for providing 'handclaps' on Gary Numan's *Telekon* album.

'Don't You (Forget About Me)' is not a Simple Minds' original but was written by producer Keith Forsey specifically for the film *The Breakfast Club* and he had already unsuccessfully tried to persuade both Billy Idol and Bryan Ferry to record it. Simple Minds recorded it in three hours during the recording sessions for 'Once Upon A Time' simply to stop Forsey pestering them!

The name Simple Minds is taken from a line in David Bowie's song 'Jean Genie'.

1986

Snapshot

The first significant computer virus, 'Brain', starts to spread ● France and the UK reveal plans for the Channel Tunnel ● The Soviet Union launches the Mir space station ● Hampton Court Palace is severely damaged by fire ● The world's worst nuclear disaster occurs at Chernobyl when one of the power station's nuclear reactors explodes ● Around five million people join hands across the USA in the charity 'Hands Across America' event ● Argentina wins the World Cup, beating Germany 3-2 in the final ● The UK's bestselling single of the year is Nick Berry's 'Every Loser Wins'. ● Prince Andrew marries Sarah Ferguson ● Phil Lynott and Cary Grant pass away ● Singer stops making sewing machines ● The *Independent* newspaper is launched ● A worldwide ban on whaling begins ● The bestselling UK album of the year is Madonna's *True Blue* ● Martina Navratilova defeats Hana Mandlikova at Wimbledon and Boris Becker beats Ivan Lendl ● The space shuttle *Challenger* explodes on take off, killing all seven crew members ● *The Oprah Winfrey Show* goes on the air in the US ● The Coca Cola company celebrates its 100th anniversary ● Desmond Tutu is elected archbishop of Capetown ● *Top Gun* is the highest-grossing US film ● Elvis Presley, Chuck Berry, James Brown, Ray Charles and Buddy Holly are among the first artists to be inducted into the Rock & Roll Hall Of Fame ● John McEnroe marries Tatum O'Neal ● The Greater London Council is abolished

'My ultimate eighties' album is *Please* by the Pet Shop Boys. I was at a friend's house and he said, "Listen to this!" It was so different to anything I was listening to at the time. I loved it instantly.'

FLASH

'The butchering rendition of Nik Kershaw's "Wouldn't It Be Good" in *Pretty In Pink* is, to this day, unforgivable!'

MICHAEL WILDER

Sounds like. . .1986

It's a year of revision, college applications and interviews, more revision and then A-levels and the end of school; a long social summer; then leaving Essex for the bright lights of Reading, and starting at the university there. During the revision, college applications and A levels part of this year A-Ha will continue to dominate the charts, reaching number five in June with 'Hunting High & Low', the sweeping title track from their debut album, as well as with a pair of top-ten singles, 'I've Been Losing You' and 'Cry Wolf' from their next album, *Scoundrel Days*, which reaches number two. The Pet Shop Boys will have a similarly successful year. Their debut album *Please* will reach number three in April and they will release three more singles from it – 'Love Comes Quickly', 'Opportunities (Let's Make Lots Of Money)' and 'Suburbia' – as well as an album of remixes, *Disco*.

Depeche Mode will release their darkest album to date, *Black Celebration*, in March and it will peak at three, launching three singles, 'Stripped', 'A Question Of Lust' and 'A Question Of Time'. I will finally see them in concert for the first time at Wembley Arena in April. *Black Celebration* will be a revision favourite (especially when using the relentlessly commercial pirate-radio station Laser 558 as background noise gets too much), as will Talk Talk's

top-ten album *The Colour Of Spring*, featuring perhaps their best-known hit 'Life's What You Make It', and The Cure's *Standing On A Beach* compilation which follows in May, preceded by a remixed version of their brilliant 'Boys Don't Cry' single.

The Blow Monkey's *Animal Magic* album will also be on my revision playlist, particularly the two singles from the album, 'Digging Your Scene' and 'Wicked Ways', alongside Hipsway's eponymously titled album and their single 'The Honeythief'. Another record that will forever be associated with revision is 'Captain Of My Heart' by Dutch act Double, which will be a hit in January and which will always remind me of being in a car with my friends, escaping from our books by driving to Rayleigh in Essex to spend nights at a club called the Pink Toothbrush. When it goes to number one in March I will think that Cliff Richard and The Young Ones' version of 'Living Doll', recorded for Comic Relief, is brilliantly funny. Funny enough to buy it when it's released, although it's appeal will very quickly wane on repeated listens. Oddly enough it's the opposite to the way I feel about another number one record this year, Doctor & The Medics' version of Norman Greenbaum's 'Spirit In The Sky', which I hate while it's at its commercial peak but will come to like

'The ultimate eighties' album has to be *Black Celebration* from Depeche Mode, because I like every single song in it. I remember I cried the first time I played it. It was like they were talking to me.'

YANNIS

1986

Number One Singles

Pet Shop Boys 'West End Girls', A-Ha 'The Sun Always Shines On TV', Billy Ocean 'When The Going Gets Tough (The Tough Get Going)', Diana Ross 'Chain Reaction', Cliff Richard & The Young Ones 'Living Doll', George Michael 'A Different Corner', Falco 'Rock Me Amadeus', Spitting Image 'The Chicken Song', Doctor & The Medics 'Spirit In The Sky', Wham! 'The Edge Of Heaven', Madonna 'Papa Don't Preach', Chris De Burgh 'The Lady In Red', Boris Gardiner 'I Wanna Wake Up With You', The Communards 'Don't Leave Me This Way', Madonna 'True Blue', Nick Berry 'Every Loser Wins', Berlin 'Take My Breath Away', Europe 'The Final Countdown', The Housemartins 'Caravan Of Love', Jackie Wilson 'Reet Petite (The Sweetest Girl In Town)'

'Ultimate eighties' album . . . my, what a toughy! *Black Celebration* by Depeche Mode. That album has never sounded dated and the lyrical content still applies today.'

BENNY

'The ultimate album I guess would have to be The Smiths' *The Queen Is Dead*. The reason? Well it's just pure genius.'

MARK FROM YORK

'My ultimate album is Wham!'s *The Final* - it always cheers me up and gets me dancing around the house!'

ALI CARVER

'Ultimate album is *The Queen Is Dead* by The Smiths, for obvious reasons. I just remember buying it when it came out and thinking music doesn't get any better than this, and I was only 15 at the time.'

JULIA

when I hear it less often!

Sigue Sigue Sputnik will briefly become the enfants terrible of electronic music when they release their brilliantly bleepy rock 'n' roll debut 'Love Missile F1-11' in March. It will reach number three in the charts and the band will embark on a chaotic and controversial UK tour around the release of their debut album *Flaunt It*, which will also reach the top ten. Equally controversial this year are Scotland's The Jesus & Mary Chain – notorious for playing very short and incendiary concerts – whose breakthrough single 'Some Candy Talking', from their 1985 album *Psychocandy*, will be their first hit in August.

During my long social summer, the part of the year that is divided between earning money by day and going out at night, I will divide music into private and personal, the private being the records I listen to for myself and the public music covering the records that are playing as the soundtrack to this social summer. My personal soundtrack will of course include The Smiths, who will release their third album, the brilliant *The Queen Is Dead* – preceded by 'Bigmouth Strikes Again' – in June, which peaks at number two. The Smiths however will seem fairly unperturbed by this and in August and November will release two brilliant new singles, 'Panic' and 'Ask' respectively, from their next album, the 1987 compilation *The World Won't Listen*. Furniture's only hit 'Brilliant Mind', It's Immaterial's 'Driving Away From Home' and The Lover Speaks' almost-hit 'No More "I Love You's" will also fall into this 'personal' category.

Publicly though, it will be a summer of pop hits, a few of which will always stick in my mind, forever associated with pubs and parties and sunshine, among them Bananarama's 'Venus', Owen Paul's 'My

Favourite Waste Of Time', Nu Shooz's 'I Can't Wait' and Haywoode's 'Roses'. Robert Palmer will enjoy a pair of top-ten singles with 'Addicted To Love' and 'I Didn't Mean To Turn You On'. Madonna will dominate the year when her *True Blue* album becomes her second number one album, in July, propelled to the top by a number one single 'Papa Don't Preach'. It will be the UK's biggest selling album this year. Janet Jackson will follow the success of her debut hit 'What Have You Done For Me Lately' with a top-ten album, *Control* and two summer singles hits, 'Nasty' and 'When I Think Of You'. But it's Wham! who will truly provide one of the songs of the summer with a final number one single, 'The Edge Of Heaven'. A greatest hits compilation – *The Final* – and a triumphant farewell concert at Wembley Stadium on 28th June will follow before the duo finally split up for good.

Queen are also an essential part of the summer soundtrack and will release a number one album, *A Kind Of Magic* in June – following a singles hit for the track of the same name in March – which they will follow with a pair of dramatic singles: 'Friends Will Be Friends' and 'Who Wants To Live Forever?' *A Kind Of Magic* was loosely written for the soundtrack to *Highlander* (in the end six of the songs from the album will be used in the movie) and took its name from a phrase frequently used in the film by the main character Connor MacLeod, played by Christopher Lambert.

Another soundtrack to do well this year will be for *Top Gun*; the soundtrack album will peak at number four and will launch one of the year's biggest hit singles with 'Take My Breath Away', a number one for US act Berlin. A second Top Gun single, 'Danger Zone' by Kenny Loggins, will follow, peaking at just 45. Genesis will also have a film-related hit single this year when

'The Final by Wham! is my ultimate eighties' album. Who could not dance and sing to this fantastic album? And who cares about toilet antics when you can get the crowd moving like George Michael does!'

ANNETTE

'In Too Deep', which is featured on the soundtrack to the British film *Mona Lisa*, reaches number nineteen in September. The track is also featured on Genesis' own chart-topping *Invisible Touch* album, along with two more singles hits, 'Invisible Touch' and 'Land Of Confusion'.

Pretty In Pink, however, will undoubtedly be my favourite film this year, partly due to a brilliant soundtrack featuring a number of hits from some favourite artists (OMD's 'If You Leave', Psychedelic Furs' 'Pretty In Pink', New Order's 'Shellshock', Suzanne Vega's 'Left Of Centre', Echo & The Bunnymen's 'Bring On The Dancing Horses', one of The Smiths' finest moments ('Please Please Please Let Me Get What I Want') and an inexplicable and frankly inexcusable cover of Nik Kershaw's 'Wouldn't It Be Good' by the Danny Hutton Hitters), but mostly because of Molly Ringwald!

Chris De Burgh's 'The Lady In Red' will go to number one in July. Publicly I hate it, of course; privately I will go out and buy the album *Into The Light* for my Walkman because I'm going away for a couple of weeks over the summer and it will remind me of a girl. She's my first love and I will always associate her with many of the major ballads of 1986 – 'Lady In Red' in particular, I'm afraid, but also Cyndi Lauper's gorgeous 'True Colors', Spandau Ballet's plaintive 'Through The Barricades', Simply Red's 'Holding Back The Years' and Everything But The Girl's 'Come On Home'. Fortunately for me a major ballad that I will never associate with this relationship is Nick Berry's 'Every Loser Wins', a number one single for the *EastEnders*' actor in October and the bestselling UK single this year. It's the second *EastEnders*

record this year, after Anita Dobson's vocal interpretation of the show's theme, 'Anyone Can Fall In Love'.

In September I will start university in Reading and two records in particular will forever remind me of my first year in the halls of residence there: Erasure's 'Sometimes' – my personal favourite – and Cameo's 'Word Up', the favourite of the student two doors along the corridor from me which he will play, at high volume, for the entire year I live there. The track will become a staple at the Friday-night student discos where, aided by pints of cheap lager, my little group of friends and I will gradually forget that we can't dance and will be seduced by the beat of the latest releases, invariably ending the night formation dancing to The Housemartins' 'Happy Hour', punching the air to Europe's 'The Final Countdown', throwing strange shapes to the B-52s 'Rock Lobster', Egyptian dancing to The Bangles' 'Walk Like An Egyptian' or demonstrating our nimble footwork to the strains of The Communards' 'Don't Leave Me This Way'.

Away from the dance floor the tapes playing on my Walkman will include The Pretenders' fourth album *Get Close*, which will reach number six in November in the wake of their upbeat single hit 'Don't Get Me Wrong'; Peter Gabriel's chart-topping album *So*, which will also launch a pair of hit singles, the upbeat 'Sledgehammer' and the fragile Kate Bush duet 'Don't Give Up'; The Communards' top-ten debut album *Communards*, which will include three great singles in 'Disenchanted', 'So Cold The Night' and the classic 'Don't Leave Me This Way' (which will top the singles charts in September). There will be

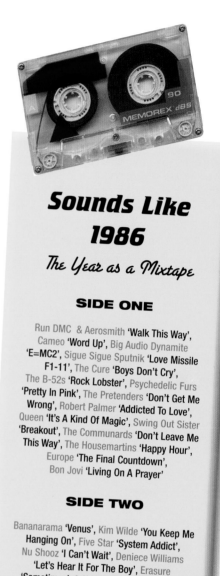

Sounds Like 1986
The Year as a Mixtape

SIDE ONE

Run DMC & Aerosmith 'Walk This Way', Cameo 'Word Up', Big Audio Dynamite 'E=MC2', Sigue Sigue Sputnik 'Love Missile F1-11', The Cure 'Boys Don't Cry', The B-52s 'Rock Lobster', Psychedelic Furs 'Pretty In Pink', The Pretenders 'Don't Get Me Wrong', Robert Palmer 'Addicted To Love', Queen 'It's A Kind Of Magic', Swing Out Sister 'Breakout', The Communards 'Don't Leave Me This Way', The Housemartins 'Happy Hour', Europe 'The Final Countdown', Bon Jovi 'Living On A Prayer'

SIDE TWO

Bananarama 'Venus', Kim Wilde 'You Keep Me Hanging On', Five Star 'System Addict', Nu Shooz 'I Can't Wait', Deniece Williams 'Let's Hear It For The Boy', Erasure 'Sometimes', A-Ha 'Hunting High & Low', Spandau Ballet 'Through The Barricades', Peter Gabriel & Kate Bush 'Don't Give Up', The Lover Speaks 'No More "I Love You"s' Furniture 'Brilliant Mind', Berlin 'Take My Breath Away', The Bangles 'Manic Monday', Madonna 'True Blue', Wham! 'The Edge Of Heaven'

'Ultimate single is definitely "Through the Barricades", quite simply the greatest song Gary Kemp ever wrote and sadly almost forgotten today. A travesty.'

MARK FINNEGAN

1986

Number One Albums

Various Artists Now That's What I Call Music 6, Dire Straits Brothers In Arms, Various Artists Hits 4, Bryan Ferry & Roxy Music Street Life – 20 Great Hits, Peter Gabriel So, Queen A Kind Of Magic, Genesis Invisible Touch, Madonna True Blue, Various Artists Now That's What I Call Music 7, Five Star Silk & Steel, Paul Simon Graceland, The Police Every Breath You Take – The Singles, Various Artists Hits 5, Various Artists Now That's What I Call Music 8

'Ultimate album has gotta be Five Star *Silk & Steel*. They released most of the album as singles and had the majority go into the top ten singles chart and the album itself stayed in the album charts for over a year, hitting number one for a few weeks – how amazing is that?!'

NORMAN WHITTAKER

a much overdue return to the charts for the Human League with their *Crash* album. It peaks at seven in September, preceded by the album's essential single 'Human'. Another welcome return will come in November when a streamlined Duran Duran (now consisting of Simon Le Bon, Nick Rhodes and John Taylor) break their silence and release a new single 'Notorious'. This will reach number seven, although the album of the same name will peak, disappointingly, at just sixteen in December.

Because of my Walkman I will buy most of my music on cassette for the next few years, but the new-fangled CD format is already closing in. A friend will buy his first CD player this year and I will admit that it does sound good even if the choice of

music on CD isn't quite broad enough for me yet. Along with the obligatory Dire Straits *Brothers In Arms* CD he will also buy two of this year's equally middle of the road albums, Huey Lewis & The News' *Fore* (featuring the hit singles 'The Power Of Love', 'Stuck With You' and 'Hip To Be Square') and Paul Simon's chart-topping *Graceland*, which will give us the hit singles 'You Can Call Me Al' and 'The Boy In The Bubble'.

Rock music will return to the charts in a big way this year, led by Bon Jovi who will become one of the late eighties' definitive rock acts. The US band will release their third album, *Slippery When Wet*, in September in the wake of their first UK hit single, 'You Give Love A Bad Name', which reaches number fourteen in

'Duran Duran's "Notorious" is my ultimate single and album. The excitement I felt as a Duranie seeing the teaser advert in *Smash Hits* for the single, then hearing it and realising that DD were back after the split is something I'll never forget. Every track on the album is excellent, the artwork and the look of the band at the time is second to none.'

CRAIG TALLENTIRE

'Bon Jovi's *Slippery When Wet* is the ultimate eighties' album and the single is their "Living On A Prayer". The album and single just captured the mood of atmosphere of my age and the hopes that me and my friends aspired to.'

GREGOR RAVENHILL

the singles charts in August. *Slippery When Wet* will peak at number six in the albums charts and will go on to launch a second single, 'Living On A Prayer', which will become, perhaps, the band's best-known song. However, this year even Bon Jovi's rock success will be eclipsed in the charts when Swedish rockers Europe chalk up a number one single with the anthemic 'The Final Countdown' and a top-ten album of the same name. US rap act Run DMC will also help to reopen the doors for rock music when their version o f Aerosmith's 'Walk This Way' – with Aerosmith's Steven Tyler and Joe Perry guesting on vocals and guitar – hits the UK top ten in September. The collaboration will give both acts their first UK chart success and is arguably the first hit to combine rock with hip-hop.

Combining rock with pop to great effect is Kim Wilde, who will have a number two hit in November with 'You Keep Me Hanging On' – her biggest hit since 'Kids In America' in 1981 – and US band The Bangles, who will have four singles hits from their *Different Light* album this year. The biggest of the four is the Prince cover 'Manic Monday', which reaches number two, but September's 'Walk Like An Egyptian' will become the one they are most remembered for. Five Star, meanwhile, will combine pop with more pop and have their best ever year with four top-ten hit singles and a number one album *Silk & Steel*. I'm not supposed to like Five Star of course, but 'System Addict' will get into my head and seduce me into submission like all great pop records should!

Among the year's oddities, novelties and one-hit wonders will be Nick Kamen, whose debut single 'Each Time You Break My Heart', co-written and produced by Madonna, and used in a Levi's commercial, reaches number five in the UK singles charts, Jermaine Stewart, whose 'We Don't Have To Take Our Clothes Off' peaks at two and Falco, whose 'tribute' to Mozart – 'Rock Me Amadeus' – will be a number one record. Page 3 model Samantha Fox will also launch a music career with two top-ten hits, 'Touch Me (I Want Your Body)' and 'Do Ya Do Ya (Wanna Please Me)', and her debut album *Touch Me*, which will peak at seventeen. More to my taste is Lick The Tins' cover of 'I Can't Help Falling In Love With You', which doesn't quite make the top forty. Lovebug Starski's 'Amityville', however, will be more to the nation's commercial taste and will peak at number twelve.

'Bon Jovi was and still is my favorite band. They started it all, the original "hair band"! They were fun and fine looking and the music was great. And they're still kicking ass 20 years later! The ultimate album is *Slippery When Wet*, of course. And "Living On A Prayer" was the best song of the eighties hands down. It sounded great and had lyrics of hope!'

LYNNE

'The Human League are the ultimate eighties' act, probably because they are the style and music squashed into one band. They just represent the eighties with their beautiful timeless synthesizer classics.'

ROSE

Neighbours

Neighbours is still in production and celebrated its 20th Anniversary in 2005, by which point 5000 episodes had been made. The show is Australia's most successful drama series, and is still watched by 30 million viewers a day in more than 20 countries.

Jason Donovan's father, Terence Donovan, played Doug Willis on the show and his half-sister, Stephanie McIntosh, plays Sky Mangel.

Neighbours' actors who have gone on to further fame as actors or musicians include Kylie Minogue, Jason Donovan, Russell Crowe, Natalie Imbruglia, Craig McLachlan, Guy Pearce, Delta Goodrem and Holly Valence.

Ian Smith, who plays Harold Bishop, is the longest-serving member of the *Neighbours'* cast and joined the show in 1987, but the only original cast member to still feature on the show is Paul Robinson (played by Stefan Dennis), who returned to the show in 2004 after almost ten years away.

Celebrities who have appeared in *Neighbours*, either as characters or as themselves, include Derek Nimmo, Pet Shop Boys' Chris Lowe, Barry Sheene, Emma Bunton, Julian Clary, Matt Lucas and David Walliams.

I can only remember two TV events during the time I was at University that absolutely everyone watched. One was Nelson Mandela's release from prison in February 1990 and the other was the 523rd episode of *Neighbours* – Scott and Charlene's wedding – in November 1988. Only one of these events was videoed by my future wife and watched by her and a friend again and again, provoking fresh tears at every viewing – the same one that attracted record daytime TV viewing figures and launched two of the late eighties' most successful music stars: Jason Donovan and Kylie Minogue.

Neighbours was first aired in Australia in 1985 and came to the UK a year later, making its UK debut on October 27th 1986. The early episodes revolve around the lives of two families, the Ramsays and the Robinsons, living in the fictitious Melbourne suburb of Erinsborough, although the storylines quickly extend to the other families living on and around Ramsay Street. Early storylines that helped the show to its regular late-eighties' peak of around 14 million viewers seemed to centre largely around romances and weddings (Scott and Charlene, Des and Daphne, Paul and Terry, Paul and Gail, Harold and Madge, Jim and Bev, Joe and Kerry), the arrival of new characters (Harold, Henry, Bronwyn, Joe, Kerry), births (Jamie), deaths (Terry, Daphne, Noelene), mysterious character changes (Scott Robinson, who was played by Darius Perkins before Jason Donovan took

over the part, and Lucy Robinson who was played by Kylie Flinker until 1987, after which she was played by Sasha Close and then by Melissa Bell!), departures (Max, Scott, Shane, Charlene) and car crashes (Shane & Danny and then Paul, Scott & Mike).

I was never a fanatical *Neighbours'* viewer but I did watch it often enough to keep up, right up until the point where I started having to work for a living when I lost sight of the show because it was only broadcast at lunchtime and teatime, in other words when I was at work. In particular I remember Bouncer's dream – pretty much an entire episode given over to the dog Bouncer's dreams about Rosie, the sheepdog next door – Joe Mangel calling everyone 'mongrels' and Melanie Pearson accidentally joining Paul and Gail on their honeymoon and laughing like a seal at every opportunity!

Scott and Charlene haven't appeared on *Neighbours* for almost twenty years but the characters still get occasional mentions on the show. If you're curious, they are still happily married and are now living in Brisbane with their two children, Daniel and Madison. Incidentally, the wedding song was 'Suddenly' by Angry Anderson.

THE MIR SPACE STATION

First I wanted to be a soldier; then I wanted to be an astronaut. By early 1986, however, when I was preparing to head off to university to do a design course, there may have been a tiny part of me that still really wanted to be a spaceman because I followed the story of the Mir space station with a mixture of interest and envy. When I was a kid in the seventies I thought my future would be full of flying cars and personal rocket packs, and although these things hadn't materialised (and still haven't, damn it!) Mir – which means 'peace' or 'world' in Russian – was certainly the next best thing: the first permanently inhabited space station. For me this was science fiction come to life, and I'd read a lot of science fiction!

It took ten years for the Soviet space agency to build the Mir space station, which was assembled from a series of different modules, each one launched separately and assembled in space. The first module, the Core, consisted of living quarters and the station controls, and was sent up in February 1986 and after the event, in line with Soviet leader Mikhail Gorbachev's new policy of 'glasnost' (political and social openness), the world was shown television footage of the launch – the first ever Soviet launch to be televised.

The station was almost immediately inhabitable. In fact, it would be almost continuously occupied for 4594 days (almost ten years), generally by a crew of three but on occasion by up to six people. In March 1986, just weeks after the launch of the Core module, the first Mir crew took off to the new station, and this time the Soviets broadcast the launch live. An astronomy module was sent up in 1987, followed by an updated life-support system module in 1989 and a scientific module for material processing, incorporating a geophysics and astrophysics laboratory, followed in 1990.

In the spirit of cooperation between Russia and America after the Cold War two more modules were launched in 1995, one to house joint experiments and another as a docking station for the American space shuttle. The final module, equipped with remote sensing equipment, was sent into space in 1996.

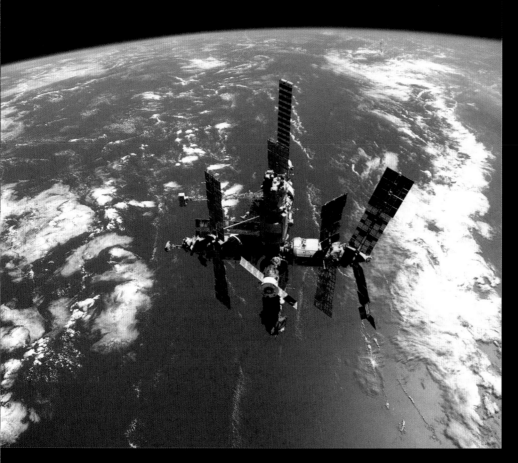

The Mir Space Station ... Up To Date!

The station was finally closed down and deliberately taken out of orbit in 2001, superseded by the International Space Station project, by which time it had orbited the Earth almost 90,000 times, travelling 2,260,840,632 miles in the process. The International Space Station (ISS) is a research facility currently being assembled in orbit around the Earth. It is a joint project between five space agencies: NASA, the Russian Federal Space Agency (Roskosmos), the Japan Aerospace Exploration Agency (JAXA), the Canadian Space Agency and the European Space Agency.

She's the most successful female recording artist of all time, having sold more than 250 million records. She has had over fifty top-ten singles in the UK, including twelve number ones. She has also had seventeen top-ten albums in the UK, nine of which went to number one. She is the wealthiest female music artist in the world and her net worth is estimated to be around half a billion dollars. She is five feet four and a half inches tall. She was born on 16th August 1958. She was supported on her first American tour by the Beastie Boys. In 1985 she married actor Sean Penn but filed for divorce in 1989. The mixture of eroticism and Catholic symbolism in her 'Like A Prayer' video was denounced by the Vatican as blasphemous. Her first greatest hits collection, *The Immaculate Collection* was dedicated to the Pope. She was voted one of *People* magazine's twenty-five Most Intriguing People In The World for 1989. In 1991 she attended the Oscars with Michael Jackson, wearing over $20 million worth of diamonds. She has appeared in twenty films and starred in the highest-grossing musical film of the nineties, *Evita*, which made almost $150 million. She has been romantically linked to Warren Beatty, Lenny Kravitz, Sandra Bernhard, Vanilla Ice, Billy Zane and Anthony Kiedis. In 2000 she married film director Guy Ritchie. She has won the Razzle Award for Worst Actress twice for her roles in *Shanghai Surprise* and *Who's That Girl?* and in 2000 was awarded another for Worst Actress Of The Century. She turned down Michelle Pfeiffer's role as Catwoman in *Batman Returns*. She has published six children's books and a book of explicit pictures of herself. In 1996 she gave birth to a daughter, Lourdes and in 2000 to a son, Rocco. She has won five Grammy Awards. In 2003 she caused controversy when she kissed Britney Spears and Christina Aguilera on stage at the MTV Awards. Along with Kylie Minogue she is the only female artist to have had a number one UK album and single in three different decades. In 2006 she controversially adopted a Malawian baby boy. Her Confessions Tour, which played to over a million people in 2006, was reported by *Billboard* as the top-grossing tour ever by a female artist, and it estimated that she personally made over $50 million from the tour. In 2007 she signed a new ten-year deal, said to be worth around £120 million, to cover albums, tours and sponsorship agreements.

She is Madonna, she is the eighties, the nineties and the noughties. We should salute her!

'I do admire the way Madonna dressed back in the day, she had style. Not much class but style none the less.'

CARLA

'Madonna is the ultimate eighties' artist because she has changed her look right thru the eighties (and beyond). She's a symbol of the times and of freedom of expression and sexuality for women! Sex on a stick!'

LISA DICK

'Madonna was and is a chameleon and makes great pop music to this day. I think if you were like myself, a girl of 12 in the mid-eighties, you were a fan. She is still great today, my ultimate eighties' artist, and has worked hard to achieve it.'

SALLY MIDLER

'Ultimate artist of the decade? Without question . . . MADONNA! She was the first artist who made me want to read the lyrics to songs, because despite everything, she will be remembered for her musical legacy. And over the past 20 plus years she has evolved as an amazing artist and still moves me like the first time I heard her sing.'

JOHN CARDONA

MADONNA

On Saturday 26th April 1986 a steam explosion in one of the reactors at the Chernobyl Nuclear Power Plant, located near Pripyat in the Ukraine, started a fire that led to a series of explosions, in turn causing a nuclear meltdown. The incident is still said to be the worst accident in the history of nuclear power and resulted in a cloud of radioactive fallout – estimated to be over one hundred times more radioactive than the atom bombs dropped on Nagasaki and Hiroshima – drifting over parts of the Soviet Union, Eastern and Western Europe, Scandinavia, the UK, Ireland and even eastern parts of North America. Over a quarter of a million people were evacuated from the areas of worst contamination, largely located in Ukraine, Belarus and Russia, and eventually over 300,000 people had to be permanently resettled.

There are two main but conflicting theories over the cause of the accident, one blaming the management of the power plant, the other blaming flaws in the reactor design, but either way it is clear that the emergency services called to deal with the accident were both ill-prepared to tackle such a situation and ill-informed about the scale of the incident. Over two hundred people were immediately hospitalised after the accident, mostly fire and rescue workers, of whom thirty-one died, twenty-eight of them from acute radiation exposure. The Ukrainian government estimates that over two million people have since suffered from health problems as a result of the accident.

The accident also contaminated land, water, plants and animals – and therefore agricultural crops and milk – and the area remains highly radioactive. However, since 1986 its status as an exclusion zone for humans led to the area become a thriving habitat for wildlife and scientists have been surprised by the dramatic revival of its ecosystem. It still remains to be seen whether there will be any long-term ecological effects.

The Chernobyl power plant continued to produce electricity until December 2000.

THE CHERNOBYL DISASTER

Chernobyl ...Up To Date!

Chernobyl remains one of the most radioactive spots on Earth and a 30-kilometre exclusion zone is still in place around the power plant. The true extent of the effects of the accident still aren't known, although official UN figures predict around 9000 fatalities, mostly from cancer caused by exposure to radioactive fallout. Greenpeace, however, predict the figure will be in excess of 90,000, and possibly double that number once other attributable illnesses – intestinal, heart and circulation, respiratory and immune system problems – are added to the equation.

1986 ICON
▶▶ *A-Ha*

It all starts with a girl in a coffee shop. She's reading a comic about motorcycle racing, the reason for this unusual choice of reading material quickly becoming apparent when a dashing young hero wins the race. The hero winks from the page and, as the girl registers her surprise, he reaches his arm out of the book and pulls her into his comic-book world. There's a chase, a fight, a flickering struggle between reality and fantasy and an epic escape as the girl re-enters the real world, simultaneously bringing her hero to life.

It was our first look at A-Ha, the video for the brilliantly poppy 'Take On Me' in 1985, a video so ahead of its time that everyone at school is talking about it, and anyone who hasn't seen it is desperate to see what all the fuss is about. The song has already been recorded several times and has been released twice before, but this time everything is right: the music, the video, the image and the timing. 'Take On Me' peaks at number two (number one in the USA). The band release another single, 'The Sun Always Shines On TV', which reaches number one, and an album, *Hunting High & Low*, will reach number two in the UK, going on to sell eight million copies. A-Ha are suddenly one of the biggest bands in the world.

In 1986 A-Ha will score two more top-ten singles hits from *Hunting High & Low*, including the gorgeous title track, before switching their attention to a second hit album *Scoundrel Days*, which again reaches number two in the UK albums charts and will also provide three more hit singles for the band, including 'Cry Wolf' and 'I've Been Losing You'. The theme to 1987's James Bond film *The Living Daylights* was the first hit to come from the band's third album, a successful attempt to move away from the disposable pop sounds of their first two albums; 1988's *Stay On These Roads* will produce a further four UK hit singles.

The band would release further albums in 1990 (*East Of The Sun, West Of The Moon*) and 1993 (*Memorial Beach*), which both made the UK top-twenty, as did a succession of singles from those albums. Although their more fickle pop fans started to fall away, an incredibly loyal and dedicated fanbase remained who voraciously support A-Ha to this day.

Internal conflicts and frustration with their record label led to A-Ha splitting in 1994 to work on solo projects, but the band eventually reunited in 2000 to record a critically acclaimed new album, *Minor Earth Major Sky*. Two years later they would release *Lifelines*, and a 2004 compilation album put them back in the UK albums charts for the first time for four years.

In late 2005 A-Ha released *Analogue*, for me their best album to date, along with a top-ten single of the same name in early 2006 which quickly became my favourite ever A-Ha single and was one of my favourite singles by any artist in that year. I got the chance to interview the band about the project in January 2006. Unusually for me I didn't do the interview on the telephone. Instead I went to London to meet the band at their hotel and spent an extremely enjoyable half hour talking with a chatty, animated Magne Furuholmen about the new release and about the band in general, who by that point had sold almost 80 million records worldwide.

'The ultimate eighties' band was A-Ha. I have to admit this was initially based heavily on a huge crush on Morten Harket (which has never quite left me!), but they were never quite right in the teeny / boyband box. I liked that they weren't full of shit, and were anti "sex, drugs and rock'n'roll", just wanting it to be about the music.'

LESLEY JEAVONS

HOW DIFFERENT IS A-HA TODAY FROM THE A-HA WE FIRST SAW IN THE EIGHTIES? DO YOU STILL 'CONNECT' WITH THE OLD YOU, THE ONE IN THE OLD PICTURES AND VIDEOS AND EVERYTHING?

Yeah, I see a very scared rabbit-caught-in-the-headlights person, who is compensating for the sheer panic of it all by you know, being very over the top and outgoing. Our biggest flaw as a band in the early eighties, our biggest problem area if you like, is that we are polite, polite people brought up in a society where politeness works, but it doesn't work so well in this business! You get caught in situations where somebody says smile and you smile, and you feel like an idiot but you still do it, and you are the one who has to say 'fuck this, I'm not going to stand here like an idiot and have my picture taken'. That's where our upbringing came into conflict with how we felt, and in the end if that gap becomes too wide you start to rebel against your own creation, and that's what

Coldplay are such big fans of A-Ha that they play on Magne Furuholmen's solo album *Past Perfect Future Tense*, which was released in 2004.

In 1991 A-Ha played a show at the Rock In Rio Festival in Brazil which attracted a paying audience of 198,000 people, the world record for the largest paying audience at that time.

we did, we started to bring it down and try to destroy it…For me the beauty of coming back is that before, the media and the critics and the industry would have one image of the band and we'd have another and it has taken time for these two images to start to overlap and marry up. The way that people look at our band and our work now is different to the way it was in the eighties so you do feel that every new thing you do is a little bit to do with restoration of your history.

I THINK YOU CAN HEAR THAT IN THE MUSIC, THE FIRST TIME I HEARD THE 'ANALOGUE' SINGLE I COULDN'T QUITE PUT MY FINGER ON WHO IT WAS AND WHEN I FOUND OUT IT WAS YOU I WAS EQUALLY SURPRISED AND NOT SURPRISED, IF THAT MAKES ANY SENSE?

I don't know if that's something you can orchestrate. I don't know if it's better if it's not willed to strongly and just kind of happens; we have worked with people who have done that and even on this album Martin Terefe, one of the producers, would say 'oh that's so A-Ha, that's such an A-Ha moment' and we always resist that to a certain degree because we don't want to be caricatures of ourselves. We don't want to mimic anyone else but we certainly don't want to go in to make 'another A-Ha album', we're interested in pushing it and it's always the material that decides where you go … the record company are always asking for that big A-Ha single and we just go, you know, these are the songs, this is what we are doing now and you just need to live with that. But

like you said, I would always rather people wonder what it is rather than have people say 'oh yes, another A-Ha record' … I don't know, I'm more interested in the stuff we haven't done than the stuff we have done!

DOES THAT MAKE EVERYTHING FRUSTRATING, SITTING HERE NOW TALKING ABOUT SOMETHING THAT IS DONE, WHEN YOU'VE GOT ALL THIS NEW STUFF INSIDE WAITING FOR A TIME TO COME OUT?

No … it's difficult to explain something that is meant to be felt, that's not actually me saying that, it's a quote from Frank Black of The Pixies in a book I just read but I think it's a good one … you can describe music as much as you want but unless you hear it it's not going to make sense to you, so I think really you can only talk about what you have done and you can't really say anything about the stuff you haven't done. Sometimes it offers chances for rare moments of self-insight you know, when you think about it and talk about it, but I don't think we've ever been that good at really selling a record – I think we've been better at making them than selling them, but I think we were perceived as a band who were very good at selling them and we were very frustrated about that.

YOU HAVE A NEW RECORD LABEL ON BOARD THIS TIME AROUND – HAS THAT AFFECTED THINGS A LOT?

Hugely. I think our previous record label – as good as they were – thought that we were just too much hassle, had too much

'A-Ha are the ultimate eighties' band because they are timeless and their music is awesome. Their music is the soundtrack of my life and it doesn't matter what happens, they are always close to my life.'

ANA GRAMA

history, plus we were signed in America and nobody felt a real commitment, nobody felt like it was their project. I guess we were just at odds with the record company because they looked at the success as something positive and we looked at it as something we wanted to leave behind, so we were on a crash course with that! I guess that now this is a kind of honeymoon period with the new label and they have been great and as I said, they've kind of given us a second wind here.

DID THE NEW LABEL AND THIS RENEWED SENSE OF COMMITMEMT MAKE A DIFFERENCE TO THE MAKING OF THE *ANALOGUE* ALBUM AT ALL?

That's the strange thing because I think you have the same high expectations every time. Every time I've made a record I've always felt 'gotta get this out there, gotta get this out' and it's a tough thing because unless you have a career that's a non-stop string of perfect hits you're going to have ups and downs over a twenty-year period – I defy anyone not to! You have to learn to live with the letdown of certain parts of your work not catching people's attention, not catching the imagination of people, and you come through the other side stronger because of it. In the end you have to decide for yourself why you're in this game and what you're doing this for and I think you see that very clearly after a while and I think you come to terms with the fact that not everything can just be taken for granted. I think that when your

first single goes to number one in twenty countries and sells millions of copies, and you're just a kid who's really trying not to lose your footing, struggling just to stay upright, you take it all for granted. You get a Grammy nomination, you get eight MTV Awards the first year you're out there and you don't know what the fuck it all means. If we got that now we'd be appreciative of it in a different way, and if we don't get it then that's OK too because we're doing it for the love of the material and because we really believe in what we're doing.

YOU'VE HAD SOME TIME TO LIVE WITH THE NEW ALBUM NOW, TO STAND BACK FROM IT AND ALSO TAKE IT ON THE ROAD … HOW DO YOU FEEL ABOUT IT NOW WITH THAT ADDED PERSPECTIVE?

It feels pretty good. The songs pretty easily made it into the live set, pretty effortlessly actually and that's always a good sign, when the new stuff sounds good when you're playing it. Looking back at it, I do think that of the 'comeback' stuff – the material we have put out since we got back together – it's the first one where the talents of the three of us are no longer necessarily pointing in opposite or different directions, you can sort of discern the three voices in the choir, perhaps more clearly than on the old stuff. I'm happy with the record, some of the moments on the record anyway … I think it has always been the case with A-Ha that we have touched on some great things on all the records but there isn't that one defining record, in my view, that is the great piece of work.

People always ask me which is my favourite record and I think that *Scoundrel Days* is really the one I mention when I talk about making something cohesive, but I think this one – for me – this is the best that I could do and the best I've done.

WHICH IS HOW IT SHOULD BE SURELY?

Yeah, but it's still out there … that one defining A-Ha record, and it's that irritation makes you want to go and record again. There's always been good songs and good moments on all the records but never that one complete record …

IS THAT EVEN POSSIBLE?

We are too headstrong as individuals, you know? There's not one dominating voice in the band and I think it must be easier if you have a band where just one person is the creative centre and it's easier to make a record then. There's too much ambition wanting to go into the record, I don't know, maybe it will seem different in ten years time but for me we're closer with this one than we were with the last one and that's inspiring, that's something I like to think is a good sign!

'I wrapped black speaker-wire around my wrist for a short time in 1985, mimicking the style of Morten Harket from A-Ha!'

JOHN BOLSAR

1987

Snapshot

Michael Jackson has the bestselling UK album of the year with *Bad* and Rick Astley' 'Never Gonna Give You Up' is the bestselling single ● British Airways is privatised ● Brett Easton Ellis publishes his second novel, *The Rules Of Attraction* ● Margaret Thatcher is elected to her third term as Prime Minister ● T'Pau's 'China In Your Hand' is the 600th UK number one single ● Terry Waite is kidnapped in Beirut and won't be released until 1991 ● *Going Live* replaces *Saturday Superstore* ● One hundred and eighty people drown when a cross-channel ferry, the *Herald Of Free Enterprise*, capsizes outside Zeebrugge ● Timothy Dalton becomes James Bond in *The Living Daylights* and A-Ha record the title track ● A nineteen-year-old German pilot lands a light plane in Moscow's Red Square ● Prozac becomes available in the USA ● Liberace, Patrick Troughton, Andy Warhol, Lee Marvin and Fred Astaire die ● Italian born star Cicciolina is elected to the Italian parliament ● Carrie Fisher publishes her book *Postcards From The Edge* ● The Docklands Light Railway in London opens ● The New York Giants beat Denver 39-20 to win the Superbowl ● TV show *Morse* is aired for the first time ● Wall Street experiences Black Monday on 19th October and stock values around the world plummet ● At Wimbledon Pat Cash beats Ivan Lendl in the men's singles and Martina Navratilova defeats Steffi Graf in the women's ● Bruce Hornsby & The Range wins the Grammy for Best New Artist ● Mikhail Gorbachev announces plans for 'Perestroika' (economic reform and restructuring) and 'Glasnost' (the beginnings of free speech) in Russia ● Bamber Gascoigne's *University Challenge* finishes (although it will be revived in 1994) ● Bill Gates becomes computing's first billionaire ● The year's new films include *Dirty Dancing*, *The Lost Boys*, *Fatal Attraction*, *Lethal Weapon* and *Wall Street* ● Digging starts on the Channel Tunnel project ● *The Simpsons* is broadcast in the US for the first time

'The ultimate artist is Def Leppard. I've been a fan of the band for 20 years and I love every Def Leppard song!'

BECKY

Sounds like...1987

The year will open with a reissue of Jackie Wilson's 1957 hit 'Reet Petite (The Sweetest Girl In Town)' at number one, propelled there after being used in a TV advert for Levi's Jeans. This kind of use of classic singles from the fifties is a trend that will continue throughout the year and will see Ben E. King top the charts with 'Stand By Me' and Percy Sledge's 'When A Man Loves A Woman' peak at two, both on the back of Levi's commercials. Similarly Nina Simone will reach number five in October with a reissue of her classic 'My Baby Just Cares For Me' following its use in an advert for Chanel No. 5 perfume.

Bon Jovi, who re-opened the floodgates to rock in late 1986 with the release of their *Slippery When Wet* album, will release two more hits ensuring their place at the cutting edge of the new rock revolution, which this year will also see US veterans Kiss peak at number four in both the singles and albums charts with their 'Crazy Crazy Nights' single and *Crazy Nights* album respectively, their highest ever UK chart positions. New US rock act Guns N' Roses will be less fortunate when they release their debut UK single 'Welcome To The Jungle' and see it peak at just 67, one place higher than their first album *Appetite For Destruction*. Def Leppard will enjoy their most successful year of the eighties with the release of their

fourth album *Hysteria,* which will go to number one in August on the back of a top-ten single 'Animal', the first of three hit singles for the band this year. Whitesnake will have a similarly successful year with two top-ten singles and a top-ten album – 'Is This Love' and 'Here I Go Again' and *Whitesnake* respectively. Both Def Leppard and Whitesnake will go on to far greater

'The ultimate single is Beastie Boys' "(You Gotta) Fight For Your Right (To Party)". School disco, say no more . . .'

KIERON

'Strangely my fave eighties' album is Johnny Hates Jazz's *Turn Back The Clock*. I still play it to this day because it's ultimate cheese but I do think they weren't given enough credit back then.'

KARLA SKINGSLEY

'Ultimate album . . . geez, Sisters of Mercy's *Floodland* – they helped me get out my frustrations – yeah baby!'

KAGSY

'Prince's *Sign O' The Times* is the ultimate album of the eighties because it truly represents the spirit of experimentation, of genre (and gender) confusion and fun of that decade.'

DANIELE FROM ROME

'George Michael is the ultimate artist because he moves with the times and spans different music categories, he isn't stuck in one category and all his music sounds different.'

ALI CARVER

success in the US, where Whitesnake will eventually sell over eight million copies (giving the band their sole US number one hit 'Is This Love' in the process) and *Hysteria* almost 14 million.

On the tails of Run DMC's success with Aerosmith in 1986 the Beastie Boys' punk, rock and hip-hop hybrid explodes into the UK this year with four hit singles including the brilliant '(You Gotta) Fight For Your Right (To Party)' and 'No Sleep 'Til Brooklyn', both of which will become student disco anthems, while their debut album *License To Ill* will be one of the albums of the year. The Beastie Boys will also find themselves at the centre of a media frenzy this year when their Licensed To Ill tour reaches the UK amid controversy over inciting riots and their use of a giant inflatable penis on stage, although even these misdemeanours will pale next to the indignation that surrounds the nationwide vandalising of Volkswagen cars by fans desperate to own VW logos to hang round their necks! Beastie Boys' success will also help open the doors for another act on their fledgling Def Jam label, Public Enemy, whose debut UK single hit will be 'Rebel Without A Pause', although the accompanying album *Yo! Bumrush The Show* will fail to chart. M|A|R|R|S will be equally influential when they release a single 'Pump Up The Volume' in August that goes on to be a number one record in the UK, the first British-made house hit.

Rock influences will also creep into hits from some far more mainstream bands. The Proclaimers' irritatingly catchy debut single 'Letter From America' will reach number three in June, T'Pau will have a fantastic number one single and album with 'China In Your Hand' and *Bridge Of Spies* respectively, while Johnny Hates Jazz will have three epic pop-rock hit singles with 'Shattered Dreams', 'I

Don't Want To Be A Hero' and 'Turn Back The Clock' this year, followed by a number one album, *Turn Back The Clock*, in early 1988. Australia's Mental As Anything and the UK's Scarlet Fantastic will both enjoy their sole UK hits with 'Live It Up' (from the soundtrack to the film *Crocodile Dundee*) and 'No Memory' respectively, while American act Timbuk 3's 'The Future's So Bright I Gotta Wear Shades' will complete a great trio of 1987 rock-influenced one-hit wonders. More straightforward rock hits this year include Zodiac Mindwarp & The Love Reaction's gloriously grungy single 'Prime Mover' and Spear Of Destiny's epic 'Never Take Me Alive' single and *Outland* album. For me both will be pushed into the margins by the Sisters Of Mercy's debut hit 'This Corrosion', which will reach the top ten in

'In the mid-eighties I liked George Michael's stubble look, but as a 17-year-old I just looked like a scruff. I dropped this look very quickly!'

FLASH

seeing Olivia Newton-John undergo the transformation from girl-next-door to sexy temptress in *Grease!* Treading a similar path to Prince (although without the Sheena Easton-style sidekick!) is Terence Trent D'Arby, whose debut album *Introducing The Hardline According To Terence Trent D'Arby* will go to number one. D'Arby will also have three hit singles this year including two of his best known hits – 'If You Let Me Stay' and 'Wishing Well' – which will both make the top five, establishing him as one of the world's hottest new artists.

It will be a good year for some established acts too. George Michael in particular will shed some of the lightweight poppiness that marked his Wham! days and reinvent himself as a more grown-up artist, releasing his debut solo album *Faith* in October on the back of two singles hits: a number one duet with Aretha Franklin, 'I Knew You Were Waiting (For Me)', and a number three hit in the summer with 'I Want Your Sex'. Eventually six singles will be taken from *Faith*, propelling the album to number one in the UK and the USA and going on to sell well over 20 million copies, establishing George Michael as one of the biggest stars of

October, preceding the brilliant *Floodland* album which reaches the top ten at the end of the year.

Prince will release a double album, *Sign O' The Times*, in March, which will peak at number four in the UK albums charts – his highest chart placing to date – preceded by a top-ten hit single of the same name and followed by a further three hit singles this year including 'U Got The Look', a duet with Sheena Easton, who has been out of the UK charts since 1983 although she has enjoyed significant US success. It's a great track but for me the true revelation will be Sheena Easton's utter transformation to sexy dance siren, an experience similar to

1987
Number One Albums

Kate Bush The Whole Story, Paul Simon Graceland, London Stage Cast The Phantom Of The Opera, Hot Chocolate The Very Best Of Hot Chocolate, U2 The Joshua Tree, Various Artists Now That's What I Call Music 9, Curiosity Killed The Cat Keep Your Distance, Swing Out Sister It's Better To Travel, Simple Minds Live In The City Of Light, Whitney Houston Whitney, Terence Trent D'Arby Introducing The Hardline According to Terence Trent D'Arby, Various Artists Hits 6, Def Leppard Hysteria, Michael Jackson Bad, Bruce Springsteen Tunnel Of Love, Sting Nothing Like The Sun, Fleetwood Mac Tango In The Night, George Michael Faith, T'Pau Bridge Of Spies, Rick Astley Whenever You Need Somebody, Various Artists Now That's What I Call Music 10

'The ultimate single would be any S/A/W produced song . . . pure 80s-tastic!'

LOUIS KEIGHLEY

'I'd choose "Always On My Mind" by Pet Shop Boys as the ultimate single because of its wonderful extended dance version with the most driving intro that always and still causes such feelings when listening to it!'

ALEXANDER ALTHON

'Erasure are the ultimate eighties act. The first time I heard them in 1986 I was thunderstruck by their energy.'

JENS

the late eighties and beyond. Boy George will also reinvent himself this year and will score four hit singles from his debut solo album *Sold*, including a number one single 'Everything I Own'.

Even George Michael's massive success this year won't be enough to outsell Michael Jackson, whose *Bad* album will go on to sell over 30 million copies, setting a US record (unbroken to this day!) in the process for featuring five number one singles ('I Just Can't Stop Loving You', 'Bad', 'The Way You Make Me Feel', 'Man In The Mirror' and 'Dirty Diana'). The singles won't perform quite as well in the UK with only 'I Just Can't Stop Loving You' making the top spot and 'Bad' and 'The Way You Make Me Feel' both reaching number three, but *Bad* will still be the year's bestselling album in the UK.

Madonna won't release a new album this year but will still reach the top five with *You Can Dance*, an album of dance mixes of her hits to date, and rake up four UK top-ten singles hits including number ones for 'La Isla Bonita' from the *True Blue* album, and 'Who's That Girl?' from the soundtrack to her movie of the same name. Madonna's success this year will be rivalled by that of another US singer – Whitney Houston – who will enjoy a number one album, *Whitney*, a number one single, 'I Wanna Dance With Somebody (Who Loves Me)' and two further singles hits in 'Didn't We Almost Have It All' and 'So Emotional'.

As Madonna moves away from the blatantly commercial pop of her early hits, Stock, Aitken & Waterman's 'hit factory'

will go into pop overdrive this year, chalking up number one singles for Mel & Kim with 'Respectable' and Rick Astley with 'Never Gonna Give You Up' – as well as top-ten hits for Pepsi & Shirley ('Heartache'), Samantha Fox ('Nothing's Gonna Stop Me Now'), Sinitta ('Toy Boy') and Bananarama ('Love In The First Degree'). But it's Rick Astley who will go on to be one of the biggest success stories of the year; his *Whenever You Need Somebody* album will top the albums charts, 'Never Gonna Give You Up' will be the UK's bestselling single this year and two further singles – 'Whenever You Need Somebody' and 'When I Fall In Love' – will also make the top three. 'Never Gonna Give You Up' will also be a number one single in the USA.

It will be a pretty good year for pop away from Stock Aitken & Waterman too. ABC will release 'When Smokey Sings' – my favourite ever track from them – an album, *Alphabet City*, and a second classic single, 'The Night You Murdered Love'. Swing Out Sister will follow the success of 1986's 'Breakout' single with their brilliant chart-topping debut album *It's Better To Travel*, and three more great singles, 'Surrender', 'Twilight World' and 'Fooled By A Smile'. Both albums will be Walkman essentials this year, as will the Pet Shop Boys' second album *Actually*, which will peak at number two in September and feature two number one singles, 'It's A Sin' and 'Always On My

New Order's Substance is my ultimate album because I begged for $$ from my friends and family to buy the LP import and I was so proud of owning something that was sooo ahead of it's time and having people over to hear it for their first time and being amazed like I was.'

SARCASZZ

Mind', as well as a duet with Dusty Springfield ('What Have I Done To Deserve This?'), which will reach number two and 'Rent', which will peak at eight.

Another favourite on my Walkman this year will be Erasure's second album *The Circus*, which will make the top ten in the first half of the year. Erasure will also release three singles from the album, including a pair of top-ten hits: 'Victim Of Love' and 'The Circus'. 'Cry Wolf' will be a hit for A-Ha at the beginning of the year (despite being released in late 1986) and will peak at number five, the final single from the band's successful *Scoundrel Days* album. A-Ha won't release their third studio album until 1988 but will neatly bridge that gap this year with the release of the title track for the James Bond film *The Living Daylights*, which will also peak at five.

Depeche Mode meanwhile will release a top-ten album *Music For The Masses*, one of my favourite albums this year, and two singles, 'Strangelove' and 'Never Let Me Down Again'. The Cure and New Order will both release double albums *Kiss Me, Kiss Me, Kiss Me*, and *Substance* respectively. Despite my love for The Cure their *Kiss Me* album is too long for me, although it does feature some fantastic tracks, among them one of my all-time favourite singles 'Just Like Heaven', the fragile 'Catch' and the upbeat single 'Why Can't I Be You?', which will be a staple of student discos and indie clubs for years to come. New

Order's album is a compilation of mostly 12" versions of all the band's singles to date launched by a brand new single, 'True Faith', which will climb to number four in the UK singles charts, another alternative dance floor classic and their biggest singles hit to date. New Order will end the year with another single, one of my favourites from them, 'Touched By The Hand Of God', taken from the soundtrack to the film *Salvation*, which will become a top twenty hit in early 1988.

I will spend my summer this year teaching on a children's summer camp in the USA followed by a month of travelling and I will always remember *Substance* as the main soundtrack to the summer, along with *Louder Than Bombs*, a double-album US compilation from The Smiths, which I buy while I'm there. While I'm in the USA The Smiths will split up following the release of a final studio album, *Strangeways Here We Come*, which will achieve a number two position in the albums charts. The Smiths will also release four singles in 1987 including 'Sheila Take A Bow' from the compilation *The World Won't Listen*, which reaches number ten, tying with 1984's 'Heaven Knows I'm Miserable Now' as The Smiths' highest singles chart position of the decade.

The year will close to the sounds of The Pogues & Kirsty MacColl's beautiful 'Fairytale Of New York' single, which is destined to become a true classic and probably my favourite Christmas song of all time.

'*Kiss Me, Kiss Me, Kiss Me* by The Cure is my ultimate eighties album. It's so varied, loud and unforgettable.'

KEVIN GUEST

Madonna's hit 'La Isla Bonita' was originally written for Michael Jackson's *Bad* album by Patrick Leonard and Bruce Gaitsch. When Jackson turned it down it was offered to Madonna who wrote the lyrics and recorded it for her *True Blue* album.

'New Order's "True Faith" is my ultimate single, because this song is extremely magical, and makes you feel all-powerful and positive when singing at full blast!'

MARK MATTERN

'I used to love *The Tube*. It was one of the only real music programmes that dealt with and addressed my obsession with music and being a rebel. Everything else seemed to be so mainstream. Most programmes from that era just blur and blend in, but *The Tube* stands out as one of the most pivotal shows of the 80s.'

ALAN

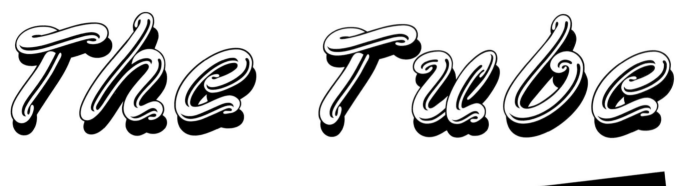

Launched in 1982 *The Tube*'s combination of live music, interviews, videos, comedy and chat positioned it perfectly as edgier than *Top Of The Pops* and more contemporary than *The Old Grey Whistle Test* (which in turn responded by changing its name to the snappier and altogether more contemporary *Whistle Test* in 1983 as part of a vague revamp to meet the challenge posed by this punky new pretender). *The Tube* was to *Top Of The Pops* what *Tiswas* was to *Swap Shop* – a mischievous, chaotic and slightly anarchic alternative to 'proper television', which of course was a big part of why we loved it. The music was live, the interviews were spontaneous and haphazard, and the presenters, comedians and guests could usually be counted on to say something mildly risque or controversial.

Predominantly a music show, *The Tube* was careful to represent a wide variety of bands and artists at all stages of their career, presenting the UK debut TV appearances for people like Madonna, Frankie Goes To Hollywood and Terence Trent D'Arby, alongside performances from more established acts across musical genres, from Scraping Foetus Off The Wheel to Wham!.

Jools Holland, Paula Yates and Muriel Gray were the show's core presenters, a fairly disparate bunch. Jools Holland was in Squeeze and brought a dry, intelligent wit to the show. Muriel Gray was similarly witty and intelligent, the polar opposite to Paula Yates who presented herself as lightweight and provocative and is best known for her flirtatious interviews, most notably perhaps for the show in which she persuaded Sting to remove his trousers! Other presenters included Leslie Ash, who would go on to star in *Men Behaving Badly*, and teenage model Felix Howard, who had appeared in Madonna's 'Open Your Heart' video and went on to a successful career as a songwriter for a number of well-known artists including Kylie Minogue and Sugababes.

Jools Holland's use of the phrase 'groovy fuckers' during a live trailer in January 1987 was the beginning of the end for *The Tube*, which had previously received complaints for similar incidents and was already fighting internal Channel 4 politics and falling viewing figures. The show was taken off the air for three weeks as a result of Holland's spontaneity and led to the producers' resignations due to 'stifling bureaucracy and heavy handed moralism' on the part of Channel 4. The fifth series finished in April 1987 and *The Tube* was never recommissioned.

> '*The Tube* was my favourite. No other live television programme introduced as many live acts that meant so much to me.'
>
> NEIL HARLAND

> *The Tube* was the best ever music programme! I wish they would broadcast the whole five years of shows again now.'
>
> SHAUN TRANTER

> 'I loved *The Tube* – it seemed so degenerate, disorganised and scruffy. Like a breath of fresh air!'
>
> LINDA KING

Bands and artists who appeared on *The Tube* included Art of Noise, Aztec Camera, Big Country, Culture Club, The Damned, Duran Duran, Echo & the Bunnymen, Elvis Costello, Frankie Goes to Hollywood, Human League, INXS, Killing Joke, Level 42, Lloyd Cole & The Commotions, Madonna, Motorhead, Paul Young, Psychedelic Furs, REM, Simply Red, Siouxsie & the Banshees, Squeeze, Style Council, Tears for Fears, Terence Trent D'Arby, The Smiths, The Cult, The Cure, The Jam, The Pretenders, The Stranglers, U2, Ultravox, Wham!, XTC and Yazoo.

Allegedly, when Dawn French used the word 'blowjob' as part of a comedy routine for *The Tube* she was the first person to ever use the word on British TV.

The Tube ... Up To Date!

Jools Holland has presented *Later With Jools Holland* since 1992, as well as continuing to record and tour under his own name. Muriel Gray went on to start her own production company, Ideal World, in 1989 and became a bestselling horror novelist in 1995 with *The Trickster,* which she has since followed with *Furnace* and *The Ancient*. She was also the chair of the judges for the 2007 Orange Prize for Fiction. Paula Yates divorced her husband Bob Geldof in 1996 for INXS singer Michael Hutchence. She died of an accidental heroin overdose in 2000. *The Tube* was revived briefly in 2006 as a radio show for Channel 4 radio hosted by Blur's Alex James, Factory Records' Tony Wilson and Blue Peter's Connie Huq.

GR££D IS GOOD

When I was growing up the image of a yuppie was of a sharp-suited businessman with a flashy car who had slicked-back hair and constantly barked 'buy' and 'sell' into an oversized mobile phone. Yuppies were everywhere in the media – on the television, in the news, in films, in books – working hard and playing hard, demonstrating their success conspicuously by buying great 'stuff' – cars, clothes, gadgets, houses, holidays, the lot – and inhabiting a materialistic world of prosperity and glamour, a world of trading floors, winebars and nightclubs. The yuppies were Thatcher's children, always ambitious, frequently ruthless and usually selfish, and have become symbolic of the self-serving, shallow side of the eighties.

Yuppies were an emerging generation of ambitious young adult professionals who graduated into the eighties' boom of economic growth and prosperity and quickly earned inflated salaries as a result. Their relative youth meant they had few responsibilities and therefore much of their income could be spent on themselves, and their lifestyles often became extravagantly competitive as they pursued status, material wealth and pleasure.

The term 'yuppie' stems from 'Young Urban Professional' or 'Young Upwardly Mobile Professional' and was first coined by American journalist Alice Kahn in 1982 as a term to describe the antithesis of 'hippie'. The term didn't really reach the public consciousness until 1984, which *Newsweek* magazine declared The Year of the Yuppie. For a few short years yuppies seemed to be everywhere, gleefully documented by the media through books like Jay McInerney's *Bright Lights Big City* and Tom Wolfe's *Bonfire Of The Vanities*, both of which were made into successful films, although perhaps not as successful as the ultimate yuppie film – 1987's *Wall Street*.

Wall Street – responsible for two of the ultimate eighties' film quotes: 'greed is good' and 'lunch is for wimps' from Michael Douglas' Gordon Gekko character – became the archetypal portrayal of eighties' excess when it was released at the end of 1987, just weeks after Wall Street's 'Black Monday' saw share prices plummet and the beginning of the end of the yuppie. When the markets crashed companies were forced to close or downsize, leaving many former yuppies unemployed and deeply in debt. The yuppie dream was finally over.

During the yuppie years a number of other terms came into use to describe the various social yuppie types, including 'dinkys' (double income, no kids yet), 'guppies' (gay urban professionals or gay upwardly mobile professionals) and 'buppies' (black urban professionals or black upwardly mobile professionals). 'Puppies' however remains the term for young dogs.

In the film *Wall Street*, over-enthusiastic sound effects ensure that even when Gordon Gekko is walking around in his socks you can still hear the sound of his shoes on the floor.

Yuppies ...Up To Date!

The term 'yuppie' has survived to this day although it has become a highly critical term for the irresponsible, self-indulgent lifestyle of wealthy young professionals from the eighties to today, and indicative of the greed, self-absorption and lack of social conscience of the eighties in general.

– THE YUPPIES

Dirty Dancing

'*Dirty Dancing* was fantastic –
a great feel-good movie.'

DELYTH

'*Dirty Dancing* was one of my
favorites because it was fun to
watch, and dramatic, and who
wouldn't want to see Patrick Swayze
strut his stuff on a dance floor???'

ASHLEY DEAN

'*Dirty Dancing* was a favourite
because of the great dancing and
music, and was just fab all round!'

SALLY MIDLER

'I will always remember *Dirty
Dancing* - my first time at the
pictures with a boy!'

TRACEY, 37

My only problem with the film *Dirty Dancing* is actress Jennifer Grey, and my problem with Jennifer Grey comes from her part in the film *Ferris Bueller's Day Off*. I suppose it's credit to Grey's acting skills that she so thoroughly portrayed Ferris' sister Jeanie as being obnoxious and unlikeable, but it means that every time I see her as Baby in *Dirty Dancing* I just can't quite shake my dislike of Jeanie for long enough to really see the new character!

I'm not sure it's a cool thing to say but *Dirty Dancing* is a great film, and was justifiably the surprise hit of 1987 despite the fact that neither of its stars, Patrick Swayze or Jennifer Grey, were particularly well known at the time. Patrick Swayze was born in Texas and under the guidance of his mother, who was a choreographer and dance teacher, he trained as a dancer, and made his first professional appearances. His first film role was in 1979's *Skatetown USA* but prior to *Dirty Dancing* his most memorable roles were in *Red Dawn* and *Youngblood*. Jennifer Grey was born in New York City and before starring in *Dirty Dancing* her most high profile role was as Jeanie in *Ferris Bueller's Day Off*, although she also had small roles in *The Cotton Club, American Flyers* and in *Red Dawn* with Swayze.

Here's the story (look away now if you haven't seen the film) … it's the sixties and Frances Houseman (Grey), a slightly sulky teenager known to all as 'Baby', goes to spend the summer with her family at Kellermans, an expensive upstate New York holiday resort. Once there she is expected to join in with the activities and make friends with the 'right' people, but when she spies the dance teacher, working-class rebel Johnny Castle (Swayze), engaging in the new fashion for 'dirty dancing' out of hours, she develops summer ideas of her own. Baby and Johnny grow close when he teaches her how to dance after Baby helps Johnny's dance partner Penny to pay for an abortion (the baby was fathered by Robbie, the rich boyfriend of Baby's sister Lisa, who refuses to take responsibility for his actions) which goes horribly wrong until Baby calls on her father – a doctor – to save the day. Consequently Baby is banned from seeing Johnny, but with Penny indisposed Johnny needs a partner for a local dance competition if he's to win enough prize-money to look after Penny over the winter, and only Baby can save the day!

Dirty Dancing was filmed in Virginia and North Carolina and cost a modest $6 million dollars to make, a good investment against box-office receipts of over $213 million and that's without the success of the soundtrack album, which featured a mix of sixties' classics and contemporary songs (including the hit 'She's Like The Wind', written and composed by Patrick Swayze) and went on to be one of the bestselling soundtracks of all time, spending eighteen weeks at number one in the USA and selling over eleven million copies.

'*Dirty Dancing* was the best! A great soundtrack AND Patrick Swayze!'

LISA

Dirty Dancing ...Up To Date!

Patrick Swayze went on to star in a string of films following *Dirty Dancing*, most notably playing Sam Wheat in *Ghost* and Bodhi in *Point Blank*. In 2004 he appeared in the film *Dirty Dancing: Havana Nights*, a 're-imagined' version of the original film, set in Cuba against the backdrop of the revolution. Jennifer Grey also appeared in a succession of TV and film roles including roles in *Friends*, *The Player* and 2006's *Road To Christmas*, in which she co-starred with her real-life husband, the actor Clark Gregg. The film has made the transition to stage musical, a production that has been a hit around the world, as well as to the world of reality TV in a show which sees hopeful dancers compete to become the ultimate *Dirty Dancing* dance champions.

THE HiT FACTORY

They are what links Judas Priest to Bananarama, Cliff Richard to Dead Or Alive and Sigue Sigue Sputnik to Big Fun. They are the most successful songwriting and producing partnership of all time, with over two hundred UK singles hits to their name. They are Stock, Aitken & Waterman.

The SAW story starts at the beginning of 1984 when producer Pete Waterman invited Mike Stock and Matt Aitken to work with him on a couple of records going through his production company PWL. Both singles – Divine's 'You Think You're A Man' and Hazell Dean's 'Whatever I Do' – would become hits in July of that year, after receiving a highly commercial Hi-NRG sheen from the partnership, the beginnings of a formula that would bring them all fame and fortune.

The trio went on to produce Dead Or Alive's *Youthquake* album, and quickly had artists and labels queuing up to work with them after Dead Or Alive's single 'You Spin Me Round (Like A Record)' went to number one in 1985. Bananarama were next to benefit when the SAW team took over the production duties for two songs on their *True Confessions* album, including 'Venus' which became Bananarama's biggest international hit in 1986 when it went to number one in the US, Canada, Australia, New Zealand, South Africa, Mexico and Switzerland. SAW then took over all production and co-writing duties on Bananarama's next album – 1987's *Wow!* – which featured the international hit singles 'I Heard A Rumour', 'Love In The First Degree' and 'Nathan Jones', whilst simultaneously working with a number of other artists, giving SAW the label The Hit Factory. Two of those artists included Mel & Kim and Rick Astley, who would give them their second and fourth UK number one singles in 1987 with 'Respectable' and 'Never Gonna Give You Up' respectively (their third number one was for the Ferry Aid charity single 'Let It Be'). 'Never Gonna Give You Up' was also an American number one for Rick Astley in 1987, as was 'Together Forever'.

In 1988 Stock, Aitken & Waterman had their first success with Kylie Minogue when her debut single, 'I Should Be So Lucky', went to number one in February, the first of thirteen consecutive top-five hits for the former *Neighbours* actress, including four UK number one singles. In December Kylie would share a number one single, 'Especially For You', with her then boyfriend, fellow *Neighbours* actor Jason Donovan, who would himself go on to enjoy a stellar run of hits with SAW.

The trio split in the early nineties and Mike Stock and Matt Aitken spent years locked in legal actions with Pete Waterman over copyright and royalty disputes, although they were eventually forced to drop their cases. Stock, Aitken & Waterman worked with well over a hundred different artists during their extraordinary career and had thirteen number one singles, although their work with Judas Priest towards the end of the eighties has yet to see the light of day.

STOCK, AITKEN & WATERMAN ...UP TO DATE!

Since their partnership dissolved Mike Stock has started a new label, Better The Devil Records, and has written a 2004 book about SAW called *The Hit Factory: The Stock, Aitken & Waterman Story*. Matt Aitken retired from music for a while, preferring to raise his family and enjoy life, although he has since returned to music. Pete Waterman continues to run PWL but has extended his lifelong interest in railways by starting a model railway company called Just Like The Real Thing. Rumours continue to circulate that SAW will put aside their differences and start working together again but at the time of writing no official announcements have been made.

Stock, Aitken & Waterman had number one singles with Dead or Alive's 'You Spin Me Round (Like A Record)', Mel & Kim's 'Respectable', Ferry Aid's 'Let It Be', Rick Astley's 'Never Gonna Give You Up', Kylie Minogue's 'I Should Be So Lucky', 'Especially For You (with Jason Donovan), 'Hand On My Heart' and 'Tears On My Pillow', Jason Donovan's 'Too Many Broken Hearts' and 'Sealed With A Kiss', 'Ferry Cross The Mersey' (a charity single to help those affected by the Hillsborough disaster), Sonia's 'You'll Never Stop Me Loving You' and Band Aid II's 'Do They Know It's Christmas?'

1987 ICON

Swing Out Sister

I was a student when Swing Out Sister's second single 'Breakout', which I absolutely loved, became their first hit at the very start of 1987, and when their debut album *It's Better To Travel* was released in the spring, after the success of another fantastic single 'Surrender', I loved that too. I loved it on a number of levels: for it's poppy effervescence; for its jazz influences, which I thought were so sophisticated; and also for Swing Out Sister's singer, Corinne Drewery, who – with her vampy, black, bobbed hair, flashing smile and unique style – ticked all the boxes in my list of criteria for the perfect woman. Even with my hormones pushed firmly to one side *It's Better To Travel* will always remind me of the summer of 1987, when I was nicely established in my student life, my final exams were still a couple of years away and I had a friend with a car who would drive us out of Reading into the Berkshire countryside to spend afternoons in rural pub gardens, all to a constant Swing Out Sister soundtrack. Even today when I hear those songs I'm transported back to those days.

Swing Out Sister formed in the mid-eighties and originally consisted of vocalist Drewery, a former fashion designer; keyboard player Andy Connell, who had formerly been part of Manchester's critically acclaimed A Certain Ratio; and drummer Martin Jackson, who had previously played with Magazine and The Chameleons. After the release of *It's Better To Travel* the band released two more singles from the album – 'Twilight World' and 'Fooled By A Smile' – and in 1988 were nominated for the Grammy for Best New Group after 'Breakout' became a top ten hit in the States.

The band's second album, *Kaleidoscope World*, was released to great acclaim in 1989, by which time the line-up had slimmed down to just Drewery and Connell, and took Swing Out Sister in a more laidback easy-listening direction. By the time they released Get *In Touch With Yourself* in 1992 (and Corinne Drewery had grown out her bobbed hair!) I lost sight of the band, although they would release a further four albums exploring a range of musical styles over the next decade and the duo are still active today.

I interviewed Corinne Drewery in 2004 to talk about Swing Out Sister's eighth studio album, *Where Our Love Grows*, and what you see here is taken from that interview. Corinne is friendly, chatty, down to earth and interesting. I don't tell her about my 1987 crush on her (by then I had already met and married my perfect woman and yes, she does have black bobbed-hair, a flashing smile and a unique style!), but we do talk a lot about *It's Better To Travel* and I do tell her that it is still one of my favourite albums.

HOW DID SWING OUT SISTER COME ABOUT? WAS IT A BUNCH OF FRIENDS WITH A VISION, OR WAS IT ALL DONE THROUGH THE CLASSIFIED ADS IN THE *MELODY MAKER* OR SOMETHING?

Well I did answer several *Melody Maker* ads and the first band I went to audition for were Working Week, who I did sing with for a bit although that didn't really work out … then a friend who managed a musical duo was looking for someone to sing with them and I said I'd do it, but he said 'oh no you're far too old and ugly …' but in the end they couldn't find a singer so he said, well you could always try and write some songs with Andy and Martin and if any of them work out we can always get a proper singer in. I think I was too keen to be offended, and they never did find another singer so I ended up staying with them!

HOW DID THOSE EARLY SESSIONS GO?

I think it worked well that none of us really knew each other; Andy had been in A Certain Ratio, Martin had been in Magazine and I had been in Working Week for about a week, but it was our musical influences and tastes that came together and it was quite tricky to make that work. Andy was coming from a kind of Brazilian avant-garde jazz background, Martin was coming from a rock and indie background and I just liked pop music – Motown, Northern Soul and those great sixties divas … that whole thing of a little symphony being rolled into three minutes was kind of where I was coming from – great orchestration, drama and catchy tunes. So it was a bit difficult and we just went with the first thing that came together as a song – none of us had worked together before so we were quite pleased to achieve a result. It was quite difficult but it was fun at the same time. It was quite exciting to see what would actually happen.

'BREAKOUT' WAS YOUR FIRST HIT, DID THAT COME TOGETHER QUICKLY OR WAS THERE A LOT OF WORK GETTING TO THAT POINT?

We did write a few songs before 'Breakout' but they were all pretty much written on the back of an envelope and were done quite separately in a way because Andy and Martin lived in Manchester and were in different bands at the time, and I lived in London. We all had to somehow do our little bit separately and then get together to get it finished off! With 'Breakout' we had a two-single deal and we'd already released one, which had been a bit of a 12" club hit called 'Blue Mood', so the second single had to be a hit or we were going to get dropped, so there was a lot of pressure on us to get it right. Andy was off on tour with ACR, Martin was up in Manchester and I was in London and they kept phoning and asking if I'd finished the lyrics to this song and I got really worried because I wanted it to be perfect. At that stage I didn't have any ideas and I was just sitting in this squat that I was living in, with a microphone plugged into the back of a stereo, trying things out. I ended up with half an hour to go and the bike was due to pick up the tapes! But maybe that lack of time just forced the best thing out – I just had to record something there and then – I think if anyone had seen how it all came about they would never have taken it seriously! I can remember having the idea the night before but I couldn't record it then because it would make too much noise, but the thing that made me remember it was thinking of a chicken clucking combined with Michael Jackson's 'Thriller'!

AND THEN 'BREAKOUT' LED TO *IT'S BETTER TO TRAVEL*, WHICH WAS A NUMBER ONE ALBUM!

Yes! No one was more surprised than us, although deep in my heart I did kind of expect it because it was what I had been dreaming about since I was a few years

old! But Andy and Martin had come from a completely different angle – schlepping around, playing the tiny venues and doing University tours and everything. They had a real underground background and I had no background at all but somehow it all worked out!

DO YOU FEEL THAT YOU'RE A NATURAL POP STAR?

Not really … I don't know if that's what I am! I'm not a diva, I like getting mucky and I like down-to-earth things. I'm probably not all that comfortable with being a pop star … it's what I always wanted to be, but as soon as we had a number one record I think I just wanted to be completely anonymous, which was a real shock! I wasn't sure that I really wanted all that attention. I'm quite happy with the way that things are now, things have calmed down now.

IT MUST HAVE THEN ALL GONE FROM ONE EXTREME TO ANOTHER THOUGH, FROM JUST HANGING ON TO YOUR DEAL TO BEING NUMBER ONE!

Well, even when we recorded the song a few people said 'that's never going to work … it sounds like a swing band or something' and nobody could really make head nor tail of it because it just didn't sound like anything that was around at the time. As far as the label were concerned, they didn't really know what to do with it! But even though it was different it was fresh and people responded to it in a different way.

IT'S FUNNY, I'VE ALWAYS THOUGHT THAT SWING OUT SISTER'S MUSIC IS SOMEHOW TIMELESS, IN THAT IT NEVER FITS ANY SORT OF PREVAILING FASHION, YET IT STILL MANAGES TO BE QUITE EFFORTLESSLY CONTEMPORARY.

I'm really glad you think that because I

think that's all we ever intended to do – not to fit in with any particular fads or trends at any particular time, but just to encapsulate good things from the past and the present – just to create something that can be enjoyed at any time. We're probably too contrary to fit in with any current trends, and if anything we'd probably try to fight against them.

I SUPPOSE THAT IT'S VERY EASY TO DRAW PARALLELS WITH SIXTIES' SINGERS AND JAZZ ARTISTS, BUT PRESUMABLY TO MAKE THE KIND OF SOUNDS YOU MAKE YOU MUST BE BRINGING IN AN AWFUL LOT OF CONTEMPORARY INFLUENCES AS WELL?

Yes that's true – while we are recording we are listening to whatever is going on; with this record that would include people like Beyonce and Alicia Keyes, Outkaste and the whole Neptunes production thing, Missy Elliot, Timbaland … those are things that we listened to as well, and maybe they are not so apparent but you hear all these sounds and production techniques – probably the freshest music around at the moment is rap and hip-hop and I like what's happening at the moment where that's starting to cross over with pop. I think that the places where two types of music crossover are the interesting bits and I think that there are some parallels there to us – the music that has influenced our past fusing with new influences.

ARE YOU PROLIFIC WRITERS?

Not really … I don't know, I think we're quite prolific when we start recording for an album, and I think that Andy is a lot more prolific than I am, he'll sit and play the piano and come up with things, but I don't know … I think I'm a bit of a receptacle – I just keep on taking things in and then when I have to finish something I will. I think that as long as you're thinking about things then strong ideas will stick and there

are always certain phrases in my mind, certain ideas that I've thought of and haven't used yet. But I think that the way we write, it's not like the words are particularly important or are saying anything, and even though I write the lyrics I wouldn't say they were the most important thing … I think they are the vehicles for the listeners to kind of attach themselves to the songs, so I like the lyrics to be unobtrusive and more like an instrumental part. Someone who does that but to far more extremes is Liz Fraser from The Cocteau Twins and her voice is an instrument and you can make out sounds and imagine what the words might be, and I like that, I like the words to be quite abstract.

IS IT DIFFICULT TO DRAW THE LINE AND SAY 'THAT'S IT, THIS RECORD IS FINISHED' WHEN YOU'RE IN THE PROCESS OF FINISHING AN ALBUM?

It's incredibly difficult – that's why it takes us so long to make an album. We're all equally indecisive – including Paul Staveley O'Duffy our producer who has written our last two albums with us – but that's partly due to the nature of recording; the process of writing a song and demo-ing it, and then going into the studio to start again and produce it … you lose some of the spontaneity of the process. We found, working with Paul from the start, that we kind of record and produce as we write, which is slightly different but it's more inspiring than sitting there with a voice and a piano where everything sounds pretty much the same in the beginning – whereas if you start off with strings or the odd sample thrown in I think you can send yourself in a different direction. We have to surprise ourselves in order to keep up our enthusiasm in order to keep up the listeners' enthusiasm – if we know what we're getting before we've

started then we're going to be bored and so are the listeners. We have to trick ourselves sometimes, into writing a song before we've written it if you know what I mean, otherwise the process is always going to be the same.

IS THE GOAL ALWAYS TO MAKE A DIFFERENT ALBUM FROM THE LAST ONE?

Make an album different for the sake of it? We couldn't really work that way and that's probably why it takes us so long to do it; we wait until we're fired up and ready. I do think that we try to explore a different area each time though, and that gets harder as time goes on because if you're true to yourself and you're exploring areas of music that are important to you, you can start to feel that you've used all the options up! But I think we just then dig a little deeper … there are so many things to be inspired by. I think that every time we make an album we feel that it won't be possible to do any better than this and I think it always comes back to getting new ideas and new enthusiasm and just going off in a different direction.

'I'd say Swing Out Sister are the ultimate eighties' act – although they are still going – for creating an uplifting and more sophisticated pop sound than previously associated with the eighties. Their aesthetic and lyrics suggest a dreamy escapism that I find both inspiring and exciting.'

JAMIE

1988

Snapshot

The Soviet Union begins its Perestroika programme of economic reform ● The films *Beetlejuice, Die Hard, Who Framed Roger Rabbit?, A Fish Called Wanda* and *Rain Man* are released ● The Winter Olympics are held in Calgary, Canada and the Summer Games are held in Seoul, South Korea ● *The Last Emperor* wins nine Oscars ● Sonny Bono is elected mayor of Palm Springs, California ● Wimbledon win the FA Cup, beating Liverpool 1-0 ● Section 28, outlawing the promotion of homosexuality in schools, becomes UK law ● A concert at Wembley Stadium celebrates the seventieth birthday of imprisoned ANC leader Nelson Mandela ● TV shows *Crossroads, The Incredible Hulk* and *Play School* all air their final episodes ● Cliff Richard's 'Mistletoe & Wine' is the UK's bestselling single ● The war between Iran and Iraq ends after eight years of conflict ● The world's first Fairtrade label, Max Havelaar, is launched in the Netherlands ● A cyclone in Bangladesh leaves five million people homeless. Kenneth Williams, Roy Orbison, Divine and car-maker Enzo Ferrari die ● Soviet forces withdraw from Afghanistan ● Salman Rushdie's *The Satanic Verses* is published. Michael Jackson buys a ranch in Santa Ynez, California, which he rechristens 'Neverland' ● Jody Watley wins the Grammy for Best New Artist ● Sony stops the manufacture of Betamax video recorders ● An intergovernmental panel consisting of representatives of thirty different nations meets for the first time to examine whether global warming is the result of changes in atmospheric gases caused by human activity ● TV shows *The Wonder Years, Home And Away* and *Red Dwarf* are aired for the first time ● Kylie Minogue's debut album *Kylie* is the UK's bestselling album ● Disposable contact lenses go on sale for the first time ● Steffi Graf beats Martina Navratilova at Wimbledon to become the Women's Champion while Stefan Edberg beats Boris Becker in the men's competition ● CDs outsell vinyl records for the first time ● McDonald's opens its first restaurants in Moscow

'I loved Kylie, I suppose because of the songs, but I also liked the way she looked.'

FACHE

Sounds like. . .1988

Belinda Carlisle will lead a particularly good year for female artists when she takes the first new number one singles spot of the year with her epic song 'Heaven Is A Place On Earth', her only number one single. An album, *Heaven On Earth*, will make the top ten and a further five singles will be released throughout the year, most notably the top-ten hits 'I Get Weak' and 'Circle In The Sand'. Vanessa Paradis' hit 'Joe Le Taxi' will follow hot on Belinda Carlisle's heels, peaking at number three a few weeks after the success of 'Heaven Is A Place On Earth', while Carlisle's former Go-Go's bandmate Jane Wiedlin will also have her sole UK singles hit this year when 'Rush Hour' makes number twelve in September.

Kim Wilde will have her best year in the singles charts since 1981 with a run of three successive top-ten hits, including 'You Came' and 'Four Letter Word', while Tiffany's *Tiffany* album will reach number five and give the seventeen-year-old US singer four hit singles, including her classic 'I Think We're Alone Now' which will reach number one. The similarly youthful Debbie Gibson will also enjoy four top-twenty singles this year including 'Shake Your Love' and 'Foolish Beat', and a top-thirty album *Out Of The Blue*.

It's Kylie Minogue however who will dominate the pop world this year, her debut album *Kylie* will be the bestselling album of the year, peaking at number one and remaining in the charts for well over a year, kept there by an incredible run of five hit singles: two number one hits, 'I Could Be So Lucky' and 'Especially For You' (a duet with boyfriend Jason Donovan) and three number two hits, 'Got To Be Certain', 'The Loco-Motion' and 'Je Ne Sais Pas Pourquoi'. Kylie will have no serious challengers for the crown as queen of pop this year; Madonna will have a year away from the charts and although there are some great pop records from female artists, none will quite match her phenomenal success.

Tracy Chapman will catch the world's attention this year when she appears on the bill of the Nelson Mandela 70th Birthday Tribute Concert at Wembley Stadium in July, and will have a number one record with her debut album *Tracy Chapman* and a top-five single with 'Fast Car' as a result. The year will also see debut hits for Sinead O'Connor and Tanita Tikaram. Sinead O'Connor's first singles hit is 'Mandinka', which will make the top twenty ahead of a top thirty placing for her debut album *The Lion & The Cobra*, although greater things are round the corner for the outspoken Irish artist. Nineteen-year-old

'The best single of the eighties is Tiffany's "Could've Been". The first love song that meant something to me.'

LISA

1988

Number One Singles

Belinda Carlisle 'Heaven Is A Place On Earth', Tiffany 'I Think We're Alone Now', Kylie Minogue 'I Should Be So Lucky', Aswad 'Don't Turn Around', Pet Shop Boys 'Heart', S'Express 'Theme From S'Express', Fairground Attraction 'Perfect', Wet Wet Wet 'With A Little Help From My Friends', The Timelords 'Doctorin' The Tardis', Bros 'I Owe You Nothing', Glenn Medeiros 'Nothing's Gonna Change My Love For You', Yazz & The Plastic Population 'The Only Way Is Up', Phil Collins 'A Groovy Kind Of Love', The Hollies 'He Ain't Heavy He's My Brother', U2 'Desire', Whitney Houston 'One Moment In Time', Enya 'Orinoco Flow (Sail Away)', Robin Beck 'The First Time', Cliff Richard 'Mistletoe & Wine'

'Bros were the best group going, Matt and Luke Goss were the best and they still are today! I had nearly everything on them. They were the best looking ones of the eighties, well I think they were and still are!'

KARIN MORGAN

'Bon Jovi was and still is my favorite band. They started it all, the original "hair band". They were fun and fine looking and the music was great. And they're still kicking ass 20 years later!'

LYNNE

Tanita Tikaram on the other hand will enjoy her most commercially successful year, releasing a top-three album *Ancient Heart* and two hit singles, 'Good Tradition' and 'Twist In My Sobriety'. Enya's *Watermark* album – featuring the number one single 'Orinoco Flow (Sail Away)' – meanwhile will spend almost two years in the albums charts, going on to sell over eight million albums worldwide.

The Primitives will release a single,

'Crash', in February which I will always consider one of the greatest pop singles of all time (along with Thomas Dolby's 'Airhead', also released this year), an opinion partly vindicated when 'Crash' reaches number five in the UK charts and number three in the US Modern Rock chart. Their debut album, *Lovely*, will make number six and position The Primitives firmly among a handful of alternative bands making great indie-pop records this

'Best single is Voice of the Beehive's "I Say Nothing". I danced around my house constantly to this, and it's such a pick me up if you're feeling down. And the video is such fun, and they're such an energetic live band.'

LESLEY JEAVONS

'*Appetite For Destruction* by Guns N' Roses came at a time where heavy metal was becoming too "nice". Nothing shocking was coming out of rock until this album made its way into the record stores. It brought back the energy that hard rock was meant to have.'

MATRACAS

year, alongside acts including Transvision Vamp (whose *Pop Art* album and 'I Want Your Love' single will make numbers 4 and 5 respectively), The Darling Buds (whose 'Hit The Ground' single will reach number 27 and album *Pop Said* 23), the much-hyped Eighth Wonder – fronted by actress Patsy Kensit – whose biggest single 'I Don't Care' will reach number seven in the spring, and Voice Of The Beehive, who will have two singles hits with 'Don't Call Me Baby' and 'I Walk The Earth' from their top-fifteen album *Let It Bee*.

Pop is order of the day and is a term that will cover a vast spectrum of music – from Michael Jackson's continued working of his 1987 *Bad* album (he will release a further four singles from the album this year including top-ten hits 'Dirty Diana' and 'Smooth Criminal') and Milli Vanilli (who will have their biggest UK hit

with the number three single 'Girl You Know It's True') to The Pasadenas, who will release three hit singles, including 'Tribute (Right On)' and 'Riding On A Train', and a top three album *To Whom It May Concern*. However, the core pop market this year will truly be dominated by Kylie Minogue, whose successes are outlined above, Rick Astley, who will release three top-ten singles and an album, *Hold Me In Your Arms*, which will peak at eight, and Bros, the newest band on the pop block.

Bros – consisting of twin brothers Matt and Luke Goss and Craig Logan – will have five top five singles this year ('When Will I Be famous?', 'Drop The Boy', 'I Owe You Nothing', 'I Quit' and 'Cat Among The Pigeons') as well as a number two album, *Push*, which will sell a quarter of a million copies in the UK in its first week of release. The band are a true pop phenomenon and will dominate the pages of *Smash Hits* this year as well as launching an army of fanatical identikit fans, 'Brosettes', who will copy the band's style of ripped jeans, bomber jackets and Doc Martens shoes (with Grolsch bottle top attached to the laces!) and roam town centres in packs.

At the other end of the scale rock music will continue to prosper and Bon Jovi will score their first number one album in October with *New Jersey* and two more hit singles: 'Bad Medicine' and 'Born To Be My Baby'. Guns N' Roses will make up for their lack of success in 1987 by releasing two classic rock singles – 'Sweet Child O' Mine' and 'Welcome To The Jungle' – which will both peak at twenty-four in the UK singles charts, while a reissue of their 1987 album *Appetite For Destruction* will peak at fifteen in the albums chart. Iron Maiden will enjoy their second

Sounds Like 1988

The Year as a Mixtape

SIDE ONE

Salt-N-Pepa '**Push It**', Neneh Cherry '**Buffalo Stance**', Yazz & The Plastic Population '**The Only Way is Up**', S'Express '**Theme From S'Express**', Prince '**Alphabet Street**', New Order '**Fine Time**', Michael Jackson '**Smooth Criminal**', The Primitives '**Crash**', Eighth Wonder '**I'm Not Scared**', Kim Wilde '**You Came**', Kylie Minogue '**I Should Be So Lucky**', Tiffany '**I Think We're Alone Now**', Belinda Carlisle '**Circle In The Sand**', Bros '**I Owe You Nothing**', Erasure '**A Little Respect**'

SIDE TWO

Guns N' Roses '**Welcome To The Jungle**', INXS '**Need You Tonight**', U2 '**Desire**', Deacon Blue '**Real Gone Kid**', Aztec Camera '**Somewhere In My Heart**', Tracy Chapman '**Fast Car**', Prefab Sprout '**Cars & Girls**', Kylie Minogue & Jason Donovan '**Especially For You**', Tanita Tikaram '**Twist In My Sobriety**', Terence Trent D'Arby '**Sign Your Name**', Enya '**Orinoco Flow (Sail Away)**', Morrissey '**Every Day Is Like Sunday**', Echo & The Bunnymen '**People Are Strange**', Sinead O'Connor '**Mandinka**', Public Enemy '**Don't Believe The Hype**'

1988

Number One Albums

Wet Wet Wet Popped In Souled Out, Johnny Hates Jazz Turn Back The Clock, Terence Trent D'Arby Introducing The Hardline According To Terence Trent D'Arby, Morrissey Viva Hate, Various Artists Now That's What I Call Music 11, Iron Maiden Seventh Son Of A Seventh Son, Erasure The Innocents, Fleetwood Mac Tango In The Night, Prince Lovesexy, Various Artists Nite Flite, Tracy Chapman Tracy Chapman, Various Artists Now That's What I Call Music 12, Kylie Minogue Kylie, Various Artists Hot City Nights, Bon Jovi New Jersey, Chris de Burgh Flying Colours, U2 Rattle & Hum, Dire Straits Money For Nothing, Various Artists Now That's What I Call Music 13, Cliff Richard Private Collection 1979–1988

'Ultimate band? INXS! I remember exactly when I got into them. My best friend at the time was watching MTV and "The One Thing" video came on. From that moment on we had to find out who this band was and find out everything about them.'

REBECCA SANCHEZ

'Ultimate act would have to be U2. They completely redefined music and the eighties' sound, then continue doing the same today.'

JAMES BONACCI

number one album in May when they release *Seventh Son Of A Seventh Son* and will have three top-ten singles, including their highest ever singles chart success when 'Can I Play With Madness' reaches number three.

Taking rock in a more mainstream direction this year are Scotland's Deacon Blue, who will enjoy their first singles success at the start of the year with 'Dignity' and finish with a top-ten hit with 'Real Gone Kid', on the way chalking up a number fourteen album for their debut album *Raintown*. Steering a similar course, Ireland's Hothouse Flowers will enjoy their biggest singles hit when 'Don't Go' reaches number eleven, followed by a debut album *People*, which narrowly misses topping the albums charts in June, peaking at two and staying in the charts for almost six months. Their fellow country-men U2 will enjoy their first number one single in October when 'Desire' tops the charts, ahead of a second number one album of live recordings and rarities entitled *Rattle & Hum*.

REM's album *Green*, meanwhile, will reach 27 on the albums charts, their most successful UK album to date, but singles success will still elude them despite the release of two fine songs, 'The One I Love' and 'Finest Worksong', which peak at 51 and 50 respectively. A band to have similarly struggled with chart success until this year is INXS, who start the year with their first UK hit 'New Sensation' and finish it with their biggest ever hit, the classic 'Need You Tonight', which will reach number two. In between the two releases the band will put out two more singles – 'Devil Inside' and 'Never Tear Us Apart' – as well as re-promoting their 1987 album *Kick*, which will go to number nine. INXS will be even more successful in the US, selling over ten million copies of *Kick*

there and collecting five MTV Awards for 'Need You Tonight'.

Success will also elude Faith No More this year when their debut single 'We Care A Lot', a potent mix of rock and rap, will fail to break into the top forty in February. Less commercial than Run DMC and Aerosmith's collaboration 'Walk This Way', the song nevertheless highlights the way that the influence of rap music is starting to be absorbed across the genres and opening doors to hip-hop. *It Takes A Nation Of Millions To Hold Us Back* by Public Enemy will be the first true rap album to break into the UK mainstream and will rise to number eight in the albums charts in August this year on the back of two successful and innovative singles, 'Bring The Noise' and 'Don't Believe The Hype', although both will be significantly less successful than Morris Minor & The Majors' novelty hit 'Stutter Rap (No Sleep Til Bedtime)', which will reach number four in January, and The Fat Boys' equally lightweight collaboration with Chubby Checker, 'The Twist (Yo Twist)', which will reach number two in the summer. Both will be irritating but Starturn On 45 (Pints)' 'Pump Up The Bitter', which will reach number twelve in May, will probably be my personal worst record of the year, although Pat & Mick's 'Let's All Chant' will give it a good run for its money…

The acid house scene will also become popular this year, going mainstream most successfully with Yazz & The Plastic Population's 'The Only Way Is Up', a number one single in the summer, followed by 'Stand Up For Your Love Rights' which will peak at two and a number three album, *Wanted*. For me 'The Only Way Is Up' is just a great pop record, which adds 'waving hands in the air' to my limited repertoire of dance moves at Friday night student discos, the acid house connection eluding me completely. It's the

same with S'Express's euphoric number one 'Theme From S'Express', just another great party record. It will be difficult, however, for even me to miss the acid house connection in D-Mob's 'We Call It Acieed' when it peaks at number three in October. I will also read enough interviews with New Order to know that their December single 'Fine Time', the first from their forthcoming 1989 album *Technique*, is directly influenced by acid house. 'Fine Time' will sometimes be my favourite ever New Order single.

In my defence regarding this complete lack of understanding of acid house, I spend this 'second summer of love' in the USA, teaching before travelling around the country with only my Walkman for company. My personal soundtrack this year will include four new albums alongside my favourite tapes: Prefab Sprout's *From Langley Park To Memphis*; Aztec Camera's *Love*; Erasure's *The Innocents*; and Morrissey's *Viva Hate*.

From Langley Park To Memphis will reach number five in the first half of the year, launching 'Cars & Girls', one of my all-time favourite singles, as well as Prefab Sprout's biggest ever hit 'The King Of Rock 'N' Roll' (and yes, I will walk the streets of New York with 'Hey Manhattan' playing as my private soundtrack!).

Aztec Camera actually first released *Love* in 1987 but I missed it the first time around, and won't pick up on it

again until after the success of the single 'Somewhere In My Heart', which will go to number three in spring 1987, quickly followed by a reissued *Love* which made the top ten. Erasure's *The Innocents*, on the other hand, I will buy on the day of its release in April, having already loved the album's first single 'Ship Of Fools'. *The Innocents* will become Erasure's first number one album in the UK – the first of five successive chart-topping albums for the duo – and will launch two further hit singles, 'Chains Of Love' and 'A Little Respect'. *Viva Hate* meanwhile will be the first solo album from Morrissey after the demise of The Smiths, and despite my misgivings about the end of one of my favourite groups, it is a pleasant surprise, in particular the two strong singles from the album: 'Suedehead' and 'Every Day Is Like Sunday'.

Terence Trent D'Arby's *Introducing The Hardline According To Terence Trent D'Arby* will return to the top of the albums charts on the back of the success of 'Sign Your Name', the final single to come from the album and the most successful of D'Arby's career, which will peak at number two. Prince will enjoy his first UK number one album in May when he releases *Lovesexy* on the back of a top-ten single 'Alphabet Street', his most commercially successful single for several years. Neither artist however comes close to selling as many records this year as Cliff Richard, whose Christmas single – his 99th UK single – 'Mistletoe & Wine' will be number one for four weeks, selling almost a million copies in the process. The end of the year will also provide a hint of pop things to come when Kylie Minogue's boyfriend, fellow *Neighbours* actor Jason Donovan's debut single 'Nothing Can Divide Us' goes top five and his duet with Kylie, 'Especially For You' tops the charts.

'My ultimate eighties' album has to be Public Enemy's *It Takes A Nation Of Millions To Hold Us Back*. It was one of the first rap albums I bought, and even though I had known about their first album, this is the one that blew them up to be the rap stars they were (and are). There were so many fantastic tracks on the album, and with the political lyrics as well the fun of Flava Flav, it really opened my eyes up to new music and also what was going on in the world - drugs and America's system of brushing stuff under the carpet.'

JAMES WATSON

'Erasure's *The Innocents* is the ultimate album. The best produced pop album of all times. Stephen Hague was a god!'

STEFANO VIGORELLI

'Prince is the ultimate artist because of his sound, look and overall talent. His music helped define the eighties, change the way people view "popular music" and is influencing major artists today.'

NATHAN BENDITZSON

ACID HOUSE
THE SECOND SUMMER OF LOVE

'Oh my God! I know the 80s are remembered for the dodgy fashions but some of the things I wore when I was a raver are the worst clothes of the decade and that's really saying something!'

NATASHA

The Second Summer Of Love, 1988. We were all there, but we all remember it so differently. Are you one of the people who considered those acid house days as revolutionary, liberating and pure? A time when everyone was united by music, becoming one on the dancefloor? Or were you on the other side of this particular fence? The side where acid house was a nonsense, a period of dubious fluorescent fashion, when clubbing was unnecessarily over-reliant on glow-sticks and whistles and there was a constant risk of sweaty builders launching themselves at you and wanting to be your new best friend?

If you were part of the whole revolution then it was an exciting time. Real dance music was back for the first time in years and the whole DIY culture that sprang up around the scene was exciting and creative – similar to punk in that everyone was equal and there were no 'stars'. Everything was about the message, the message in this case being one of self-expression, liberation and hedonism. Drugs were involved of course, although everyone was adamant that it wasn't about the drugs – it was really about music and people, about having fun. Early raves were informal, haphazard and almost always peaceful and good-natured, often taking places in fields, warehouses or vacant buildings, attracting vast crowds by word of mouth and going on all night.

Of course vast crowds of people waving glow-sticks and dancing all night in fields attracted attention, and the authorities quickly become intolerant of the movement. Landowners and local councils either opposed events or charged huge amounts of money for the licences to stage them, forcing rave culture to truly make the transition from the underground to the mainstream. Similarly the music started to appear in the charts in 1988 when records like Yazz & The Plastic Population's 'The Only Way Is Up', Bomb The Bass's 'Beat Dis' and S'Express's 'Theme From S'Express' quickly found their way into the mainstream and made stars of bands like The Shamen, 808 State, A Guy Called Gerald, Technotronic, Primal Scream and The Beloved.

The media naturally had a field day. *The Sun* originally tried to jump on the acid house bandwagon, even going so far as to offer a 'groovy and cool' acid house T-shirt to readers for just £5.50 in 1988, but like the rest of the media they quickly turned on acid house, gleefully running a series of headlines condemning the dangers of ecstasy and the evils of acid house parties.

The Second Summer Of Love ... Up To Date!

The acid house scene started to fragment in the early nineties, launching a series of smaller scenes including jungle, drum n' bass, techno and happy hardcore, and by the end of the nineties the term 'raving' went out of fashion, replaced by the more general word 'clubbing'. However the rave days are looked back on affectionately and there are a number of recent compilation albums on the market, as well as a small but enthusiastic retro rave scene dedicated to re-creating that late eighties magic.

'I loved the whole acid house scene... I had smiley everything, even smiley boxer shorts and smiley socks! We spent hours driving around the M25 every weekend waiting for someone to find the next party. It was brilliant.'

DANNY 'GLOW-STICKS' ASHER

Red Nose Day

'I think some of the comedians from the 80s were better than anything around today... I have never laughed so much as when The Young Ones did that spoof "University Challenge" for the very first Comic Relief!'

CAPTAIN JACK

'When I think of comedians from then I just think of Lenny Henry wearing a suit with red noses all over it, shouting at people with that big daft grin on his face!'

JESSICA S

A guide to the red noses issued by Comic Relief over the years: 1988 – The Plain Red Nose; 1989 – The Smiley Face (a nose with a face, made from rose-scented plastic); 1991 – The Stonker Nose (a nose with hands and face); 1993 – The Tomato Nose (with stalk and face); 1995 – The Colour Change Nose (changed colour from red to either yellow or pink); 1997 – The Furry Nose; 1999 – The Big Red Hooter (with gold glitter, which hooted when squeezed); 2001 – The Whoopee Nose (red face with inflated cheeks, and when squeezed the tongue inflated); 2003 – The Big Hair Do (with a tuft of hair and eyes that squeezed out); 2005 – Big Hair & Beyond (with smiley face and elastic hair); 2007 – The Big One (expanding foam nose).

Back in 1988 it was almost unthinkable that the BBC would agree to chuck an entire Friday night's BBC1 schedule into the bin to make way for a night of comedy and music to raise money for Comic Relief, but on 5th February 1988 that's exactly what happened, and I can still remember how exciting that night was. Comic Relief had already been around for a few years at that point. In fact it was launched live on Noel Edmonds' BBC TV show *Late Late Breakfast Show* on Christmas Day 1985, and had already earned a great deal of money through that appeal plus a number of comedy concerts and events, as well as a book and records (Cliff Richard & The Young Ones' 'Living Doll' in 1986 and Mel & Kim - comedian Mel Smith and Kim Wilde - with their version of 'Rocking Around The Christmas Tree' in 1987). This was different though. It put Comic Relief up there with Children In Need but was a lot more anarchic, a lot funnier, and there was a plastic red nose to wear to show your support!

That night in 1988, entitled *A Night Of Comic Relief*, was hosted by Lenny Henry and Griff Rhys Jones – with assistance from Harry Enfield's Stavros ('Hello everybody peeps!') – and included 'A Question Of Spit' (in which team members from *A Question Of Sport* competed against their Spitting Image puppets); '73 Of A Kind' (73 celebrities appearing is short filmed sketches) and special editions of *Blackadder* and *The New Statesman* alongside live comedy from new and established comedians (including Little & Large, Jim Davidson, Phil Cool and Jasper Carrott) and shows from the BBC archives including *Dad's Army, Steptoe & Son* and the film *The Bedsitting Room*. The comedy was sharply contrasted by filmed reports of celebrities in Africa, talking about some of the popular misconceptions about what was happening there. The show was watched by 30 million people and raised an amazing £15 million pounds.

In addition to just watching the show, people were encouraged to raise money locally, often by means of bizarre stunts the strangest of which would be broadcast live as part of the show. This element of participation really struck a chord to the extent that a second show in 1989 earned almost twice the 1988 amount and it is estimated that over 20 million people around the country took part in some of the 70,000 Red Nose Day activities that took place. It also saw Dawn French, Jennifer Saunders and Kathy Burke reach number three in the UK charts with their collaboration with Bananarama, 'Lananeenoonoo'.

Since 1989, Red Nose Day has become a bi-annual event that continues to this day. To date there have been ten Red Nose Days and three Sport Relief Days, and Comic Relief remains committed to 'delivering real and long-lasting change to the poorest, most vulnerable people at home and across the world; as well as informing the public and young people in particular about global citizenship and the underlying causes of extreme poverty.'

Red Nose Day ... Up To Date!

By 2007 Comic Relief had raised around £425 million, every penny of which has gone towards supporting the work of a vast number of different charities at home and abroad. Comic Relief do this by using a 'golden pound' principle, where all operating costs, salaries, etc. are covered by corporate sponsors or interest earned while money raised is waiting to be allocated to charitable projects.

FREE NELSON MANDELA!

Nelson Mandela was seventy in 1988 and to mark the occasion a huge 'Mandela Day' concert took place at London's Wembley Stadium on 11th July, watched by a live audience of 72,000 people and a TV audience of around 600 million from sixty countries across the world. Simple Minds, Whitney Houston, Peter Gabriel, Phil Collins, George Michael, Dire Straits, Stevie Wonder, Sting and Eurythmics were among the vast bill of performers paying tribute to one of modern politics' most iconic figures. Nelson Mandela himself couldn't be there of course, because on 11th July 1988 he was in prison in South Africa, exactly as he had been every day for the previous twenty-five years. 'Mandela Day' was a birthday celebration but it was also one of the biggest political protests ever staged, and the event was quickly dubbed the 'Free Nelson Mandela Concert'.

I wore an anti-apartheid badge back then because it seemed so simple; inequality because of colour was just wrong. But If I'm honest I didn't really know much about Nelson Mandela. I knew he was in prison, a political prisoner – the Special AKA had taught me that much when they released their 'Free Nelson Mandela' single in 1984. I knew his imprisonment was 'wrong' but I didn't know the details, and until now, to my shame, I didn't even think to ask.

Nelson Mandela was born Rolihlahla Mandela in South Africa in 1918 and was the first in his family to attend school, where his teacher called him Nelson – after Lord Nelson – after having problems pronouncing his real name. Involved in politics from his student days he became increasingly politically active after the National Party, with their policy of racial segregation, were elected in 1948. He ran away from his family, after leaving university, to avoid entering into an arranged marriage, and started to work as a legal clerk. By 1955 Mandela was leading the armed division of the ANC (African National Congress), engaged in a guerrilla campaign of sabotage against government and military targets. In 1962 he was charged with inciting workers to strike and was sentenced to five years in prison, during which time he was additionally tried for sabotage, treason and planning armed action, for which the ANC was banned and Mandela was sentenced to life imprisonment.

Nelson Mandela spent the next eighteen years on Robben Island working in a lime quarry and living in very basic conditions. In 1985 President P.W. Botha offered Mandela release if he would renounce the ANC's armed struggle. Mandela refused the offer and in doing so strengthened his position as the international focal point of all anti-apartheid activities. President Botha suffered a stroke in 1989 and was replaced by Frederik W. de Klerk, who lifted the ban on the ANC and announced that Mandela was to be freed. Nelson Mandela was finally released on 11th February 1990 after spending 27 years in prison, going on to become South Africa's first black president in 1994, a post he held until his retirement in 1999.

I will always remember watching his release live on TV; the coverage seemed to go on for hours, and right up to the last minute it seemed possible that the South African authorities would change their minds and keep him imprisoned. Up to the moment of his

Nelson Mandela's prison number – 46664 – has been used for a series of huge concerts around the world to promote awareness of the spread of HIV/AIDS in South Africa.

Nelson Mandela makes an appearance in Spike Lee's 1992 film Malcolm X, playing a teacher reciting one of Malcolm X's famous speeches.

'I was in my early teens in the 80s so politics didn't really feature for me. And being brought up in South Africa I just remember being so cut off from the rest of the world. We weren't even allowed to see photographs or pictures of Nelson Mandela when I was growing up. I still have a copy of a *Number 1* magazine from 1984 when the Special AKA brought out the song "Free Nelson Mandela". The article of course explained about Mandela and they printed a picture, but each and every copy of the magazine had been censored – the distributor had to blacken the photograph out. It's so odd considering he is one of our national treasures today.'

ALAN FOLEY

release it felt like the world was holding its breath, and when he finally emerged a free man it felt like the world had suddenly become a better place.

Nelson Mandela ...Up To Date!

Although his life has not been without its controversies Nelson Mandela is generally seen as a tireless supporter of social and human rights causes, and has received a vast number of awards for his work from nations across the world, including the Nobel Peace Prize, the American Presidential Medal Of Freedom and the UK's Order Of Merit and Order Of St John. Mandela has never stopped working for the causes he believes in and in 2006 was awarded Amnesty International's Ambassador of Conscience Award.

'I was too young and too uninterested to get involved in politics, but I certainly agreed with and was influenced by left-leaning politics espoused in songs and interviews, Free Nelson Mandela, etc. PS. I never got my free Nelson Mandela!'

HAYDEN

Miami Vice

Designer stubble, espadrilles (no socks), Wayfarer sunglasses, pastel colours, jackets over T-shirts (sleeves rolled up) … it's a pretty powerful picture of mid-eighties' fashion isn't it? Add a Florida setting, drug crime, prostitution and a pair of undercover cops and we have *Miami Vice*, possibly the ultimate eighties' TV show. Parodied in *Friends, The Wedding Singer, The Simpsons, Sesame Street* ('Miami Mice'!) and in the video game 'Grand Theft Auto: Vice City', it's also perhaps one of the most successful and influential shows of the decade, fortunately for more than just it's sense of style.

Miami Vice made stars of its two main actors – Don Johnson and Philip Michael Thomas – who play two Vice Squad police officers, James 'Sonny' Crockett and Ricardo 'Rico' Tubbs, working undercover in the seedy underworld of eighties' Miami, tackling a range of crimes from drug dealing to gambling and prostitution to murder. To do this they have to fit into the flashy world of Miami's criminals, hence the opportunity for the snappy wardrobes, sports cars and speedboats! It's a world of dilemmas; who are the true criminals in this seedy underworld? Who are innocents caught up in situations they can't control? And how far will Tubbs and Crockett go in pursuit of personal revenge?

The show's heavy reliance on contemporary music led to the series being dubbed 'MTV Cops' – Jan Hammer would even score a US number one (five in the UK) with his theme for the show and have a second international hit with 'Crockett's Theme' – and such was the influence of the show at its peak that artists and record labels actively petitioned for their music to be used, and occasionally (in the case of Phil Collins, Glenn Frey and Ted Nugent for example) artists would guest star on the series. Sheena Easton would even join the cast as Crockett's wife, although her character, Caitlin Davies, would quickly be brutally murdered (allegedly to prevent a character from coming between Crockett and Tubbs). The show also attracted a host of guest stars from the worlds of film and television, among them Bruce Willis, Julia Roberts, Wesley Snipes and Helena Bonham-Carter.

Miami Vice started in 1984 and ran to five seasons, attracting its peak US audience in 1985 and 1986. By 1988 however the show's ratings had gone into a considerable decline and the fifth series, which started this year, became its last. Don Johnson and Philip Michael Thomas were also keen to move on and explore the film and television offers that their *Miami Vice* success was attracting.

I have to confess that I don't think I ever saw a single episode in the eighties (although I will be seeking out the Helena Bonham-Carter episode in the name of research!), and I've certainly never worn a pastel colour in my life, but the legend and influence of *Miami Vice* – alongside shows like *Cagney & Lacey* and *Hill Street Blues* – is still with us today.

Miami Vice ... Up To Date!

Don Johnson went on to appear in a number of TV and film roles, most notably as Nash Bridges in the crime drama of the same name and David Simms in the 1996 romantic comedy *Tin Cup*. In 2007 he made his London stage debut as Nathan Detroit in the musical *Guys & Dolls*. Philip Michael Thomas went on to appear in a number of TV movies and also briefly appeared in *Nash Bridges* as Don Johnson's sidekick. In 1994 he became the spokesman in a series of TV adverts for psychic services. Both however will be forever associated with their *Miami Vice* roles. The show enjoyed a brief resurgence of interest in 2006 when a film version was released, and every episode of the TV series is now available on DVD.

'I loved *Miami Vice*, I loved the style and the extravagant lifestyles, oh . . . and the music was so cool!'

MICKELLE PATIENCE

'I enjoyed *Miami Vice*. I had a crush on Don Johnson and I liked the music!'

JULIANA HERNANDEZ

'I loved *Miami Vice* but I wouldn't admit it to anyone.'

MARILU

1988 ICON

Terence Trent D'Arby

There are few records that so strongly remind me of a certain time and place in my life as Terence Trent D'Arby's *Introducing The Hardline According To Terence Trent D'Arby*. The album – part Sam Cooke, part Prince, part Stevie Wonder – was released in 1987. I didn't buy it but I did know it, in fact everyone knew it. It would go on to sell over twelve million copies and was responsible for an over-excited media proclaiming that here was the next big thing, here was an artist to rival Prince and Michael Jackson, an artist who would take over the world. I liked the singles ('Sign Your Name', 'If You Let Me Stay', 'Wishing Well' and 'Dance Little Sister') but the hysteria surrounding the album was enough to turn me off without even hearing it.

In summer 1988 I was teaching printing on a creative arts Summer Camp in America. My partner-in-print had *Introducing The Hardline …* on tape and we only had a few tapes so it was played a lot, and I came to love it. I bought it when I got back to England and even today when I listen to those songs it reminds me of that summer.

Then, I guess like many people, I just lost sight of Terence Trent D'Arby. A second album, *Neither Fish Nor Flesh: A Soundtrack of Love, Faith, Hope & Destruction*, followed in 1989 and it did well, selling over two million copies, but it was experimental and uncommercial and lost D'Arby the support of the media and his own record company. A third album, *Symphony or Damn: Exploring the Tension Inside the Sweetness*, wouldn't follow until 1993. Although it was a return to the more accessible musical styles of his debut the relationship between Terence Trent D'Arby and his label had become untenable, and after delivering a final album – *Terence Trent D'Arby's Vibrator* – for Sony in 1995, he was finally able to leave the label in 1996.

The new decade coincided with the start of a new lease of life creatively, spiritually and personally and in 2001 Terence Trent D'Arby became Sananda Maitreya and released a new album, *Wildcard*, which he made available for free via his website before giving it a commercial release through Universal in 2003. By 2005 Sananda had completed work on another album, *Angels & Vampires – Volume 1*, which he had previewed on-line throughout the songwriting and recording process. *Angels & Vampires – Volume 2* came in 2006 followed by *Nigor Mortis* in 2008.

I interviewed Sananda Maitreya in 2003 for the commercial release of his excellent *Wildcard* album and thoroughly enjoyed talking to him. Contrary to my expectations he was humble, friendly and talkative, and above all he was hugely passionate about his life and his work as both Terence Trent D'Arby and Sananda Maitreya.

'I think the thing I like the best about Terence Trent D'Arby's music is that he covers so many different styles and genres – pop, rock, funk, r&b – and fuses them all together. That's what keeps him and his music interesting and so enjoyable.'

NATHAN BENDITZSON

HOW DIFFICULT WAS IT FOR YOU AS AN ARTIST, TO COMPLETE YOUR CONTRACTUAL OBLIGATIONS WITH SONY … TO GIVE THEM THEIR POUND OF FLESH AS IT WERE?

I gave them the blood that I was obligated to give, and I learned as much from it as I could during that time. But I did feel that I just had to hold too much back, and the truth about who I am is that in the deepest, deepest part of my heart I just wished to share the joy of expression that I have, in its most authentic and truest form. I'm just not comfortable compromising it and dampening it down just to help them sell more soap. As difficult as it was I can now say that I am grateful that the corporate structure that was oppressing me gave me an invaluable education and really taught me the necessity of learning as much about it as possible, and about growing up and becoming a man.

WAS THERE EVER A SINGULAR POINT OF RELEASE? A DAY OR A MOMENT WHEN YOU WERE SUDDENLY FREE AGAIN?

Really from 1990 onwards I had been trying to win my freedom from that system – a footnote to rock history is that the case that George Michael took to court had been my case previously; Sony basically just got very nervous and came back to me and I settled, because at the end of the day I just wanted to make records. I understood that they weren't going to promote them but all the same it is still better to have a canvas for your work and then people can have it who are willing to look out for it! After stepping out of it George talked to the same lawyer and decided that it all fit for him.

WHILE YOU WERE ACTUALLY GOING THROUGH THOSE DARKEST DAYS WERE YOU ALREADY STARTING TO FORMULATE PLANS AS TO WHAT YOU WERE GOING TO DO NEXT?

Yes … but you know, sometimes an artist can take credit for something that's not so much a thing you formulate as a thing you incubate. I could sense that there was some kind of other timeline that I was being magnetised towards that did mean that I had to be willing to surrender the one I was on, and that the transition could take place and basically that I could put myself in the position where I could see things from a much clearer perspective.

DO YOU FEEL THAT THE INTERNET HAS BECOME IMPORTANT IN FOSTERING THAT SENSE OF COMMUNITY? AS A MEANS OF COMMUNICATION IT HAS MADE THE WORLD SO SMALL.

It's a chance to reinstate the small voices back into the choir, and that's really important. It has certainly been empowering for me to speak directly to people who have a feeling for you, somehow as a human being it's a very gratifying experience, and I feel very grateful for it. I believe that the internet, because it can't be stopped will become the new network, so in future if you have an interesting idea you can have your own window and before you know it you can have two, three, four million people from around the world watching it because they identify with you and what you have to say.

WHICH SOUNDS LIKE A GOOD POINT TO ASK YOU ABOUT YOUR NEW RECORD!

Well, it's called *Terence Trent D'Arby's Wildcard*, and it's nineteen songs, nineteen good songs – it's not about trying to pad out a project, but right now I'm in a zone where I can offer this. We know that CDs don't need to cost what they cost, but since they do I know that I can offer more value for money. They're just songs fair to my heart.

YOU ARE CREDITED AS PRODUCER, WRITER AND ARRANGER, AND I REALLY THOUGHT –

WRONGLY AS IT TURNS OUT – THAT THE ALBUM WAS GOING TO BE SOMETHING VERY SELF-INDULGENT.

What's disheartening sometimes is the fact that we've got so mean in our minds about who we are and what we're capable of doing, that we now make people try to feel bad about having a gift that the Creator has given them and which they have a true desire to share. It's a case of 'How dare you write, produce, and arrange!' This is just me. I am offering to you who I think I am, and that is the answer to that question. We've just got so mean-spirited about our potential and who we are; we've just accepted this mindset of keep your head down and have no ambition and just do one thing. We've become a nation of specialists as opposed to what we used to be when every man was a renaissance man and every man took it upon himself to master many things, because he understood that not only would it make his life richer and more fulfilled, but that the knowledge might also come in handy some day.

AM I RIGHT IN THINKING THAT YOU ENJOYED MAKING THIS ALBUM?

It is one of the true, true joys of my existence to be able to do what comes naturally from my heart and to be able to offer it. It's like being a painter and being let into this room where there's all these endless colours and all these endless canvases.

IT CERTAINLY SOUNDS LIKE THERE'S JOY IN IT.

Well I'm glad you mentioned that because when people ask me about the album that's the one thing that I try to say; if they listen to it with an open mind then they will actually feel better afterwards. It is uplifting, an energy, and that's what I want to share. Right now we need that kind of thing from as many artists as we can

possibly get it from … we need more expression of that which speaks best of us.

I'M AWARE THAT THIS INTERVIEW IS WITH SANANDA MAITREYA, SO WHO IS TERENCE TRENT D'ARBY NOW?
Right now I would say that he is a ghost, but a very useful ghost, although that's just describing it from my perspective. He is still something for people who have some historical reference to a person who meant something to their life, it's made me more appreciative of who I was, because the truth is that I had just completely lost perspective on it and moving away from it now has actually given me some distance to appreciate what his sacrifice was, and it definitely was a sacrifice.

HAVING HAD SOME TIME TO GET THAT PERSPECTIVE, HOW MUCH DO YOU IDENTIFY WITH HIM NOW?
You know it's funny, I just see a guy who came along for the ride, did his duty, and just walked off into another dimension. Basically now it's a layer peeled away and a truer version is there in its place. It always felt like a mask that I was wearing at the appropriate time that just fell away, and I had kind of soured of it to be honest. There was far more pain than there was joy, and I was so desperate to experience more joy in my life that I would do anything necessary to achieve it. When the opportunity came to just switch my name to something that felt like it had the power to lift me into something else I didn't hesitate … emotionally it was like a rope had been thrown to me.

IT MUST HAVE BEEN ALMOST A DANGEROUS PLACE TO BE – TO BE FEELING THAT YOU'D DO LITERALLY ANYTHING MUST BE PRETTY MUCH THE POINT WHERE SO MANY PEOPLE JUST GO OFF THE RAILS.

But it's also the point where you just completely surrender as well and just let go and trust your process because every man has to come to a crossroads where he acknowledges that there's a little bit more going on than meets the eye. It really is giving me a new lease on life, the whole idea of taking another identity is that you are anticipating a rebirth in your life, a resurrection in your life, so when I found out later what the name means it makes a lot of sense that I would want to tap into something that gave me the opportunity to be uplifted.

WHAT DOES IT MEAN?
Well it means a lot of things to a lot of different people; some of the things I've heard are 'he who walks in grace', 'love and light', 'life carrier' …

THEY'RE ALL VERY OPTIMISTIC NAMES AREN'T THEY? THEY'RE ALL VERY POSITIVE.
Definitely. Definite positive associations and that's what I like because I guess the negative weight of my past had just caught up with me – and I wasn't just going to tamper with a name that had meant so much to so many people unless it really felt like life or death to me … you just don't frivolously do those things!

AFTER EVERYTHING YOU'VE GONE THROUGH, ARE YOU HAPPY NOW?
You know what, I'm tapping into a level of happiness now that I just didn't have before, but most importantly my life is more rounded, I just seem to be in a place where I accept myself more as I am. What we're really looking for from ourselves is that one hundred per cent approval, and I'm starting to give myself that again, and I've noticed that the magic seems to be coming back.

'Terence Trent D'Arby was, and possibly still is, the most beautiful man I have ever seen.'
RAYMONDO

'I spent an entire year listening to Terence Trent D'Arby's 'Introducing The Hardline...' and pretty much nothing else. I think I know every word he sings and every note they play off by heart. Nothing else has ever touched me like that record did.'
SUZY BRAXTON

'I think there are very few 80s acts who could truly be described as 'artists' but Terence Trent D'Arby is one of them without a doubt. His body of work is sublime to this day.'
JONATHAN PRICE

Snapshot

Samantha Fox and Mick Fleetwood host The Brit Awards ● The Berlin Wall comes down ● Timothy Dalton is James Bond in *A Licence To Kill* ● The Poll Tax is introduced in Scotland ● Black Box release the UK's bestselling single 'Ride On Time' ● TV's *Emmerdale Farm* shortens its name to the far snappier *Emmerdale* ● *Baywatch, Byker Grove* and *The Simpsons* appear on television for the first time ● Jason Donovan's *Ten Good Reasons* is the UK's bestselling album ● The Solidarity movement in Poland is made legal ● Serial killer Ted Bundy is executed in Florida ● Sky TV is launched in Europe ● South African President P.W. Botha resigns after suffering a stroke ● Bill Wyman marries Mandy Smith ● Ayatollah Khomeini places a bounty on the head of *The Satanic Verses*' author Salman Rushdie ● The Hillsborough disaster leaves 96 Liverpool football fans dead ● Liverpool beat Everton 3-2 in the FA Cup Final ● Nintendo puts the 'Game Boy' on sale in Japan ● Madonna divorces Sean Penn ● Chinese students demonstrate for democracy in Tiananmen Square ● Every one of Australia's 1645 airline pilots resign in an industrial dispute ● Salvador Dali, Bette Davies, Laurence Olivier and Lucille Ball pass away ● *When Harry Met Sally, Heathers* and *Shirley Valentine* are released ● Barbie celebrates her thirtieth birthday ● Ronald Regan leaves the White House after eight years as President ● Amy Tan published her novel *The Joy Luck Club* ● Around $6 billion-worth of damage is caused by the San Francisco earthquake ● Deep Thought becomes the first computer to beat a human chess master ● TV's *The Benny Hill Show* comes to end ● The Galileo space probe is launched ● Steffi Graf beats Martina Navratilova at Wimbledon and Boris Becker beats Stefan Edberg ● Bobby McFerrin wins the Grammys for Best Song and Album of The Year for his 'Don't Worry, Be Happy' single and album

'Madonna's *Like A Prayer* is my ultimate eighties album.
It's her best album, every track is a gem.'

KEV FROM BIDEFORD

Sounds like. . .1989

I am fortunate to be living in Reading for most of this year because back in my family's home in Chelmsford my ten-year-old brother will develop a passion for novelty dance act Jive Bunny. He won't be the only one – Jive Bunny will this year become the third act in chart history to have a number one record with their first three singles (the others being Gerry & The Pacemakers and Frankie Goes To Hollywood) – but he's the only one I know who is buying the records, although they will all be trotted out at student union discos with alarming regularity. Contrary to their videos, which depict Jive Bunny as a six-foot-tall rabbit with uncanny DJ mixing skills, Jive Bunny is actually a duo whose technique of taking old classic songs, cutting them up and reassembling them 'in the mix' will see them at the top of the singles charts for nine weeks in total this year, as well as releasing an album which will peak at two.

Another ten weeks of number one singles this year will be courtesy of the Stock, Aitken & Waterman team who will chalk up three weeks at the top for Kylie Minogue and Jason Donovan ('Especially For You'), four weeks for Jason Donovan solo (two each for 'Too Many Broken Hearts' and 'Sealed With A Kiss'), a week for Kylie Minogue solo ('Hand On Your Heart') and two weeks for Sonia ('You'll

Never Stop Me Loving You'). The trio will remain at number one for a further six weeks, three weeks each, as producers for the charity records 'Ferry 'Cross The Mersey' (in aid of those affected by the Hillsborough disaster and featuring Paul McCartney, The Christians, Holly Johnson and Gerry Marsden) and Band Aid II.

Jason Donovan, who will additionally score two number two singles with 'Every Day I Love You More' and 'When You Come Back To Me', will also release the year's bestselling album, *Ten Good Reasons*, to be 1989's pop sensation. His success will soundly eclipse that of his closest male rivals this year – Bros and a new US act, New Kids On The Block. Bros will have three top-ten hits, including a number two record with 'Too Much', and an album, *The Time*, which will peak at number four. American pop-rappers New Kids On The Block, however, won't release a record until the autumn but will still finish the year with a number one single, 'You Got It (The Right Stuff)', and a number two album, *Hangin' Tough*, under their belts, transcending Bros's success and placing themselves in a very strong position when the new decade begins.

Kylie Minogue will come much closer to emulating Donovan's success, and will continue the phenomenal run of success she started in 1988 with that

'My favourite eighties band was The Bangles. They paved the way for Katrina & The Waves to get signed when they covered our song "Going Down To Liverpool". They were strong, talented and gorgeous, which was the perfect combination for a "girl group".'

KATRINA LESKANICH,
KATRINA & THE WAVES

'Depeche Mode's "Personal Jesus" for the greatest single – it had me hooked when it was released in 1989 and it still sounds great today!'

WAYNE KISBEE

number one single plus two more top-five hits ('Wouldn't Change A Thing' and 'Never Too Late') and a number one album *Enjoy Yourself*. Madonna will return to the charts this year – Kylie's closest female rival (or should that be the other way round?) – and will enjoy similar success, with a number one single, 'Like A Prayer', and three further top-five singles, including 'Express Yourself' and 'Cherish', as well as a number one album *Like A Prayer*.

Pop tinged with jazz and soul will be the order of the day on one of my favourite albums this year, Fine Young Cannibals' *The Raw And The Cooked*, which will produce two US number one singles – 'She Drives Me Crazy' and 'Good Thing' (reaching numbers five and seven respectively in the UK charts) – and will top the charts in the US and in the UK. Wet Wet Wet will tread similar water and will also have a good year when their third album, *Holding Back The River*, goes to number two and they have one of their biggest singles hits when 'Sweet Surrender' peaks at six. Equally Simply Red will enjoy their first number one album – *A New Flame* – and repeat their biggest singles success to date when 'If You Don't Know Me By Now' peaks at two, the same position as 1986's 'Holding Back The Years'.

Tina Turner will get her first number one album when *Foreign Affair* is released in September, entering the charts at the top spot on the back of the success of one of her best-known and most successful UK singles, 'The Best'. Cher will also have a good year when her 'If I Could Turn Back Time' single reaches number six and a reissue of her *Heart Of Stone* album reaches seven. Approaching the charts from the opposite end of the career ladder this year, however, will be Sam Brown,

whose debut single 'Stop' and album of the same name will both reach number four, her best ever chart positions. But as epic as these songs are none will come close to the success of another chart veteran this year, when Gene Pitney teams up with former Soft Cell singer Marc Almond for a duet of 'Something's Gotten Hold Of My Heart', which tops the singles charts for four weeks scoring both artists their only solo number one hits.

Cyndi Lauper will eclipse the chart success of what will become her best-known album *She's So Unusual* this year, when *A Night To Remember* gets to number nine and a single, 'I Drove All Night', reaches number seven, the same position Roy Orbison will reach with his cover of the song a few years later. The Bangles will also surpass their previous successes when 'Eternal Flame' from their 1988 album *Everything* reaches number one and remains there for four weeks in April and May.

But 1989 will perhaps be best remembered as the year of exhilarating dance music and will be responsible for

some of the decade's most anthemic floor-fillers, led by the bestselling single of this year, Black Box's 'Ride On Time', which even I have been known to try to dance to! It will be a favourite of one of my housemates this year and I will always remember it being a big part of the soundtrack of a party we held in the basement of our shared house, walls decorated for the event in the style of the day with spray-painted smiley faces, flowers and peace signs. The party soundtrack will be provided from a selection of party mix-tapes we will spend hours making. Technotronic will be heavily featured, their 'Pump Up The Jam' will be a number two single this year remaining on the chart for over three months, alongside De La Soul who will release 'Me Myself And I' and 'The Magic Number' (the magic number is three in case you were

wondering!) from their brilliant *3 Feet High And Rising* album, and Lisa Stansfield's collaboration with Coldcut, 'People Hold On', as well as her solo hit 'All Around The World', which will go to number one in November.

If I have to choose one record that will sum up the year – and that party – it will be Soul II Soul's number one single 'Back To Life (However Do You Want Me)' from their debut album *Club Classics Volume One*, which will top the charts in July, the summer hit of the year. The album also features two more top-five singles of this year, 'Keep On Movin' and 'Get A Life', although in the case of the latter it will seem that everyone is more interested in the B-side, 'Jazzie's Groove'. Beatmasters' 'I Can't Dance (To That Music You're Playing)' will also stick in my mind but more for the charms of their

SIDE ONE

Aerosmith 'Love In An Elevator', Alice Cooper 'Poison', Guns N' Roses 'Paradise City', Queen 'I Want It All', Midnight Oil 'Beds Are Burning', Cyndi Lauper 'I Drove All Night', Tina Turner 'The Best', Lisa Stansfield 'All Around The World', Wet Wet Wet 'Sweet Surrender', The Bangles 'Eternal Flame', Simple Minds 'Belfast Child', Madonna 'Like A Prayer', Jason Donovan 'Too Many Broken Hearts', Tears For Fears 'Sowing The Seeds Of Love', Shakespears Sister 'You're History'

SIDE TWO

Black Box 'Ride On Time', Technotronic 'Pump Up The Jam', Beatmasters & Betty Boo 'I Can't Dance (To That Music You're Playing)', Soul II Soul 'Back To Life', De La Soul 'Me Myself And I', New Kids On The Block 'You Got It (The Right Stuff)', Fine Young Cannibals 'She Drives Me Crazy', Marc Almond & Gene Pitney 'Something's Gotten Hold Of My Heart', Erasure 'Drama', Depeche Mode 'Personal Jesus', Electronic 'Getting Away With It', 808 State 'Pacific', A Guy Called Gerald 'Voodoo Ray', Stone Roses 'Fools Gold', Band Aid II 'Do They Know It's Christmas?'

1989

Number One Albums

Various Artists Now That's What I Call Music 13, **Erasure** The Innocents, **Roy Orbison** The Legendary Roy Orbison, **New Order** Technique, **Fine Young Cannibals** The Raw And The Cooked, **Simply Red** A New Flame, **Gloria Estefan & Miami Sound Machine** Anything For You, **Madonna** Like A Prayer, **Deacon Blue** When The World Knows Your Name, **Holly Johnson** Blast!, **Simple Minds** Street Fighting Years, **Jason Donovan** Ten Good Reasons, **Queen** The Miracle, **Paul McCartney** Flowers In The Dirt, **Prince** Batman (soundtrack), **Transvision Vamp** Velveteen, **Soul II Soul** Club Classics Volume One, **Gloria Estefan** Cuts Both Ways, **London Stage Cast** Aspects Of Love, **Eurythmics** We Too Are One, **Tina Turner** Foreign Affair, **Tears For Fears** Seeds Of Love, **Tracy Chapman** Crossroads, **Kylie Minogue** Enjoy Yourself, **Erasure** Wild!, **Chris Rea** The Road To Hell, **Phil Collins** ...But Seriously

collaborator on the track, Betty Boo (it's a bobbed hair thing again!), who will embark on a successful solo career next year.

Soul II Soul is not an album I will buy though, preferring to spend my student grant on old favourites: Erasure's second number one album *Wild!*, featuring their two singles hits this year, 'Drama' and 'You Surround Me'; New Order's Balearic-influenced *Technique* (their first number one album); and Depeche Mode's live double album *101*, the soundtrack to a film of their recent US tour which the band will launch at a screening at a London theatre and which I will get a ticket for, thrilled to be seated just seven rows behind the band and their guests. Depeche Mode will also release a new single, 'Personal Jesus', which will reach number thirteen in the UK single

charts, their best chart position for a single for three years, the first single from their forthcoming *Violator* album which will become one of my favourite albums of all time when it is released in 1990. Duran Duran will undergo a similar upturn in the singles charts when their 'All She Wants Is' reaches number nine and their first hits compilation, *Decade*, peaks at number five.

It will also be a great year for new electronic music emerging from the DIY culture of acid house. 808 State's 'Pacific' will reach the top ten at the end of the year beginning a run of hits for the experimental Manchester band while sometime 808 State collaborator A Guy Called Gerald will also make the singles charts with his innovative 'Voodoo Ray' EP which will peak at twelve. Electronic, a side-project for former Smiths guitarist Johnny Marr and New Order frontman Bernard Sumner will release their debut single 'Getting Away With It' – which also featured Pet Shop Boys singer Neil Tennant on vocals – in December. It will also reach number twelve, although the band's second single 'Get The Message' and debut album *Electronic* won't follow until 1991.

I will be reminded of the best bits of my early eighties rock days when Aerosmith release their epic 'Love In An Elevator', their first UK singles hit (not counting their 1986 collaboration with Run DMC) and Alice Cooper releases his biggest hit single for seventeen years, 'Poison'. Queen will enjoy their first number one studio album since 1980 when *The Miracle* hits the top spot in June on the back of their classic single 'I Want It All', and Guns N' Roses will also build on their 1988 success this year with four hit singles – including the classic 'Paradise City' and a remixed version of 'Sweet Child O' Mine', which both reach number six – propelling a reissue of their *Appetite For*

Destruction album to number five. REM will, finally, break into the top forty singles charts in June when 'Orange Crush' reaches twenty-eight, although a second single 'Stand' (which will be reissued twice this year) will fail to get higher than forty-eight. Australia's Midnight Oil are more successful when a reissue of their 1988 single 'Beds Are Burning' goes to number six, their only UK singles hit of the decade, and their reissued *Diesel & Dust* album makes the top twenty.

Rock of a very different kind will hit the singles chart in August in the shape of 'She Bangs The Drums', the debut single from Manchester's Stone Roses, quickly followed by a second single, the classic 'Fools Gold' which will go on reach number eight and an

album *The Stone Roses* that will reach the top twenty. It's the first of a series of records which will be loosely considered part of the emerging 'Madchester' movement, another key release of which will be Happy Mondays' 'Madchester Rave On' EP, featuring 'Hallelujah' as its lead track, which will reach number nineteen in the singles charts.

The ultimate album for me this year will be *Disintegration* by The Cure, which will go on to become one of my favourite albums of all time and will cross the band into a world of stadium-superstardom propelled by a trio of classic hit singles – 'Lullaby', 'Fascination Street' and the wonderfully melancholy 'Pictures Of You'.

The decade will end with Phil Collins at the top of the albums charts with his fourth solo effort *...But Seriously*, which will enter the charts at number one on the back of the success of his number two hit single 'Another Day In Paradise'. A new version of Band Aid's 'Do They Know It's Christmas?' will top the final singles chart of the eighties. This version, billed as Band Aid II, goes straight in at number one and stays at the top of the charts for three weeks. It features a new line-up of the year's most contemporary artists, including Bananarama, Bros, Cathy Dennis, D Mob, Jason Donovan, Kevin Godley, Kylie Minogue, The Pasadenas, Chris Rea, Cliff Richard, Jimmy Somerville, Sonia, Lisa Stansfield, Technotronic and Wet Wet Wet.

'I spent the bulk of the eighties completely convinced that there would never be another New Order. What other band could possibly blend the most exciting elements of alternative rock and dance music so perfectly? Then I heard "Fools Gold" by the Stone Roses. And "Step On" from Happy Mondays. Suddenly, there was hope for music again!'

STEVE-O

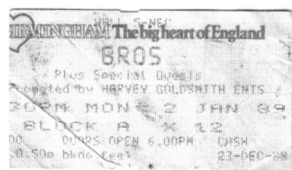

THE FALL OF THE
BERLIN
WALL

I never visited Berlin during the eighties so the Berlin Wall images in my head were borrowed from a range of other sources, predominantly the video for Pink Floyd's number one single 'Another Brick In The Wall'. I didn't actually expect there to be marching hammers, or children going through a mincing machine, but it did cast a slightly surreal tinge to my idea of the Berlin Wall.

At the end of the Second World War, Germany was divided into four occupation zones - one each controlled by the USA, Great Britain, France and the Soviet Union - and Berlin, as the seat of the newly formed Allied Control Council, was similarly divided. The onset of the Cold War however meant that the Soviet zone was excluded from the new Federal Republic of Germany, which controlled West Berlin, and instead became the German Democratic Republic, controlling East Berlin. The economies of the two Germanys then developed at very different rates, the West experiencing an incredible postwar economic recovery while the East – although performing well by Eastern European standards – recovering more slowly. This unequal economic situation meant that huge numbers of East Germans were emigrating to the prosperous West, which led to East Germany setting up the Inner German Border of which the Berlin Wall was a part.

The first 28 miles of barrier between East and West were erected in the early hours of 13th August 1961 when East German troops tore up streets and put up barbed wire and fences. The barrier was built slightly inside East German territory to ensure that no part of it stood on West German soil. The effects on Berlin were instant; some 60,000 people living in the Eastern part of the city were cut off from their jobs in the West and therefore their livelihoods, and families and friends were separated. Over the next few years a concrete wall was erected along almost a hundred miles of border between East and West Germany, with a second inner wall built a hundred yards inside East Germany. This created a clear corridor between the two walls known as the 'death strip',

which was patrolled by East German troops with instructions to shoot anyone who tried to cross.

For almost thirty years the wall remained in place, but in August 1989 Communist Hungary removed its border restrictions with Austria and an estimated 13,000 East Germans escaped into Austria via Hungary, fuelling a period of unrest in East Germany that led to mass demonstrations and the resignation of the East German president Erich Honecker. East Germans continued to flee their country and in November 1989 the decision was made to remove access restrictions through the official checkpoints and finally the two halves of the divided city were reunited. The official reunification process was complete by October 1990.

The surreal Berlin Wall images in my head that had been created by Pink Floyd were finally banished by television news pictures on 9th November 1989 of scenes of jubilation as East and West Berliners were reunited, and unforgettable images of revellers and souvenir hunters attacking the wall with sledgehammers and chisels.

The Berlin Wall ...Up To Date!

Only three small stretches of the Berlin Wall remain today, powerful symbols of the end of the Cold War, although they have been badly damaged by graffiti artists and souvenir hunters since the wall fell in 1989. Some cultural differences between East and West Berliners also remain, attributed to 'Mauer im Kopf', which translates as 'the wall in the head'.

Around 5000 East Germans escaped in the 28 years the wall was in existence, 574 of them were East German border guards.

In July 1990 Roger Waters performed Pink Floyd's *The Wall* in Berlin's Potsdamer Platz and was joined by a number of guest artists including Bryan Adams, Cyndi Lauper, The Scorpions, Thomas Dolby, Sinead O'Connor and David Hasselhoff.

The construction of the Berlin Wall cut through 32 railway lines, 3 autobahns and 192 streets, as well as several rivers and canals.

THE SIMPSONS

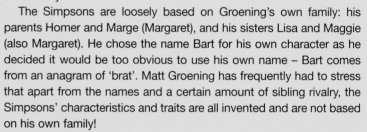

In 1985 Matt Groening, an American cartoonist who drew rabbits for a living (he is the creator of the 'Life In Hell' cartoons) was invited to a meeting to discuss making a series of short animations to be featured in the popular US TV show *The Tracey Ullman Show*. The show's producers were hoping that the cartoonist would draw rabbits for them, but Groening, fearing the loss of ownership for his beloved rabbit characters, instead decided to come up with a different idea for their cartoon. Fifteen minutes later 'The Simpsons' was born. Fifteen years later and *Time* Magazine would declare *The Simpsons* the best TV series of the twentieth century.

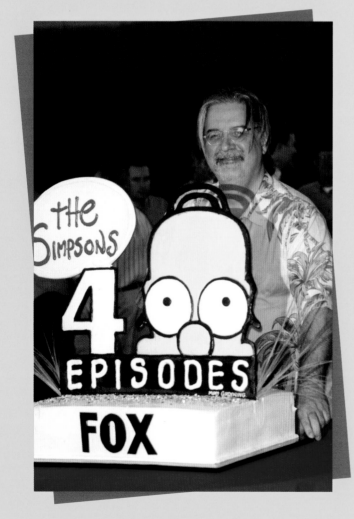

The Simpsons are loosely based on Groening's own family: his parents Homer and Marge (Margaret), and his sisters Lisa and Maggie (also Margaret). He chose the name Bart for his own character as he decided it would be too obvious to use his own name – Bart comes from an anagram of 'brat'. Matt Groening has frequently had to stress that apart from the names and a certain amount of sibling rivalry, the Simpsons' characteristics and traits are all invented and are not based on his own family!

'The Simpsons' made their TV debut in 1987 on *The Tracey Ullman Show* and quickly became enough of a hit to be developed into its own half-hour show, which debuted on 17th December 1989. The show was quickly criticised for providing poor role models for children, and Simpsons merchandise was banned from schools, which inevitably made the show even more popular and even created a bestselling Bart T-shirt – 'Underachiever (and proud of it, man!)' – in the process.

The show went from strength to strength, beating *The Flintstones* in 1997 to become the longest-running prime-time animated series in US television history and winning 22 Emmy Awards in the process. Potential guest stars are queueing up to appear on the show, as animated versions of themselves or voicing characters for the show, and the stellar cast of guests to date has included Jimmy Carter, Tony Blair, Dolly Parton, Leonard Nimoy, U2 and Britney Spears.

The show first came to the UK in September 1990 and was originally broadcast by Sky, who estimated that around a quarter of their subscribers had joined just to watch the show. There have been more than 400 episodes of *The Simpsons* made to date, each one taking around six months to produce at a cost of approximately one million dollars. Personally I think that the greatest testament to the success of *The Simpsons* is that Homer Simpson's exclamation 'd'oh!' has been included in the Oxford English Dictionary!

Homer Simpson was voted number one in a Channel 4 poll to find the 100 Greatest TV Characters.

Among favourite messages written on the chalkboard at the start of each episode of *The Simpsons* are 'A burp is not an answer', 'Goldfish don't bounce', 'I am not delightfully saucy' and 'Frankincense is not a monster'.

Time Magazine placed Bart Simpson on a 1998 list of the 100 Most Influential People of the twentieth century.

The Simpsons has featured more guest stars than any other show.

The Simpsons ...Up To Date!

Despite frequent rumours that the show is to go out of production, there has never been any official announcement to indicate that *The Simpsons* is to finish, and with a full-length film version released in 2007 and new episodes in production it seems that *The Simpsons* will be with us for some time to come.

BAYWATCH

When I was at junior school in the seventies, running in slow motion was something you did in your lunchbreak when it was your turn to be Steve Austin in *The Six Million Dollar Man*, so I can't even begin to imagine what sort of an impact *Baywatch* made on school playgrounds around the world when it first launched in 1989…

Baywatch was created by Greg Bonann who had worked as a lifeguard in Los Angeles and came up with an idea for a TV series loosely based on his own experiences, although when he first started work on the scripts he was undecided whether to make it a mini-series or a sitcom. Reactions to the idea were lukewarm initially, but Bonann's luck changed when his sister married TV producer Doug Schwartz who helped him streamline his ideas into the *Baywatch* we know today.

The first sighting of the show was a pilot movie, *Baywatch: Panic At Malibu Pier*, which was first aired in April 1989, and attracted a good enough audience for NBC to give the green light to the first season of the TV series. The series was first broadcast in 1990 and attracted respectable viewing figures, but NBC were concerned that the show was too lightweight to be sustained for further series and threatened to drop the project after just one season. *Baywatch* star David Hasselhoff stepped in personally to help save the show, and after a series of cost-cutting measures and a healthy injection of Hasselhoff's own cash the show was recommissioned, with Hasselhoff elevated to the position of Executive Producer.

Despite Hasselhoff's attempts to improve the show's storylines, *Baywatch* was quickly known more for featuring attractive people in swimwear than for its dramatic content, despite plots involving earthquakes, sharks, bombs and disasters, as well as the interpersonal relationships between the main characters. The *Baywatch* production team, however, knew what boosted their ratings and drafted a new character into the show's third season, 'C.J. Parker' played by Pamela Anderson, who became one of the show's most iconic and recognisable characters.

Baywatch gradually played to its strengths and stepped up its racier elements and themes. It even launched a spin-off series, *Baywatch Nights*, which turned the saucy content up another couple of notches. *Baywatch Nights* was originally a detective series but after just one season switched to an X-Files-style format concentrating on paranormal investigation. The show folded in 1995 after its second series. Meanwhile *Baywatch* carried on until 2001, eventually finishing after 242 episodes and eleven series. According to *The Guinness Book Of World Records*, *Baywatch* at its peak was the all-time most watched TV show in the world, with an international audience of over 1.1 billion viewers.

A *Baywatch* movie – *Baywatch: Hawaiian Wedding* – was made for television in 2003 and reunited Hasselhoff and Anderson with some of the best-known cast members from the TV series, including Carmen Electra, Yasmin Bleeth and Gena Lee Nolin.

BAYWATCH … UP TO DATE!

Baywatch is still shown on TV networks around the world and there are rumours that a brand new film based on the series, starring Jessica Simpson as 'C.J. Parker', is in production. David Hasselhoff went on to become a major music star in Germany where he has released six platinum albums, and in 2006 enjoyed a number three novelty single hit in the UK with 'Jump In My Car'. Pamela Anderson has gone on to appear in a number of TV and film projects, all of which have been eclipsed by stories of her colourful private life and the unofficial release of at least two homemade sex videos.

At its commercial peak *Baywatch* was being shown on every continent in the world with the exception of Antarctica.

In Germany, David Hasselhoff's *Baywatch* character 'Mitch Buchannon' is voiced by the same actor who provides the voice for Kermit the Frog in *The Muppet Show*.

Baywatch is the longest running show never to win an Emmy award in the USA.

Now That's What I Call Compilation Albums

'My ultimate album was a various artists one called *Modern Dance*, which included bands like Japan and early Simple Minds. I was only 14 in 1981 and you had to be blooming sure that any album was going to be good – so compilations were ideal!'

ELAINE L

'Ultimate album? That's so hard! I am gonna cheat and say one of the *NOW* compilations, probably *NOW 3*. You can still play that album today and it immediately transports you back to what you were doing at the time, it's a real time capsule of memories for me, all of them good. That stuff was on at school discos, in the pub during secret under-age-drinking Fridays, on heyday *Top of the Pops* – and of course in the arcades. Great stuff!'

SHAUN

Last night I saw a television advert for *Now That's What I Call Music 69* (by the time you read this that number will probably be a lot higher!) and obviously I had to go down the whole 'I remember when the first *Now That's What I Call Music* album came out' route; I think it must be my age!

I do remember though. It was 1983 and it came out on double-vinyl and double cassette with thirty tracks, ten of which had been number one hits. The first track was Phil Collins' 'You Can't Hurry Love' and the last track was Culture Club's 'Victims'. Alongside the track listing, the artwork featured a bizarre picture of a pig in sunglasses listening to a chicken singing. The pig didn't appear on the second compilation at all (nor did the chicken), but featured on the front cover of compilations three, four and five wearing a variety of fashionable sunglasses (and sometimes a pair of headphones). The chicken, rather mysteriously, disappeared after the first compilation.

Musically the *Now…* albums would happily mix up genres. Any track would qualify as long as it was a hit, or if it was expected to be a hit by the time the compilation was released (which in the eighties meant the inclusion of Fine Young Cannibals' 'Blue' and Billy Bragg's 'Greetings To The New Brunette', neither of which actually made the top forty). At the other end of the scale there were a number of highly specialist compilations, for example the early eighties rock compilations *Metal For Muthas* – I only mention this short-lived series because I owned volume one – and the innovative *Street Sounds Electro* series.

This 'hit' policy meant the *Now …* albums were very eclectic. On the first compilation, for example, you'll find tracks from The Cure, The Rocksteady Crew and Mike Oldfield, which also expanded their potential market. The *Now …* series was often imitated but never bettered, the closest being the *Hits* albums which followed the same formula across nine volumes between 1984 and 1988, scoring five number one albums in the process.

Compilation albums rounding up a selection of hits from different artists first started getting really popular in the seventies, and by 1989 compilations were so popular that the decision was made to give them their own chart for the first time, to free up some space in the albums charts for some actual albums. Fair enough really, when you consider that the *Now That's What I Call Music* series alone, in all its various forms, featured in the top seventy-five for 425 weeks between 1983 and the start of the compilation chart in January 1989, and was responsible for thirteen number one albums!

Compilation Albums …Up To Date!

The *Now That's What I Call Music* series is still going strong and shows no sign of slowing down, and it has also launched a number of spin-off albums, including *Now – The Christmas Album*, *Now – The Summer Album* and the extremely successful *Now Dance* series. The market for compilation albums is one of the few areas where sales of recorded music are increasing, and compilations account for approximately one in three albums sold in the UK.

1989 ICON

▶▶ *Jason*

Donovan

By 1989 I was 22. I'd almost finished my degree and the real world was just around the corner. I was aware of Jason Donovan of course – everyone knew who Jason Donovan was – I knew his hits from the radio and I'd almost certainly danced to a fair few of them at student union discos, strictly ironically of course! But I wasn't a fan as such; I was too busy working out what was next for me to pay much attention to Stock, Aitken & Waterman's latest pop sensation. So in 2007, when I got the chance to interview Jason for my website, I was surprised that I was quite nervous about talking to him, although I suppose that at the end of the eighties there was almost no one more famous than Jason Donovan and even fewer people who'd managed to sell quite so many records over such a short period of time.

Donovan has sold over three million albums in the UK alone, the majority of those sales in 1989 when he sold more albums in this country than any other artist. But even before his phenomenal success as a singer, Jason was extremely well known in the UK as the actor who gave us *Neighbours*' 'Scott Robinson', one half of one of the eighties' greatest love stories in the story of Scott and Charlene, whose eventual wedding broke daytime television audience records when it was broadcast in 1988. The other half of that story was of course Kylie Minogue, who was also Jason's real-life girlfriend at that time. Kylie was snapped up by Stock, Aitken & Waterman who put her firmly on the path to international success as a singer with the release of her chart-topping debut hit 'I Should Be So Lucky' in 1988.

It made all sorts of sense for Jason to follow in Kylie's musical footsteps and he released his debut single 'Nothing Can Divide Us' (another Stock, Aitken & Waterman production) at the end of 1988, swiftly followed by 'Especially For You', an epic duet with Kylie which saw him top the singles charts for the very first time. The bestselling album *Ten Good Reasons* and a run of huge hit singles followed, and by 1989's second album – *Between The Lines* – Jason Donovan was one of the biggest names in pop.

Donovan returned to his day job of acting in 1990,

appearing in his first feature film *Blood Oath* and then appearing in London's West End for the first time in 1991, playing *Joseph in Joseph & The Amazing Technicolor Dreamcoat* for a few years while enjoying a high profile London social life. Marriage and children tamed his hedonistic streak and he began to pick up more serious acting roles, including a high profile part in the hit Australian medical-legal drama *MDA*, before returning to the West End to play Caractacus Potts in the stage adaptation of *Chitty Chitty Bang Bang*.

An appearance in the 2006 series of the reality TV show *I'm A Celebrity Get Me Out Of Here* returned him to the public eye and the success of a greatest hits album made him turn his attention back to music; he announced a comeback tour in 2007 as well as an autobiography 'Between The Lines'. I interviewed him just after he'd announced the shows and found him to be friendly, funny and open, and above all passionate about what he does and excited about the future.

YOU'RE GOING ON TOUR AGAIN AREN'T YOU? THERE'S GOING TO BE LOTS OF PEOPLE GETTING OVEREXCITED, LOTS OF TEARS AND SCREAMING…

There is! Maybe I should be sponsored by Kleenex Tissues or something like that … or maybe Tesco's cheap-brand tissues!

ALL THAT EMOTION FOR 'ESPECIALLY FOR YOU'! WILL YOU PLAY THAT OR DOES IT HAVE TO BE IN A DUET?

Well you know, you are allowed to perform it on your own! But to be honest it's all still a while off and I haven't quite got into the nuts and bolts of what would be the appropriate thing to do with that song, but it's a classic song and it still stands up. I have done it on my own and I have done it in duet with someone other than Kylie … who knows, but it will definitely be part of the set!

WHO DO YOU THINK WILL BE IN YOUR AUDIENCE THIS TIME AROUND?

I'd imagine that most of the mullets will have been cut off by now but I think the ripped jeans are about to come back in! I don't know yet, I mean I imagine that most people will be recapturing their childhood and most of my fanbase is around twenty-five, thirty … we'll see!

HOW DO YOU APPROACH SOMETHING LIKE THIS TOUR, THAT'S KIND OF A STEP FORWARD BUT ALSO A LOOK BACK?

You're right, that's exactly what it is … I don't quite know how you work out how it's going to play out because I've yet to get to that stage. What I do know is that a lot of people will be buying tickets so they can look back, and one of the greatest things in my life is to have been part of some recordings that really captured kids' hearts and minds, and that is a very strong connection to have … music can capture people's imaginations like no other thing, it's like heroin … probably! It's like a strong drug and I feel very fortunate to have been part of that emotion. So let's be honest, the looking back is going to be a big part of the show, but also I would be fooling myself if I didn't aim to move forward a little bit too, be a little bit self-indulgent and play a few songs that I've been working on recently … and that's the other twenty-five, thirty per cent of the show.

THERE ARE SOME NEW SONGS ON YOUR MYSPACE PAGE AT THE MOMENT – ARE THEY REPRESENTATIVE OF WHERE YOU ARE NOW MUSICALLY?

I think it's reasonably representative. I mean there's always room for improvement, and I'm never completely satisfied on every level, but there is one particular song called 'Share My World' which I'm extremely proud of. That hasn't been put on MySpace for obvious reasons … hopefully, if things go well, we should see some of those things being released in

the summer and then we'll take it from there. I mean my writing is a hobby rather than a profession for me and I think where my real talents lie is in the interpretation of the music itself, but I do write songs. Although if I'm honest with you I don't necessarily know yet if I have articulated something that is sufficiently special and interesting and different and groundbreaking…

HOW INVOLVED WERE YOU IN THE WRITING OF THE CLASSIC EIGHTIES' HITS? DID YOU HAVE A HAND IN WRITING THEM OR WAS IT ALL DOWN TO STOCK, AITKEN & WATERMAN?

No I wasn't, unfortunately not … God, if I had I would be far, far wealthier! Seriously, I am extremely lucky to have had any part of that stuff, but at the same time I suppose it would have been nice to have just a little slice of the writing credits in there! In all honesty, if you went in and said to them 'actually I can write a better one than you' they would probably have said 'well OK, play it to us', and if they had agreed with you – and this is one of Stock, Aitken & Waterman's enduring qualities, and they knew how to write the hits – I'm sure they would have put it on the record. At the end of the day it only helps them, and it helps you and it helps the whole machine, but unfortunately I wasn't that prolific at that point in time, I was more caught up in trying to deliver on other elements and projects.

'I have to admit that I was a huge fan of Jason Donovan at the end of the eighties and in the early nineties. And I like him still. I had a whole wall full of posters of him and they still are in a folder on a shelf. I also have all the records, videotapes, etc. and I managed to get my hands on some special stuff over the last few years from record fairs, the internet, etc.'

MARTINA

> '**Jason Donovan is probably more responsible than anyone else for what I still think of the perfect man – blonde, boyish hair and a cheeky smile with beautiful white teeth... I must have missed the chance of meeting so many nice guys just because they didn't remind me of Jason.**'
>
> ANIKA FROM SWEDEN

WHAT SORT OF MUSIC DO YOU LISTEN TO FOR YOURSELF?

I'm pretty varied in my musical tastes, I can listen to anything from The Killers – who I love, I saw their performance on The Brits and it was so strong and full on and that really attracts me – I like strength. I've always been a massive U2 fan because I like their intelligence and their bittersweet sort of melancholy. I love pop music too, I like classical, I love Ella Fitzgerald, so it's hard to say 'this is where my music tastes are' because they're everywhere really!

DOES SEEING THINGS LIKE THE KILLERS ON THE BRITS MAKE YOU JUST WANT TO GET BACK OUT THERE, TO GET BACK ON THE MUSIC STAGE AGAIN?

Yeah it does … it is inspiring, but having already been through the ins and outs of the whole thing once you have to kind of take that into perspective; to imagine myself as a twenty-two-year-old getting up there with my band is probably not a true representation of where I am at the moment, but it all helps.

WITH ALL THE MUSICAL THEATRE WORK YOU'VE BEEN DOING, DO YOU THINK YOU'LL BE A BETTER PERFORMER THIS TIME AROUND? HAVE YOU PICKED UP ANY LITTLE TRICKS OR ANYTHING?

Well I think I'm probably more confident in myself – more confident than I've ever been in my life actually – and I'm more comfortable as a performer than I've ever been, so hopefully that will just kick in … but everyone gets a sense of anxiety: I did an audition this morning and I'm still apprehensive in that situation.

YOU STILL HAVE TO DO AUDITIONS?

Yeah. I think to a certain degree, when you're investing a lot of money into a production you want to be sure you've got the right person and people do change. To drag yourself out there to do them can be sort of tough, but at the same time if I was a producer I would want to meet people and see what their possibility is, see what they can do … but I'm not at the cattle-call audition stage, I'm at the higher-up meetings, kind of at the 'are you right for us?' stage. It's understandable. I think that people do need to have a sense of knowing you to make sure that you're the right thing for their investment. I mean these shows cost a lot of money, so there's a lot of money to be lost.

BUT DOESN'T EVERYONE KNOW YOU ALREADY? OR IS THAT THE PROBLEM, THAT PEOPLE PIGEONHOLE YOU AS SOMETHING YOU'RE NOT? A SORT OF SCOTT ROBINSON MEETS JOSEPH CHARACTER…

Well … I guess I have slowly had the opportunity to … well, grow up! That's maybe the best way to articulate it. I don't think that in my life I necessarily have anything to prove, that's the first thing – I have been fortunate enough to do some things that not many people get to do and to live a dream that not many people get to live in their lives. But you can only work the loincloth for so long! I have to say that for the last four or five years I think I have been getting that message across, that the boy everyone used to know is now a man! You need to create a new story for yourself.

HOW WERE YOU ABOUT GROWING UP? DID THAT COME VERY NATURALLY OR ARE YOU SOMEONE WHO HAD TO BE DRAGGED THERE, KICKING AND SCREAMING?

Not kicking and screaming no … God, what's happened to me in my life I'm very proud of, I'm not trying to run away from the truth, but you want to reach a point in your life where you can change – I mean, we all change! As much as I'm proud of Scott Robinson and my Stock, Aitken & Waterman days, and Joseph and all those different things, I have a different story now. But unfortunately in life you do tend to get remembered for those moments … but I can think of worse things to be associated with, put it that way! I've never been squeaky clean so I have been able to screw with the canvas a little bit!

WHEN YOU WERE DOING *NEIGHBOURS*, WHEN THE WHOLE MAD PERIOD OF FAME STARTED, WERE YOU AWARE OF JUST HOW BIG YOU WERE IN THE UK?

That didn't really happen I suppose until the whole Scott and Charlene thing kicked off and Kylie had all that success with her record, which really started to get some momentum then.

IF KYLIE HADN'T MOVED IN THAT MUSICAL DIRECTION, WOULD YOU HAVE GONE IN THAT DIRECTION YOURSELF?

I don't know! It's a good, good question but I can't answer that one … I mean history has happened so it's all hypothetical and to be honest it's not really an issue for me, do you know what I mean? It's like sort of saying 'what if I had done that audition and got that part' … it's already happened!

ARE YOU HAPPY?

Everything I do I put my full effort into; I enjoy what I do in my life! I've been freelancing for twenty-five, thirty years and I have managed to pay the bills so far and I have a reasonably good life … we get to go on some nice holidays and the kids get to go to a decent school, so I can't really complain!

Index

Page numbers in italics denote photographs.

References

In writing this book the one title that I referred to again and again was *The Complete Book Of The British Charts: Singles and Albums* by Tony Brown, Jon Kutner, Neil Warwick (Omnibus Press, 2002) and all the chart information I have used in this volume is taken from that book. Tony, Jon and Neil I salute you!

Other than that I used the writing of this book as an excuse not only to re-read a lot of books from my own shelves, but also to justify the purchase of a few more, and although I haven't used them as direct sources they all deserve a mention for the information they provided, the facts they allowed me to check, and the memories they triggered;

MUSIC - GENERAL

Rip It Up And Start Again - Postpunk 1978-1984 by Simon Reynolds (Faber & Faber, 2005)
The Virgin Encyclopedia Of 80s Music by Colin Larkin (Virgin Books, 2003)
Black Vinyl, White Powder by Simon Napier-Bell (Ebury, 2001)
Wheels Out Of Gear - 2 Tone, The Specials And A World In Flame by Dave Thompson (Helter Skelter, 2004)
The Hit Factory: The Stock, Aitken & Waterman Story by Mike Stock (New Holland, 2004)
I Wish I Was Me - The Autobiography by Pete Waterman (Virgin Books, 2000)
80s Chart Toppers by Sharon Davis (Mainstream Publishing, 1999)
The Best of 'Smash Hits' by Mark Firth (Little Brown, 2006)
Guinness Hits Of The 80s by Paul Gambaccini, Tim Rice and Jonathan Rice (Guinness Publishing, 1990)

MUSIC - BANDS & ARTISTS

Take It Like A Man - The Autobiography Of Boy George by Boy George with Spencer Bright (Sidgwick & Jackson, 1995)
Straight by Boy George with Paul Gorman (Century, 2005)
Prince - A Thief In The Temple by Brian Morton (Canongate, 2007)
True - The Autobiography Of Martin Kemp by Martin Kemp (Orion, 2000)
Siouxsie & The Banshees - The Authorised Biography by Mark Paytress (Sanctuary, 2003)
Luke Goss - My Story by Luke Goss (Grafton, 1993)
If I Was... The Autobiography by Midge Ure (Virgin, 2004)
Duran Duran - The Unauthorised Biography by Steve Malins (Andre Deutsch, 2005)
Praying To The Aliens (An Autobiography) by Gary Numan with Steve Malins (Andre Deutsch, 1997)
To Cut A Long Story Short by Tony Hadley (Sidgwick & Jackson, 2004)
Stand & Deliver - The Autobiography by Adam Ant (Sidgwick & Jackson, 2006)
Blitzed! The Autobiography Of Steve Strange by Steve Strange (Orion, 2002)
Blondie - From Punk To The Present by Allan Metz (Musical Legacy Publications, 2002)
The Stranglers - No Mercy by David Buckley (Hodder & Stoughton, 1997)
Living Out Loud by Toyah Willcox (Hodder & Stoughton, 2000)
Never Enough - The Story Of The Cure by Jeff Apter (Omnibus, 2005)
Pet Shop Boys Versus America by Chris Heath (Penguin, 1994)
Is That It? by Bob Geldof (Penguin, 1986)

The Jam - Our Story by Bruce Foxton & Rick Buckler (Castle Communications, 1993)
Tainted Life by Marc Almond (Sidgwick & Jackson, 1999)
Strange Fascination, David Bowie: The Definitive Story by David Buckley (Virgin Books, 2005)
Freak Unique by Pete Burns (John Blake, 2006)
A Bone In My Flute by Holly Johnson (Arrow Books, 1994)
More Than You Know - The Autobiography by Matt Goss (Harper Collins, 2005)
Bare by George Michael & Tony Parsons (Penguin, 1990)
Depeche Mode, A Biography by Steve Malins (Andre Deutsch, 1999)
Morrissey & Marr, The Severed Alliance by Johnny Rogan (Ominbus, 1992)
The Cure, Faith by Dave Bowler & Bryan Dray (Sidgwick & Jackson, 1995)
Between The Lines: My Story Uncut by Jason Donovan (Harper Collins, 2007)

POLITICS & CURRENT AFFAIRS

Reasons To Be Cheerful by Mark Steel (Scribner, 2002)
Britain in the Eighties - The Spectator's View Of The Thatcher Decade by The Spectator (Paladin, 1989)

FASHION

The Look - Adventures In Pop & Rock Fashion by Paul Gorman (Adelita, 2006)
New Romantics: The Look by Dave Rimmer (Omnibus, 2003)

CULTURE

Once In A Lifetime - The Crazy Days Of Acid House And Afterwards by Jane Bussman (Virgin Books, 1998)
Altered State: The Story of Ecstasy Culture and Acid House by Matthew Collin (Serpent's Tail, 1998)
Videogaming by Helen Flatley & Michael French (Pocket Essentials, 2003)

FILMS & TELEVISION

Teen Dreams - Teen Film & Television From Heathers To Veronica Mars by Roz Kaveney (I.B. Tauris, 2006)
Best Movies Of The 80s by Jurgen Muller (Taschen, 2005)
TV Heaven by Jim Sangster & Paul Condon (Harper Collins, 2005)
Brat Pack Confidential by Andrew Pulver & Steven Paul Davies (B.T. Batsford, 2000)

The internet was, inevitably, an invaluable tool and in the course of writing this book I spent a staggering amount of time online gathering information and checking and comparing facts. As I can't possibly list all the websites I visited, I'm afraid a general thank you to webmasters everywhere will have to suffice.

All the celebrity quotes and interview material that appear in this book are taken from interviews I have done with those artists and celebrities. Some were done specifically for the book, the rest are taken from interviews I have conducted for my website, RememberTheEighties.com, over the last few years.

Acknowledgements & Credits

All pictures provided by the author unless indicated.

FOREWORD
Martin Fry picture courtesy of Martin Fry/Blueprint Management.

1980:
John Foxx, The Beat, Siouxsie & The Banshees badges contributed by Heather on behalf of Patrick Marsh
Blondie © David Redfern/Redferns, The Police © Fin Costello/Redferns, The Specials © BBC Photo Library/Redferns, Sheena Easton © GAB Archives/Redferns, Adam & the Ants © GAB Archives/Redferns
Space Invaders pinball machine, Peter Duncan, New Romantics (Teens at the Blitz Club, London), Mod Revival - Mods in Brighton, Dallas, Adam & the Ants (Birmingham Odeon) © Rex Features

1981:
OMD, Ultravox badges contributed by Heather on behalf of Patrick Marsh. Human League picture courtesy of the Human League/Sidewinder Management. Stray Cats tour pass contributed by Ryan Goldman. Shakin' Stevens ticket contributed by Craig Williamson.
Duran Duran © Fin Costello/Redferns, Dollar © Graham Wiltshire/Redferns, The Human League © GAB Archives/Redferns, Soft Cell © Fin Costello/Redferns, Siouxsie Sioux © Fin Costello/Redferns
New Romantics (Fantasy Ball at the Rainbow 1981), Toyah Willcox, wedding of Prince Charles & Lady Diana Spencer, Clare Grogan (Altered Images), protestors, Gregory's Girl © Rex Features

1982:
Madness, Yazoo, Bow Wow Wow, Culture Club (bottom of page 55) badges contributed by Heather on behalf of Patrick Marsh.
Flock of Seagulls © Fin Costello/Redferns, Duran Duran © GAB Archives/Redferns, Bananarama © Ebet Roberts/Redferns, The Cure © Ebet Roberts/Redferns, Grandmaster Flash © Peter Noble/Redferns
E.T., Rik Mayall, Kids from Fame T.V. series, Front page of the Sun during Falklands Campaign, Woman exercising © Rex Features

1983:
U2, Thompson Twins, Heaven 17, Eurythmics, The Police, Men At Work, Echo & The Bunnymen badges contributed by Heather on behalf of Patrick Marsh. The Police guest pass and Men At Work tour pass contributed by Ryan Goldman.
David Bowie © Ebet Roberts/Redferns, Eurythmics © BBC Photo Library/Redferns, Spandau Ballet © BBC Photo Library/Redferns, Wham! © Peter Still/Redferns, Paul Young © Mike Prior/Redferns Idols
Margaret Thatcher, Michael Jackson, Goth Teenagers hanging around, Compact Disc & laser reader © Rex Features

1984:
Howard Jones, U2, Nik Kershaw (lower of two on page 85) badges contributed by Heather on behalf of Patrick Marsh. Cyndi Lauper tour passes contributed by Lance Davis. Nik Kershaw picture (page 87) courtesy of Nik Kershaw.
Morrissey © Kirsten Rodgers/Redferns, Prince © Ebet Roberts/Redferns, Band Aid © BBC Photo Library/Redferns, Nik Kershaw © Mike Prior/Redferns Idols, Howard Jones © Mike Prior/Redferns Idols
Betamax video player, Ghostbusters, Torvill & Dean, Trivial Pursuit © Rex Features

1985:
Billy Idol tour pass contributed by Ryan Goldman. Simple Minds badges (top and bottom of page 103) contributed by Heather on behalf of Patrick Marsh. Simple Minds tickets contributed by Bart Lefevre.
Simple Minds © Virginia Turbett/Redferns, Madonna © Ebet Roberts/Redferns, Billy Idol © Mike Prior/Redferns Idols, Dead or Alive © Mike Prior/Redferns Idols, Go West © Mike Prior/Redferns Idols
Live Aid at Wembley, Paul McCartney/Pete Townshend/Bob Geldof onstage at Live Aid concert, Freddie Mercury onstage at Live Aid concert, Anita Dobson and Leslie Grantham (EastEnders actors), Molly Ringwald © Rex Features

1986:
Run DMC tour pass contributed by Ryan Goldman. A-Ha tour badge contributed by Lesley Jeavons.
Madonna © Ebet Roberts/Redferns, Bon Jovi © Ebet Roberts/Redferns, Depeche Mode © Ebet Roberts/Redferns, A-Ha © New Eyes/Redferns, 5 Star © Mike Prior/Redferns Idols
Kylie Minogue & Jason Donovan, Space station Mir, explosion of the space shuttle Challenger, derelict Chernobyl, derelict Chernobyl (interior) © Rex Features

1987:
U2 after show pass, George Michael local crew pass, Madonna tour pass and concert ticket, Michael Jackson after show pass contributed by Ryan Goldman. New Order badge contributed by Heather on behalf of Patrick Marsh.
Beastie Boys © Ebet Roberts/Redferns, Swing Out Sister © David Redfern/Redferns, Stock, Aitken & Waterman © GAB Archives/Redferns, Rick Astley © Mike Prior/Redferns Idols, T'Pau © Mike Prior/Redferns Idols
Jools Holland & Paula Yates (the Tube), Sisters of Mercy, man with large mobile telephone, Patrick Swayze/Jennifer Grey (Dirty Dancing), Michael Douglas (Wall Street) © Rex Features

1988:
Belinda Carlisle tour pass contributed by Ryan Goldman. Voice Of The Beehive badge contributed by Lesley Jeavons. Bros ticket contributed by Craig Williamson. INXS badge contributed by Heather on behalf of Patrick Marsh.
Terence Trent D'Arby © George Chin/Redferns, Tracy Chapman © Ebet Roberts/Redferns, Bros © Ebet Roberts/Redferns, Axl Rose (Guns n' Roses) © Michael Uhil/Redferns, Sinead O'Connor) © Michael Linssen/Redferns
Nelson Mandela benefit concert, Acid House party (Heaven nightclub, London), Acid House clubber (Heaven Nightclub, London), Acid House smiley face, Lenny Henry comic relief, Nelson & Winnie Mandela, South Africa, Jon Johnson & Philip Michael Thomas (Miami Vice) © Rex Features

1989:
Bros and Bananarama tickets contributed by Craig Williamson. Bon Jovi tour pass contributed by Ryan Goldman.
Bez (Happy Mondays) © Ian Dickson/Redferns, Soul II Soul © Ian Dickson/Redferns, Michael Stipe (REM) © Ebet Roberts/Redferns, the Stone Roses © Michael Linssen/Redferns, Jason Donovan © Michael Linssen/Redferns
Berliners tear down the Berlin Wall, Baywatch, The Simpsons, Matt Groening at The Simpsons 400th episode party © Rex Features

Mind-Boggling Tricky Logic Puzzles for Clued-up Kids

Managing Editor: Sarah Wells
Editor: Lucy Dear
Contributors: Fran Pickering, Philip Carter, Nick Daws,
Peter Sorrenti, Ann Marangos, Claire Redhead
Cover, page design and layout: Alan Shiner

Published by:
**Lagoon Books,
PO BOX 311, KT2 5QW, U.K.**

ISBN 1902813693

© 2003 Lagoon Books, London

Printed in Singapore

mind-boggling
TRICKY LOGIC
puzzles

GREAT PUZZLES FOR CLUED-UP KIDS • GREAT PUZZLES FOR CLUED-UP KIDS • GREAT PUZZLES FOR CLUED-UP KIDS

GREAT PUZZLES FOR CLUED-UP KIDS!

Other titles in the Mind-Boggling range include:

**KIDS MIND-BOGGLING
LATERAL THINKING PUZZLES
(For Clued-up Kids)**

**KIDS MIND-BOGGLING
BRAIN TEASER PUZZLES
(For Clued-up Kids)**

**KIDS MIND-BOGGLING
CODE BREAKER PUZZLES
(For Clued-up Kids)**

MIND BOGGLING
TRICKY LOGIC PUZZLES
FOR CLUED-UP KIDS

Logical mind? Cool under pressure?
Clever enough not to make any silly mistakes?
Then we have just the challenge for you.

In this book you'll find a series of cool but
tricky puzzles. You don't need to be great at math to
solve them, just able to think problems through logically
and not get side-tracked down any blind alleys!

The puzzles are graded in difficulty from 1
(shouldn't take someone of your caliber more
than a few minutes to solve) to 5
(be prepared for a sleepless night).

You can find all the answers at the back of the
book – but no peeking now! Before you check the
answer to a puzzle, try hard to solve it first.
Some of the puzzles in here are tough,
but they're all fair.

So do you still think you're up to it? Great!
Put a 'Do Not Disturb' sign on your door, then pick up
your pen, turn over the page, and start puzzling!

Five Sum

Difficulty Rating ☆☆

Can you write down five odd numbers
so that when added together they equal 14?

Japanese Style

Difficulty Rating ★★★★★

On Japanese trains it is forbidden to travel with
a ceremonial sword longer than 30 inches.
How did the passenger manage to travel with a
sword that measured 34 inches in length, completely
concealed, if he only had a suitcase 28 inches long,
28 inches wide and 6 inches deep?

Sequence Dilemma

Difficulty Rating ☆

1 2 4 8 ?

What number comes next?

Coded Crossword

Difficulty Rating ☆☆☆

Bird of Prey

French Coin

What comedians tell

African drum

Furious

Small light

Not a finger

Meadow

Vine fruit

Amusing

Savory snack

Striped animal

Grown up

Under

Head bone

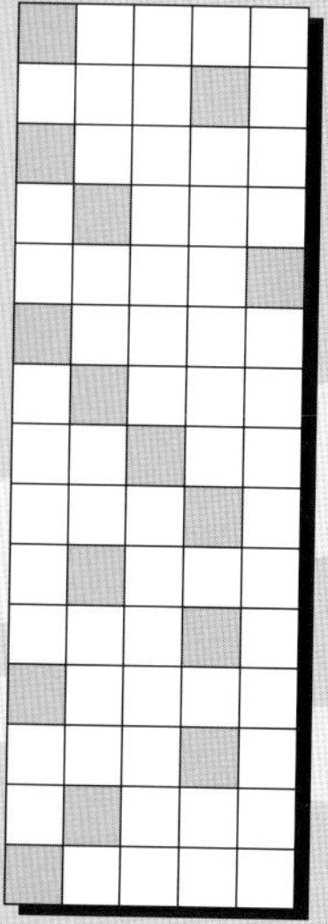

Can you work out what the 5-letter word answers to
the clues are? If you can, place them in the grid.
A secret message will be revealed in the shaded squares.
Can you see what it is?

9

Jewel Robber

Difficulty Rating ★★★★

The Sheik of Araby was in despair.
A clever thief had broken into his palace and stolen
most of his jewels. All but ten of his collection of
priceless ruby rings had been taken, 50% of his
fabulous collection of 120 tiaras, 90% of the 100
emeralds and all his priceless diamonds.
How many rings did he have left?

Money Sum

Difficulty Rating ☆☆

Peter and Jenny have $24 between them.
Peter has twice as much money as Jenny.
How much money does each of them have?

Toy Turns

Difficulty Rating ☆☆☆☆☆

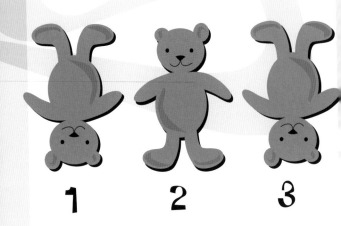

1   **2**   **3**

Can you turn these teddies over so they are all the right way up? You only have 3 moves to do it in and you must turn 2 teddies over on each move.

Square Deal

Difficulty Rating ☆☆☆☆☆

May's kitchen measured 6 square meters. Molly's was 6 meters square. Who had the larger room?

Over the Rainbow

Difficulty Rating ☆☆☆☆☆

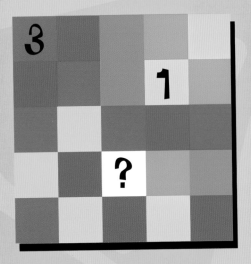

In Rainbow Land they use colors to represent numbers.
A color always represents the same number.
Which color should go in the gap, so that each row
and column, adds up to 15?
Some numbers have been put in to start you off.

Baffling Boxes

Difficulty Rating ☆

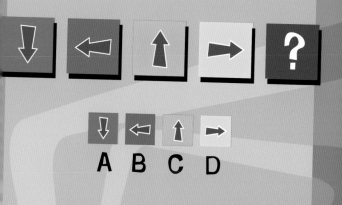

A B C D

Which box should go next: A, B, C or D?

Crazy Cube

Difficulty Rating ☆☆☆☆☆

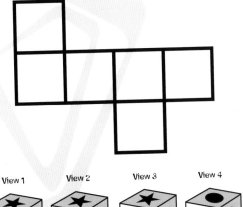

View 1   View 2   View 3   View 4

Can you fill in the squares, using the different views of the made-up cube as a guide?

Circle Conundrum

Difficulty Rating ☆☆

What number should go in the empty circle?

Missing Letter

Difficulty Rating ☆

Put one letter in the center of the circle to
make two 5-letter words.

Toy Sale

Difficulty Rating ☆☆☆☆☆

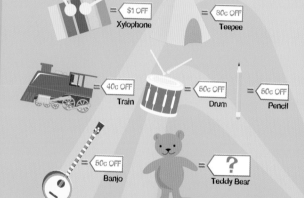

There's a sale on at the village toyshop! Different amounts have been taken off the prices of some of the toys.
Mr Plush, the toyshop owner has used a special system to work out how much should be taken off each price.
How much has been taken off the price of the teddy bear?
See bottom of page for a clue…

Number Crunching

Difficulty Rating ☆☆☆

Which of the numbers is wrong?

Card Craze

Difficulty Rating ☆☆

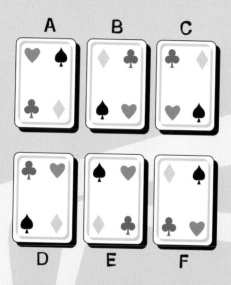

Which card is the odd one out?

Number Challenge

Difficulty Rating ☆☆

| 16 | 24 | 32 | 40 | 48 | 56 | |

Can you add a number to continue the pattern?

Holed Up

Difficulty Rating ☆☆☆☆☆

A beetle is climbing out of a hole, 40cm deep.
He climbs 7cm each day and slips back 2cm each night.
How long will it take the beetle to get out of the hole?

Star Attraction

Difficulty Rating ☆☆☆☆

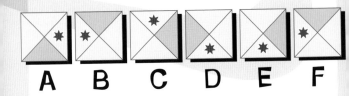

Which figure is the odd one out?

Bone Boggling

Difficulty Rating ☆☆☆☆☆

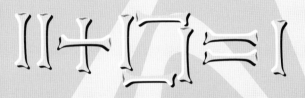

Fido, the amazing performing dog, is learning
how to do arithmetic, using his collection of bones.
Can you move one bone to make the sum work?

Square Eyes

Difficulty Rating ☆☆

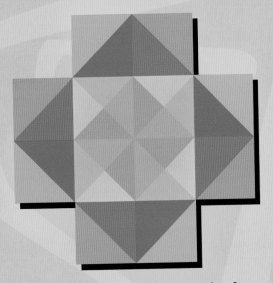

How many squares can you see here?

Back to Front

Difficulty Rating ☆☆☆☆☆

A palindrome is a word or number that reads the same backwards and forwards. For example: MADAM or 12121.

A lorry driver notices that his mile reading is 15,951 miles. If he is driving at a steady 55 miles an hour, how long will he drive before his meter shows another number that is a palindrome?

Ball Baffler

Difficulty Rating ☆☆☆

Which is the odd sport out?
TENNIS BASEBALL SOCCER BASKETBALL
VOLLEYBALL

Sweet Sensation

Difficulty Rating ★★★☆

The floss in a candyfloss machine doubles every second. If, after 5 minutes, the machine is full, when was it half full?

House Swap

Difficulty Rating ☆☆

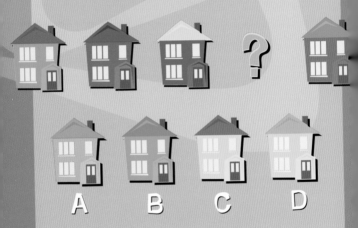

Which house fits in the gap?

Line Up

Difficulty Rating ☆☆☆

A B C D

What comes next, A, B, C or D?

Chair Challenge

Difficulty Rating ☆☆☆☆☆

Five friends went to a rodeo. Matt sat nearer to Eric than to Jo. Wilbur was between Eric and Matt. Jo was on Sid's right. Eric was not next to Sid.

From left to right, in what order did they sit?

Triangle Teaser

Difficulty Rating ☆

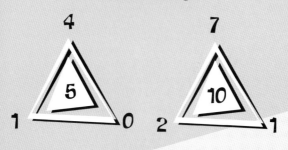

4

7

5

10

1   0

2   1

3

?

2   6

What is the missing number?

Pen Puzzle

Difficulty Rating ★★★

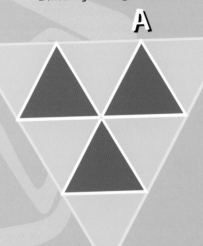

Starting at A, can you draw this shape in one go, without lifting your pencil from the paper and without going back over a line?

Animal Attraction

Difficulty Rating ☆☆☆☆☆

TIGER

SQUIRREL

FROG

RHINO

MOUSE

LION

ANTEATER

HIPPO

Which animal is 2 animals below the animal that is 5 animals above the animal that is 2 animals above the animal that is 3 animals below the mouse?

Fun and Games

Difficulty Rating ☆☆

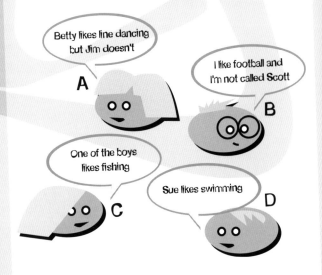

Four children are talking about their favorite sports.
Can you name each child and say what
their hobbies are?

Coin Switch

Difficulty Rating ☆☆☆☆☆

Move 1 coin to make 2 straight lines,
each with 4 coins in it.

Odd One Out

Difficulty Rating ☆☆☆☆

Cube. Pyramid. Circle. Sphere.

Carrot. Pea. Cabbage. Apple.

Zebra. Magpie. Lion. Bear.

Sausage. Chop. Egg. Steak.

Ottawa. Lisbon. Vancouver. Toronto.

Each row has an odd one out.
Write down the initial letters of the odd one out
in order, to reveal an animal.
What is the animal?

Word Mix Up

Difficulty Rating ☆☆☆☆☆

In Townsville there was a fair to raise money for the local church. The top prize of a DVD player could be won on one of the stands. Can you work out which stand it was by inserting the missing letter in the empty segment?

Jumbled

Difficulty Rating ☆☆☆☆☆

Can you find a single five-letter word which can be added to each of the following letters to make a series of six-letter words?

Sum It Up

Difficulty Rating ☆☆☆☆

$$9 \quad 3 \quad 7 \quad 7 = 20$$

Can you put in + and - signs to make the sum work?

Fruit Salad

Difficulty Rating ☆☆☆☆

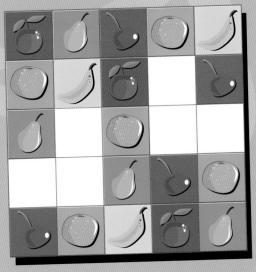

Mr Plum is arranging his fruit stand at the market.
He wants to arrange the stand so that each row
and column contains one of each fruit.
What fruits go in the empty squares?

Fifteens

Difficulty Rating ☆☆☆

1 2 3 4 5 6

Can you fit the numbers (above the grid) into the grid
so that every row and column adds up to 15.
Three have been put in to start you off.

43

Box Brain Ache

Difficulty Rating ☆☆☆☆

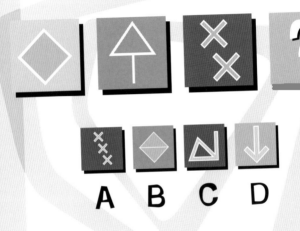

A   B   C   D

Which box logically completes the series?

Next Number

Difficulty Rating ☆

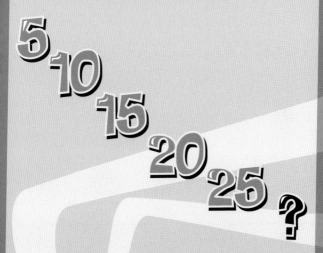

Can you add a number to continue the pattern?

Square Numbers

Difficulty Rating ★★★★

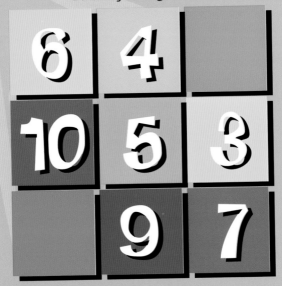

What numbers should go in the empty squares?

Monster Mash

Difficulty Rating ☆☆☆

If one green monster balances 2 purple monsters and
3 yellow monsters balance 2 green monsters,
how many purple monsters will it take to balance
6 yellow monsters?

What's This?

Difficulty Rating ☆☆☆☆☆

If
IT=3
IS=4
HI=5
HIS=8

Then
THIS=?

Doctor's Orders

Difficulty Rating ☆☆☆☆

If a doctor gives you 12 tablets and tells you to take one every two hours, starting at 10.00 a.m. that day, when will you take the last one?

Holiday Sights

Difficulty Rating ★★★★

There was a go-slow at
the airport, so we had
time to buy a fluffy purple
nylon donkey; Emma'd ridden
the real thing on the beach.
When we got back, Mum said
she'd pop a risotto in the oven.

In this extract from her essay about the holidays,
Jane has hidden the names of four of the cities she
visited with her family. Can you find them?

Birthday Bonanza

Difficulty Rating ✮✮✮

The triplets, Sophie, Sheila and Sheree,
swapped their birthday presents.
Sophie gave her skates to Sheila
in exchange for Sheila's CD.
Sophie then exchanged the CD for Sheree's necklace.
Sheila and Sheree then swapped presents.
Who had what at the end of the swapping session?

What's Up?

Difficulty Rating ☆

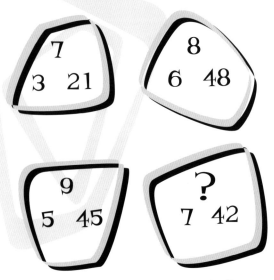

7
3 21

8
6 48

9
5 45

?
7 42

Can you fill in the missing number?

Figure It Out

Difficulty Rating ☆☆☆

How would you write eleven thousand and eleven
hundred and eleven.

Stick 'Em Up

Difficulty Rating ★★★

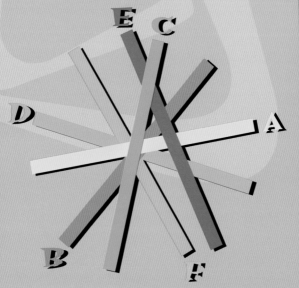

In this game of pick-up-sticks,
in what order should you remove the sticks
so that you take away the top one each time?

Pattern Puzzler

Difficulty Rating ☆☆

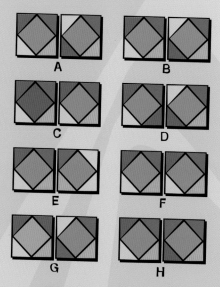

Which is the odd pair out?

Sequence

Difficulty Rating ☆☆

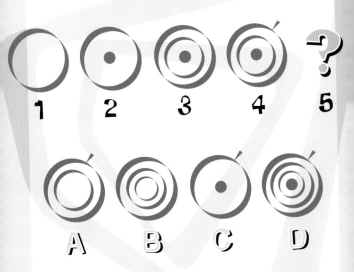

What comes next in this series?

Sum Total

Difficulty Rating ☆☆☆

Can you put in + and − signs to make the sum work?

Dancing Dilemma

Difficulty Rating ☆☆☆

Here is a poster from last week's dance contest.
Using the clues below, can you work out each team's
color and which dance they performed?

DANCING!

Dance Teams:
Ohio, Portland, New Orleans
and Wyoming.

Dances being performed:
tango, salsa, samba and square dancing.

Team Colors:
red, green, blue, and black.

- The dance teams at the contest wore different colors.
- The team dancing samba were in red and not from Wyoming.
- The team in black were square dancing.
- Ohio team were in green.
- The Ohio team were not salsa dancing.
- From where they were salsa dancing, the Portland team could
  see the green team dancing the tango.

Bullseye!

Difficulty Rating ☆☆☆☆

In a darts competition each dart scores either
40, 39, 24, 23, 17 or 16.
How many darts must be thrown to score exactly
100 points?

Square Sum

Difficulty Rating ☆☆☆☆

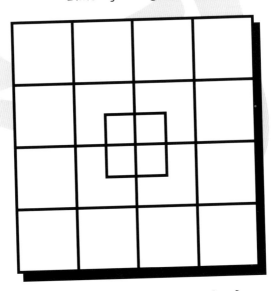

How many squares can you see here?

Number Number

5
7
10
14
19
?

Can you add a number to continue the pattern?

Backwards Thinking

Difficulty Rating ⭐⭐

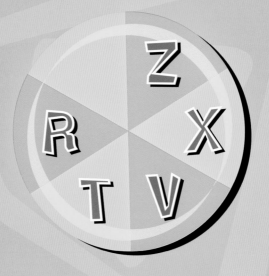

Which letter should go in the empty segment?
There is a clue to help you.

Face-To-Face

Difficulty Rating ☆☆☆☆☆

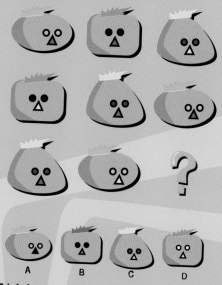

Which face logically completes the sequence?

Triangle Test

Difficulty Rating ☆☆☆☆☆

How many triangles are there?

Hint: copy or trace the figure a few times and color in each size of triangle.

Fruit Cocktail

Difficulty Rating ☆☆☆☆

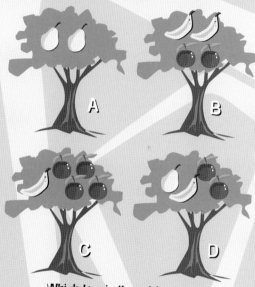

Which tree is the odd one out?

Clue: apple = 1, banana = 2, pear = 3

What's Next?

Difficulty Rating ☆☆☆☆☆

AAAAA?

Which letter comes next in this collection?

Clowning Around

Difficulty Rating ☆☆

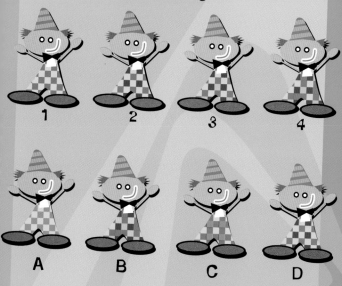

Which clown comes next?

Weekly Work Out

Difficulty Rating ★★★★

| Monday 12 | Tuesday 13 | Wednesday 14 | Thursday 15 | Friday 16 | Saturday 17 |
| | | | | | Sunday 18 |

If yesterday's tomorrow was **Sunday**,
what is the day after tomorrow's yesterday?

Turn Around

Difficulty Rating ☆☆

1 8 2 3 5 9 4 6 10 7

Which number between 1 and 10 will increase its value
by half if you turn it upside down?

Missing Link

Difficulty Rating ☆☆☆☆☆

John and Martha will be able to go home early from
their Math class if they can get this question right.
Their teacher, Mr Digit, has asked them to find
the number that needs to go into the missing segment.
Can you help them?

How Many Squares?

Difficulty Rating ★★★★

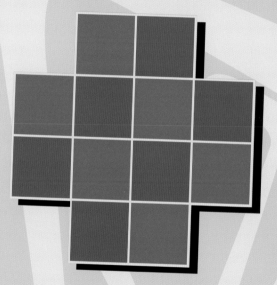

How many squares can you see here?

Math Muddles

Difficulty Rating ☆☆☆☆☆

$$7 \ 4 \ 5 \ 9 \ 8 = 7$$

Can you put in + and - signs to make the sum work?

Eye Eye!

Difficulty Rating ☆☆☆☆☆

Using the letters above in as many combinations
as you like, how many ways can you spell EYE?
You can use the 'E's twice, but not the 'Y's.

Flag It Up

Difficulty Rating ☆☆☆☆

Can you move one flag to make 3 lines
(rows, columns or diagonals) of 3 flags?

Wavy Lines

Difficulty Rating ★★

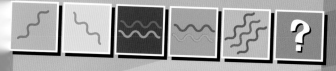

A B C D

Which square comes next, A, B, C or D?

Face Shapes

Difficulty Rating ☆☆

Which face completes the logic sequence?

Logic Letters

Difficulty Rating ☆☆☆

There is a missing letter here that will complete the
sequence. Can you work out what it is?
There is a clue to help you.

Clue: Write out the alphabet and circle the letters that you have been given.
Can you see a pattern?

Seventeens

Difficulty Rating ☆☆

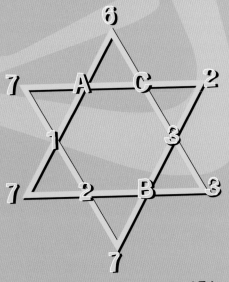

This is a magical star from the planet Zylon.
Which numbers need to replace
A, B and C so that each straight line adds up to 17?

Half and Half

Difficulty Rating ★★★

Mr and Mrs Jones have 6 children, their ages are
listed here in this circle. There is a logical pattern to
the children's ages. Can you work out what the
missing age is to fit in the empty segment?
There is a clue to help you.

Clue: Does the top half of the circle relate to the bottom half?

Sewing Sum

Difficulty Rating ★★

Jenny the dressmaker loves Math.
Can you help her by moving just one of her sewing
needles to make the sum work?

Pattern Path

Difficulty Rating ☆☆

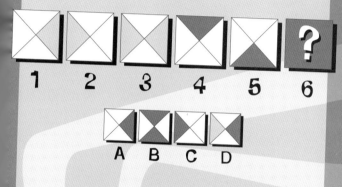

1   2   3   4   5   6

A   B   C   D

Which box comes next?

Dragon Dilemma

Difficulty Rating ★★★★★

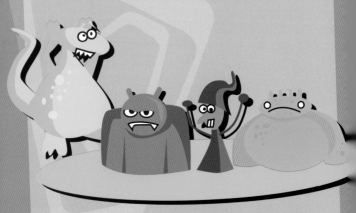

The dragon is rescuing creatures from an island in
the flooded valley. He has 3 left to save: a goblin,
a troll and an orc. He will pluck them from the island
and move them to a mountain top, until more help arrives.
He can only carry one creature at a time. However,
he has to be careful which two he leaves together.
The orc will eat the goblin. The troll will kill the orc.
The troll and the goblin get along well together.
How can he rescue them?

Color Combination

Difficulty Rating ☆

Using multiplication and addition find the combinations of blue and green numbers, always one of each, that give the following answers:

a) 17 b) 8 c) 54 d) 20

Brainy Birds

Difficulty Rating ☆

What comes next in this series?

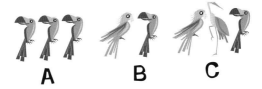

A   **B**   **C**

Magic Square

Difficulty Rating ☆☆☆

Jonathan knows that there is a pattern that will give him the missing number in this magic square. Can you work it out for him?

Solutions

Page 6 - Five Sum

```
  11
   1
   1
   1
 ----
  14
```

Page 7 - Japanese Style

He placed the sword in diagonally from corner to corner.

Page 8 - Sequence Dilemma

16.
Each number is twice the number before it.

Page 9 - Coded Crossword

Enjoy the Puzzles!

EAGLE
FRANC
JOKES
BONGO
CRAZY
TORCH
THUMB
FIELD
GRAPE
FUNNY
PIZZA
ZEBRA
ADULT
BELOW
SKULL

Page 10 - Jewel Robber

Ten.
It says in the question all but 10 of his collection of priceless ruby rings were stolen.

Page 11 - Money Sum

Jenny has $8. Peter has $16.

Page 12 - Toy Turns

Turn over 1 and 2.

Turn over 1 and 3.

Turn over 1 and 2.

Page 13 - Square Deal

Molly.
6 meters square = 6 meters x
6 meters = 36 square meters.
May's kitchen measures only 6
square meters.

Page 14 - Over the Rainbow

Red. Red = 3/ yellow = 1
/ green = 2/ blue = 4/
purple = 5.

Page 15 - Baffling Boxes

A.
Each time the arrow turns 90
degrees.

Page 16 - Crazy Cube

Page 17 - Circle Conundrum

5.
The top numbers and right-
hand numbers add up to the
left-hand number in each
group.

Page 18 - Missing Letter

A.
Ready. Grape.

Page 19 - Toy Sale

50c.
Each vowel is worth so many
cents, in order from A.
A -10c   E - 20c   I - 30c
O - 40c   U - 50c
Teddy Bear = 20c + 20c + 10c
= 50c.

Page 20 - Number Crunching
29.
It should be 31. They are the numbers of days in the months of the year, starting with January.

Page 21 - Card Craze
D.
All the others have diamonds and hearts diagonally opposite each other, and clubs and spades diagonally opposite each other.

Page 22 - Number Challenge
64.
All the numbers are multiples of 8.

Page 23 - Holed Up
8 days.
On the 8th day the beetle will climb 7cm and be out of the hole.

Page 24 - Star Attraction
E.
If you look at each square making sure the colored triangle is on the bottom (like A), E is the only one that does not have the star to the right of the colored triangle.

Page 25 - Bone Boggling

Page 26 - Square Eyes
26.

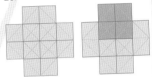

12 squares.

5 sets of squares made from 4 squares.

4 small squares and 1 large square.

4 center squares.

Page 27 - Back to Front
2 hours or 110 miles.
15951 + 110 = 16061 miles.

88

Page 28 - Ball Baffler
Soccer.
It is the only one where the ball is kicked.

Page 29 - Sweet Sensation
4 minutes 59 seconds.

Page 30 - House Swap
C.
The roof color moves down to the house color and a new roof color is added each time.

Page 31 - Line Up
C.
The figure in the first square has 1 straight line, the next has 2, and so on, so the fifth square should be a figure with 5 straight lines.

Page 32 - Chair Challenge
Sid Jo Eric Wilbur Matt.

Page 33 - Triangle Teaser
11.
The number in the center of the triangle is the sum of the numbers on the corners.

Page 34 - Pen Puzzle
A round to B, B to C, C to D, D to B, B round to E, E to C, C to F, F to E, E round to A. A to C and back round to A.

Page 35 - Animal Attraction
Frog.

Page 36 - Fun and Games
A is Sue who likes swimming.
B is Jim who likes football.
C is Betty who likes line
  dancing.
D is Scott who likes fishing.

Page 37 - Coin Switch
Move F and put it on top of B.

Page 38 - Odd One Out
CAMEL.
Circle (the others are 3 dimensional, a circle is 2 dimensional).
Apple (the others are vegetables, an apple is a fruit).
Magpie (the others are animals, a magpie is a bird).
Egg (the others are kinds of meat, an egg is not).
Lisbon (the others are cities in Canada, Lisbon is the capital of Portugal).

Page 39 - Word Mix Up
F.
Rearrange the letters to spell RAFFLE.

Page 40 - Jumbled
The word is 'angle' (bangle, dangle, jangle, mangle and tangle).

Page 41 - Sum It Up
9 - 3 + 7 + 7 = 20.

Page 42 - Fruit Salad

Page 43 - Fifteens

2	9	4
7	5	3
6	1	8

Page 44 - Box Brain Ache
C.
All the figures should have 4 straight lines.

Page 45 - Next Number
30. Numbers go up in 5s.

Page 46 - Square Numbers

6	4	8
10	5	3
2	9	7

All the rows and columns add up to 18.

Page 47 - Monster Mash
8.

Page 48 - What's This?
10.
T = 2, H = 4, I = 1, S = 3.

Page 49 - Doctor's Orders
8 o'clock the next morning.

Page 50 - Holiday Sights
Oslo, London, Madrid and Paris.
There was a go-slow at the airport, so we had time to buy a fluffy purple nylon donkey; Emma'd ridden the real thing on the beach. When we got back, Mum said she'd pop a risotto in the oven.

Page 51 - Birthday Bonanza
Sophie: necklace
Sheila: CD
Sheree: skates.

Page 52 - What's Up?
6.
The number on the right is the sum of the other two numbers multiplied together.

Page 53 - Figure It Out
11,000 + 1,100 + 11 = 12,111.

Page 54 - Stick 'Em Up
C E A B F D.

Page 55 - Pattern Puzzler
F.
It's the only set with two patterns the same.

Page 56 - Sequence
D.
Each circle has one more item than the one before.

Page 57 - Sum Total

4 + 6 − 5 = 5.

Page 58 - Dancing Dilemma

Ohio – green – tango
Portland – blue – salsa
New Orleans – red – samba
Wyoming – black – square dancing.

Page 59 - Bullseye!

Six.
Four darts scoring 17 each = 68, plus two darts scoring 16 each = 32. 68 + 32 = 100.

Page 60 - Square Sum

31.

17 squares.

4 small squares.

4 large squares made up of 4 small squares.

1 large square.

1 large square made up of 4 small squares.

4 large squares (1 at each corner), made from 9 small squares.

Page 61 - Number Number

25.
Add 2 to the first number to get the second number, then add 3 to the second to get the third, add 4 to the third, to get the fourth, and so on.

Page 62 - Backwards Thinking

P.
They are the letters of the alphabet, working backward from Z and missing out one letter each time.

Page 63 - Face-to-Face
B.
The face shape moves along one place to the left in each row, the nose color moves one place to right in each row and the eye color moves one place to the left.

Page 64 - Triangle Test
16.
ADC / ABD ABC / AGD AGF AGC AGE / GDB GDC GCB GCE GDF/ EDC FDC FAC EAD.

Page 65 - Fruit Cocktail
D.
It is the only one whose fruits do not add up to 6.

Page 66 - What's Next?
E.
They are the initials of the continents. Asia, Africa, Antarctica, Americas, Australasia and Europe.

Page 67 - Clowning Around
B.
One more color is added each time.

Page 68 - Weekly Work Out
Monday.

Page 69 - Turn Around
6.

Page 70 - Missing Link
11.
From the 6, the numbers go alternately 6 – 8 –10 – 12 and then 8 – 9 – 10 – 11.

Page 71 - How Many Squares?
17.
12 small squares. 5 large squares - made up of 4 small squares.

12 x

5 x

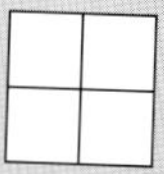

Page 72 - Math Muddle
7 + 4 - 5 + 9 - 8 = 7.

Page 73 - Eye Eye!
18.

Page 74 - Flag It Up
There are five possible answers. Move the top flag to either A, B, C, D or E.

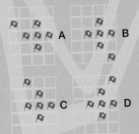

Page 75 - Wavy Lines
A.
The first 2 squares contain 1 line, the next two squares contain 2 lines and the third pair of squares should contain 3 lines.

Page 76 - Face Shapes
A.
What is round in the first column becomes square in the next. What goes up in the first column, goes down in the next. What goes down in the first column, goes up in the next.

Page 77 - Logic Letters
U.
Clockwise, they are the letters of the alphabet in order from A, but missing out one letter, then two letters, then three, and so on.

Page 78 - Seventeens

A = 3
B = 5
C = 5.

Page 79 - Half and Half

9.
Multiply the number in each bottom segment by 3 to get the number in the opposite top segment.

Page 80 - Sewing Sum

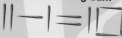

Page 81 - Pattern Path

B.
The patterns of squares 1 and 2 combined make the pattern of square 3. The patterns of squares 4 and 5 combined should therefore make the pattern of square 6.

Page 82 - Dragon Dilemma

The dragon takes the orc. He leaves him on the mountain top and comes back for the troll. He leaves the troll on the mountain top and brings back the orc to the island. He then leaves the orc and takes the goblin to the mountain top. He then goes back for the orc.

Page 83 - Color Combination

a) 9 + 8
b) 2 + 6
c) 6 x 9
d) 5 x 4

Page 84 - Brainy Birds

A.
The number of birds increases by 1 each time.

Page 85 - Magic Square

12.
Each row and column adds up to 34.

LAGOON
BOOKS